Selected Writings of August Cieszkowski

Portrait of August Cieszkowski by the Polish poet Cyprian Norwid. The legend reads:

'Water and fire too can be joined* . . . but . . . first a *steam* engine must be built!' (words of Mr August C. in a private conversation).

* (joined, harmonized)

Selected Writings of August Cieszkowski

EDITED AND TRANSLATED WITH
AN INTRODUCTORY ESSAY BY

ANDRÉ LIEBICH

Professeur de Science Politique
à l'Université du Québec à Montréal

CAMBRIDGE UNIVERSITY PRESS

CAMBRIDGE

LONDON · NEW YORK · MELBOURNE

Published by the Syndics of the Cambridge University Press
The Pitt Building, Trumpington Street, Cambridge CB2 1RP
Bentley House, 200 Euston Road, London NW1 2DB
32 East 57th Street, New York, NY 10022, USA
296 Beaconsfield Parade, Middle Park, Melbourne 3206, Australia

First published 1979

Printed in Great Britain by
Western Printing Services Ltd, Bristol

Library of Congress Cataloguing in Publication Data
Cieszkowski, August Dołega, hrabia, 1814–1894.
Selected writings of August Cieszkowski.
(Cambridge studies in the history and theory
of politics)
Includes bibliographical references and index.
I. Liebich, André, 1948– II. Title.
B4691.C52E5 1979   199'.438   77–94371
ISBN 0 521 21986 8

Contents

Acknowledgements

Above all, to Miguel Abensour who awakened my curiosity about Cieszkowski and to Zbigniew Pelczynski who proved so receptive to the idea of my undertaking the present volume.

In addition, to all those who offered encouragement, comments or help at various stages: Shlomo Avineri, Isaiah Berlin, Charles Taylor, Wiktor Weintraub and others. Also to Tadeusz Kozanecki who lent me his typescript of Cieszkowski's notebooks.

Finally, to the staff of the Cambridge University Press whose pleasant and efficient collaboration was invaluable throughout.

André Liebich

August Cieszkowski: praxis and messianism as reform

I
Cieszkowski and the antinomies of thought

More than most of his contemporaries, August Cieszkowski succeeded in formulating a world-view which can be termed typical of his period and yet can lay claim to originality. Many students of nineteenth-century intellectual history would see in Cieszkowski a characteristic figure of his age: a generous and sincere aristocrat nurtured on Hegelianism, utopian socialism and messianic nationalism, who embraced a variety of social and political causes with unrelenting optimism in the possibilities of human progress. At the same time, those students who see intellectual history through the prism of present-day schemata of classification and dominant modes of analysis would be puzzled by a thinker whose apparently contradictory commitment both to social reconciliation and social transformation makes him virtually undefinable in terms of standard ideological and intellectual categories.

If one were to compare Cieszkowski to his contemporaries one would make of him a sort of Polish Alexander Herzen, a philosophical Robert Owen or a romantic and religious Louis Blanc. Such a comparison, however, could convey only very approximately the complexity, the originality and even, in some ways, the importance of Cieszkowski's position among his contemporaries. Thus, the concern of the present essay is, in part, to trace the development of Cieszkowski's thought through a study of the milieux which influenced him and in which he was active, and consequently to define Cieszkowski historically in relation to his contemporaries and to evaluate his specific solutions to shared problems and preoccupations. On the other hand, the bibliographic essay which follows the selections in this volume will discuss the growing number of studies which have drawn attention to Cieszkowski's role as a critic of Hegel, an influence on Marx and a progressive Christian well ahead of his times.

In addition to Cieszkowski's place as a precursor and a contributor to a number of powerful intellectual movements, I would argue that his significance and originality as a thinker lie in his analysis of the crisis which his era was experiencing and in his formulation of peaceful and meliorist alternatives to revolutionary solutions. It seems to me that one of the key problems of studying Cieszkowski is precisely that of understanding why the analysis and alternatives he proposed failed to find an enduring echo. I would suggest that this failure can be best explained in terms of a certain number of contradictions, real or apparent, which mark both his writings and his activities. Inasmuch as these contradictions appear as such far more readily to the present-day reader than to Cieszkowski's contemporaries, one may wonder whether these perceived contradictions are not themselves evidence of an inability to understand Cieszkowski's age on its own terms. Whether this is or is not the case, before proceeding further it may be worth while to glance at some of the contradictions to which I have alluded as explaining either Cieszkowski's failure to win wider following or posterity's inability to understand him fully.

The most fundamental contradiction in Cieszkowski would seem to lie in the divorce between the content and the form of his thought. Whereas Cieszkowski's social and political concerns appear overwhelmingly modern and familiar the utopian and religious form in which he chooses to express them seems quite archaic. When Cieszkowski demands as he does in the *Prolegomena to Historiosophy* that philosophy not only help one to understand one's circumstances but that it contribute to shaping these circumstances in such a way as to abolish physical want and class conflict we find him readily understandable. However, when the product of practical philosophy or *praxis* turns out to be a Christian, perhaps even theocratic utopia whose operative principles are deduced from the precepts of the Lord's Prayer we do not easily identify with the outcome. Moreover, we cannot help feeling that the epic proportions of Cieszkowski's utopianism in the *Our Father* stand in glaring contrast to the sensible, moderate and practical ideas contained in both this work and in Cieszkowski's other writings. In short, the utopian and religious form of Cieszkowski's thought would seem to undermine the credibility of his system as a whole.

I would suggest that the critique of Cieszkowski which fastens upon this apparent divorce between form and content rests upon an inadequate appreciation of the nature of utopian modes of expression in general and the prevalence of utopias in nineteenth-century social philosophy in particular. Like the work of a number of better-known figures of his own time – Fourier, Saint-Simon, Cabet, to mention the most obvious – the entire corpus of Cieszkowski's writings could be said to constitute a utopia in the sense of a total and self-sufficient world-view standing self-consciously at a distance from immediate reality.[1] Indeed, even in his obsession with the details of the future Cieszkowski falls in with the mainstream of utopian thought of all periods. Here as in More, Campanella or Fourier the specification of minor elements seems to constitute some sort of guarantee of their feasibility and presumably legitimates the essential elements of the utopia. Thus, Cieszkowski's utopia joins with others in constituting a critique, a standard of measurement and a transcendence of existing reality which is itself a liberation. Above all, Cieszkowski goes even further than his contemporaries in believing that the construction of utopia is the first step towards its attainment.[2]

It is Cieszkowski's religiosity, however, even more than his earnest utopianism, which sets him apart from modern political thought. Although there is some debate as to whether he can be properly called a messianist there is no question about his eminently religious and, more specifically, Christian outlook as manifested in his pervasive use of Christian symbols and structures. Historically considered, however, Cieszkowski's religiosity too establishes him firmly within a stream of influential thinkers and tendencies which includes Lamennais, Weitling, Mickiewicz and the Saint-Simonians, with whom Cieszkowski shares the peculiarity of living in a period of transition from a religious to a secular consciousness. Whether intent on making inroads into popular beliefs by presenting new ideas in familiar religious garb or simply influenced by the romantic reaction to Enlightenment rationalism, these thinkers adopted a mode of discourse which referred back to Christian doctrine and experience. In their own time this device was tremendously appealing and one might even argue that it has left its imprint on later, strictly secular movements. I would submit that Cieszkowski's works offer one of the richest fields available for exploring those peculiar structures of thought and discourse which fuse socialist ideas with religious notions. Indeed, the *Our Father* should be considered an archetype of the genre for it is certainly more sophisticated, more thorough and more coherent than such better-known classics as *Paroles d'un croyant* or *Nouveau christianisme*.

If the apparent contradiction between form and content in Cieszkowski's

---

[1] For an extended discussion of utopia in this sense see Andrzej Walicki, *The Slavophile Controversy*, translated by Hilda Andrews-Rusiecka (Oxford, Clarendon Press, 1975), and especially its introduction.

[2] For a brilliant rehabilitation of utopia see Miguel Abensour, *Utopies et dialectiques du socialisme* (Paris, Payot, forthcoming).

thought can be resolved by a close and sympathetic examination of his historical context, a second important contradiction arises when we attempt to assess Cieszkowski in terms of the ideological categories familiar to us: where are we to situate Cieszkowski on an ideological spectrum running from 'right' to 'left'? Even a superficial reading of the selections translated here reveals that Cieszkowski fits no established mould, for we are confronted with a thinker in whom, for example, paternalism and nostalgia co-exist with a eulogy of self-help and a resolutely future orientation, cautious parliamentary strategies are pursued for the sake of revolutionary aims, and national messianism culminates in cosmopolitanism. Indeed, even the most sophisticated models of ideological allegiance, such as Mannheim's opposition between conservative 'ideology' and revolutionary 'utopia', provide little help in understanding Cieszkowski.[1] To be sure, in deference to Hegelian dialectics and in recognition of his own epoch's tendency towards polarization Cieszkowski often reduces problems to binomic terms. Nevertheless, his thought is elaborated independently of these terms, and even if his ideas may be justifiably called a synthesis, they are in no way a *juste-milieu* or a compromise. For instance, when addressing himself to the problem of social change, Cieszkowski shows that the reform he is advocating is as profound as that sought by anyone on the left. In his case, however, it is a reform solidly based on the acquisitions of the past and respectful of the need to practise an economy of suffering by paying heed to the laws of historical change. Moreover, here as elsewhere, Cieszkowski is quite aware that the consequence of this refusal to be terrorized by the false alternatives of 'ideology' and 'utopia' is to be rejected by both right and left. Surely, there is much to learn from a thinker who accepts the fate of being ignored by the leading tendencies of his times because he will not subordinate his goals to their tactical options.

II
Germany: from philosophy to praxis

August Cieszkowski was born near Warsaw in 1814.[2] As the heir of a

---

[1] See Karl Mannheim, *Ideology and Utopia*, translated by Louis Wirth and Edward Shils (New York, Harcourt, Brace and World, 1936) for the classic formulation of the difference between 'ideology' which justifies an existing order and accompanying class structure and 'utopia' which transcends that order by proposing a model defined in terms of its otherness.

[2] The most complete biographical article on Cieszkowski is Andrzej Wojtkowski's piece in Witold Jakóbczyk (ed.), *Wielkopolanie XIX-go wieku*, vol. II (Poznań, Poznańskie Wydawnictwo Państwowe, 1969), pp. 141–75.

wealthy, cultivated and aristocratic Polish family, he received a thorough private education which left him with considerable linguistic versatility. He was soon exposed to the romantic nationalism which prevailed in partitioned Poland at the time and, according to legend, participated in a non-combatant capacity in the anti-Russian insurrection of 1830–1.[1] After having matriculated in the Free City of Cracow in 1832 he spent two semesters at the philosophical faculty of the Jagiellonian University there, and then, because of ill-health, transferred to the University of Berlin for a further five semesters. It was here that Cieszkowski became acquainted with the Hegelianism which was to underlie all his writings.

It is hardly surprising that Cieszkowski should have been swept up by enthusiasm for Hegel's philosophy in the Friedrich-Wilhelm University of the 1830s. Hegel's death in 1831 had only intensified the zeal with which his disciples studied and propagated their master's ideas. Indeed, one could suggest that their ardour compensated for the self-imposed limitations of their task: inasmuch as Hegel had attained the standpoint of absolute knowledge nothing of real consequence remained to be discovered. Thus, the Hegelians saw themselves as bearers of truth but also as epigones condemned to annotating the collected works of the master.[2]

In fact, Hegel's heritage was far more ambiguous than his disciples at first cared to recognize. In two major areas, religion and politics, Hegel was equivocal enough to allow the most contradictory interpretations and conclusions. Thus, Hegel's declared adherence to Protestant Christianity stood in uneasy relation to his theogonous, even pan-logical tendency to identify the divinity with an historically unfolding, essentially philosophical Spirit.[3] Similarly, Hegel's apparent respect for his adopted state appeared to contradict his own rational criteria by tolerating both arbitrariness and political obscurantism.[4]

---

[1] Cieszkowski's first known writing is a lyrical patriotic poem of 1831 reprinted and discussed in Janina Znamirowska, 'O nieznanych wierszach Augusta Cieszkowskiego', *Ruch Literacki*, IV, 2 (February 1929), pp. 44–6.

[2] For a first-hand impression of what it meant to be a Hegelian after Hegel see the texts of Marheineke's and Förster's funeral orations for Hegel, in Johann Karl Friedrich Rosenkranz, *Georg Wilhelm Friedrich Hegels Leben* (Berlin, Duncker und Humblot, 1844), pp. 562–6. For an historical examination of the question see Karl Löwith, *From Hegel to Nietzsche: The Revolution in Nineteenth Century Thought*, translated by David E. Green (New York, Holt, Rinehart and Winston, 1964), especially pp. 53–136.

[3] Hegel's attitude and ideas on religion still allow widely divergent interpretations today. Compare Emil L. Fackenheim, *The Religious Dimension in Hegel's Thought* (Bloomington, Indiana University Press, 1967), which puts religion at the very centre of Hegel's thought, and Walter Kaufmann, *Hegel: Reinterpretation, Texts and Commentary* (London, Weidenfeld and Nicolson, 1965), which minimizes this element.

[4] One might claim that Prussia in the Restoration era, with its well-developed educa-

The potential conflict about Hegel's meaning and intentions exploded in 1835 with the publication of D. F. Strauss's *Das Leben Jesu*, an attempt to historicize the Gospels by analysing them in terms of myths reflecting the popular consciousness of early Christians. Strauss's theses were not startlingly new but his avowed dependence on Hegel brought the Hegelian school as a whole into open controversy with pietist and traditionalist theologians.[1] Soon, the logic of the polemics had led a number of Hegelians from questioning to rejection not only of orthodox Biblical scholarship but of such fundamental Christian tenets as the divinity of Christ and the doctrine of personal immortality.

To be sure, religious polemics did not immediately lead to political dissent.[2] Indeed, the original division among left, right and centre within the Hegelian school applied uniquely to theological alignments.[3] Nevertheless, it was these apparently abstract religious debates which first demonstrated that Hegel's writings allowed a multiplicity of interpretations and that the speculative method could be creatively applied, even against Hegel himself. Such iconoclastic attitudes to Hegel's legacy created another fundamental division, this time between Old Hegelians who had been Hegel's students and Young Hegelians, newcomers only mediately familiar with the master's teachings.[4] As might be expected,

---

tional system, examination-selected bureaucracy and imminent constitution, was more liberal than most existing states and more liberal than it was itself to be after 1840. The controversy over Hegel's 'Prussianism' thus continues. See Walter Kaufmann (ed.), *Hegel's Political Philosophy* (New York, Atherton Press, 1970).

[1] For a study of Strauss's work and its reception see Albert Schweitzer's classical work, *The Quest of the Historical Jesus: a Critical Study of its Progress from Reimarus to Wrede*, translated by W. Montgomery (New York, Macmillan, 1948), pp. 68–120.

[2] Most accounts follow Friedrich Engels, *Ludwig Feuerbach and the Outcome of Classical German Philosophy*, ed. C. P. Dutt (New York, International Publishers, 1935) in assuming that the transition from religious to political criticism was somehow spontaneous and automatic. They overlook the fact that university Hegelianism was protected and privileged until 1841. Rudolf Haym, *Hegel und seine Zeit* (Berlin, R. Gaertner, 1857), p. 4, writes of the 1830s as a time 'when in the eyes of the Prussian Ministry of Culture and Learning it was considered nearly a crime not to be a Hegelian'. This point has been made more recently by William J. Brazill, *The Young Hegelians* (New Haven and London, Yale University Press, 1970).

[3] Löwith, *From Hegel to Nietzsche*, p. 53, attributes the adoption of this image to D. F. Strauss, *Streitschriften zur Verteidigung meiner Schrift über das Leben Jesu*, no. 3 (1837), and Carl-Ludwig Michelet, *Geschichte der letzten Systeme der Philosophie in Deutschland von Kant bis Hegel*, vol. II (Berlin, Duncker und Humblot, 1838), p. 659.

[4] See Horst Stuke, *Philosophie der Tat: Studien zur 'Verwirklichung der Philosophie' bei den Junghegelianern und den Wahren Sozialisten* (Stuttgart, E. Klett, 1963), especially pp. 32–3, for an interesting account of the divisions among the Hegelians and a useful reminder that 'old' did not necessarily correspond to 'right' nor 'young' to 'left'. The examples of Feuerbach and Kierkegaard should suffice to make this point.

the staid veneration of the former contrasted starkly with the critical impatience of the latter.

Even so, German philosophy as perfected by Hegel constituted such a tightly knit structure that no internal criticism could upset it. Consequently, any attempt to transcend Hegel's system had to be introduced from the outside. In the case of political theory, the search for such external premisses eventually took the form of an appeal to the historical experience of contemporary France.[1] Admittedly, Hegel himself had given the cue to this interest by contrasting France and Germany as practical and theoretical nations.[2] Everything in his system, however, militated against the inversion of the relation between theory and practice towards which his bolder disciples were now tending:[3] frustrated by the limits of reverential exegesis but confident in their grasp of the absolute and fascinated by the French Revolution and its consequences, certain Hegelians looked away from theoretical knowledge to practical knowledge and from retrospective historical considerations to speculation on the future.[4]

In summary, one could characterize Cieszkowski's years in Berlin as a time when the prevailing Hegelianism was tempered by religious controversy and impatience with contemplative, theoretical attitudes was already leading to an inchoate search beyond the confines of classical German philosophy for a way out of the perceived impasse of Hegel's system. Significantly, Cieszkowski's closest mentors were two philosophers most instrumental in articulating these very trends: Eduard Gans (1798–1839) and Carl-Ludwig Michelet (1801–93).

Gans distinguished himself among Hegel's associates by his liberalism and his interest in French social thought.[5] Indeed, he took the lead

---

[1] Studies of the relations between French social thought and German philosophy in this period are far too few. See the pioneering article by Bernard Groethuysen, 'Les jeunes hégéliens et les origines du socialisme contemporain en Allemagne', *Revue Philosophique*, XLVIII, 2 (1923), pp. 379–95. Also Jacques d'Hondt, *De Hegel à Marx* (Paris, Presses Universitaires de France, 1972), pp. 121–35.

[2] Georg Wilhelm Friedrich Hegel, *The Philosophy of History, translated by J. Sibree* (New York, Dover Publications, 1956), pp. 443–4.

[3] Hegel's letter to Niethammer dated 28 October 1808 summarizes his notion of the pre-eminence of theory: 'Every day I am more convinced that theoretical work brings more into the world than the practical. If the kingdom of the imagination is revolutionized first, then reality cannot hold out'. *Briefe von und an Hegel*, edited by J. Hoffmeister, vol. I, 1785–1812 (Hamburg, Verlag von Feliz Meiner, 1952), p. 253.

[4] The earliest example that I know of such an orientation is a letter from Feuerbach to Hegel dated 1828. Ten years later such examples would abound. *Ibid.*, vol. III, pp. 244–8.

[5] See Hanns Günther Reissner, *Eduard Gans: Ein Leben in Vormärz*, Schriftenreihe

among his colleagues in drawing attention – though with some reservations – to the Saint-Simonians and in predicting the future importance of the social question.[1] As a popular lecturer, it was natural that Gans should have impressed Cieszkowski, but his influence went considerably deeper: not only did Cieszkowski read philosophy of law and philosophy of history under Gans[2] but he refers to Gans familiarly in his correspondence and it was Gans's publication of Hegel's *Lectures on the Philosophy of History* that moved him to undertake the *Prolegomena to Historiosophy*.[3] Gans's premature death thus deprived not only the Hegelians in general but Cieszkowski himself of an invaluable counsellor and teacher.

Carl-Ludwig Michelet, on the other hand, lived to be the last and most faithful of the Old Hegelians as well as Cieszkowski's most constant correspondent.[4] Their letters cover almost sixty years and offer a vivid portrait of the gradual disintegration of the Hegelian school.[5] In the 1830s, however, Michelet too was affected by the current interest in France and social issues and his loyalty to Hegel was tempered by impatience.[6] Significantly, his writings of the period evoke two themes which Cieszkowski was to make his own: first, the need to reorient philosophy towards the future so that the reconciliation already realized in thought could be effected in reality; second, the need to popularize philosophy by having it spread through all areas of knowledge and all social strata.[7]

It is through Cieszkowski's correspondence with Michelet that one can best trace the genesis of the *Prolegomena to Historiosophy*. Upon his return to Poland in 1836 Cieszkowski had already expressed his dis-

---

Wissenschaftlicher Abhandlungen des Leo Baeck Instituts, 14 (Tübingen, Mohr, 1965).

[1] Edouard Gans, *Rückblicke auf Personen und Zustände* (Berlin, Veit, 1836), pp. 91–105.

[2] August Cieszkowski, *curriculum vitae*, published in Walter Kühne, *Graf August Cieszkowski, ein Schüler Hegels und des deutschen Geistes: Ein Beitrag zur Geschichte des deutschen Geisteseinflüsse auf die Polen*, Veröffentlichungen des Slavischen Instituts an der Friedrich Wilhelm Universität Berlin, vol. xx (Leipzig, O. Harrassowitz, 1938), p. 426.

[3] Cieszkowski to Michelet, letter no. 1, 20 June 1836, *ibid.*, p. 359.

[4] For the memoirs of this youngest Old Hegelian see Carl-Ludwig Michelet, *Wahrheit aus meinem Leben* (Berlin, Nicolai, 1884).

[5] The entire correspondence is published in Kühne, *Graf August Cieszkowski*, pp. 353–425.

[6] Michelet, *Wahrheit aus meinem Leben*, p. 129.

[7] Already in 1831 Michelet was consciously inverting Hegel's image of 'the owl of Minerva' by referring to philosophy as the 'cock-crow of a newly breaking day', in the *Jahrbücher für wissenschaftliche Kritik*, cited in Stuke, *Philosophie der Tat*, p. 64. See also Michelet's *Geschichte der letzten Systeme der Philosophie*, vol. ii, especially p. 799.

satisfaction with Hegel's failure to raise the philosophy of spirit to the same dialectical perfection as his logic.[1] Some months later this criticism and the accompanying references to a projected 'Dialectics of History' took on more concrete shape as Cieszkowski specified his intention:

Has philosophy become an exact science or not? If so, the principles are given and we have but to draw the consequences . . . This is where philosophy stands, history too has traversed a good part of the road and has thus supplied us with a goodly number of exact data; thus, all invites us to make our calculations, to seek the extrapolation of this progression and to discover the *x* of the problem.

This *x*, I confess, *is the future*. The future which has so often escaped intuition and reflection and which I want to conquer for the domain of positive speculation.[2]

Michelet reacted with sceptical interest. He referred his pupil to Fichte's *Characteristics of the Present Age* and remarked that Cieszkowski seemed to be proceeding very differently from Hegel. Generally speaking, Michelet felt that the project would turn out to be utopian and abstract – unless it could be grounded in the experience of a concrete people, such as contemporary Christianity, or unless it were Cieszkowski's intention to popularize the principles of modern speculation by showing in comprehensible terms their applicability to history. If this was the case, then Michelet had no objections to the project.[3]

Cieszkowski brushed aside these queries and continued with his work. In June 1838 he read the manuscript to Michelet and another Hegelian, Karl Werder;[4] after some additions and changes it appeared that same year as a 157-page book published in Berlin by Veit and Company.

The *Prolegomena to Historiosophy* may allow schematic summary. The work as a whole consists of three chapters entitled respectively 'The organism of universal history', 'The categories of universal history' and 'The teleology of universal history'. In Cieszkowski's own words these deal in turn with the *how*, the *what* and the *why* of the organism of universal history.[5] In fact, the first chapter founds the basic principle of history as an organism, the second chapter inventories the various principles –

---

[1] Cieszkowski to Michelet, letter no. 1, 20 June 1836, in Kühne, *Graf August Cieszkowski*, p. 358.

[2] Cieszkowski to Michelet, letter no. 3, 18 March 1837, *ibid.*, p. 366.

[3] Michelet to Cieszkowski, letter no. 4, 6 April 1838, *ibid.*, p. 270.

[4] Karl Werder (1806–1893) was known as a drama critic and as tutor to a succession of Russian Hegelians, particularly Bakunin. See Dmitry Chyzhevsky, 'Hegel in Russland', in *Hegel bei den Slaven*, 2nd edn (Bad Homburg, Gentner, 1961), pp. 145–397.

[5] *Prolegomena zur Historiosophie* (Berlin, Veit, 1838), p. 77.

physical, logical, spiritual – through which we may come to know the laws of historical development, and the third chapter rounds out the exercise by extrapolating these principles into the future and thus completing the construction of the organic structure of history.

It is thus the notion of universal history as an organism that dominates the *Prolegomena*. By demonstrating that history as a whole constitutes a unity of rationally developing and interdependent elements governed by dialectical laws – what the *Prolegomena* calls an organic structure – Hegel has made possible a science of history which would encompass the future. However, Hegel himself has failed to pursue this possibility by ceding to the standing prejudice against future-oriented speculation and by resorting to an untenable tetrachotomous periodization of history which violates his own principles and which would have us believe that the course of history has been completed. In fact, applying Hegel's principles rigorously, we find that history necessarily consists of three periods; that the first two, dialectically opposite, periods – Antiquity and Christianity – have already passed and everything indicates that we are entering a third, synthetic period. Further dialectical analysis suggests that in contrast to unreflective, substantial Antiquity and contemplative but individualistic Christianity the third period will be marked by a post-theoretical and socially oriented activity which Cieszkowski calls *praxis* and whose concrete manifestation is the *deed*. In short, since mankind has understood its own history and the laws of historical development, it can act in full consciousness of its vocation, which is to construct a universal social church of humanity where goodness might reign.

The evidence on which Cieszkowski's arguments are based might appear paltry and contrived, but if one is willing to abstract from the stilted Hegelian language in which they are couched one must acknowledge that they are based on certain incontrovertible premises: that history demonstrates certain discontinuities, that the characteristics of the Christian-bourgeois world – individualism, abstraction, and other-worldliness, to name but some – have exhausted their potential for positive development, and inasmuch as these characteristics were already antithetical vis-à-vis the ancient world they will be succeeded by a series of syntheses which compensate for the deficiencies of both preceding periods. Materially speaking, human welfare can now be founded on the technical and scientific achievements of the past, but existing social, economic and intellectual institutions act as a brake on the progress which they themselves have made possible. In retrospect, we can only confirm Cieszkowski's intuition that the nineteenth century as heir to Hegel, the French

Revolution and industrialism marks a profound discontinuity with the past, and that the material basis for making the next historical period a happy and harmonious one is available.

Evaluation of the *Prolegomena* is a problem of perspective. From the vantage-point of what was to follow, the *Prolegomena* may appear timid in spirit and heavily dependent on Hegel.[1] Indeed, by 1843 Cieszkowski's central idea – to transcend philosophy through social *praxis* – was the standard fare of the entire Hegelian left.[2] From the perspective of what had preceded its publication, however, the *Prolegomena* was truly pioneering in reorienting discussion of history from the past to the future and in redirecting criticism of Hegel from religion to politics. In 1838, a work which challenged complacency by arguing that Hegel had only realized an ideal and not a real reconciliation was radically original.[3]

Hegel was undoubtedly the leading inspiration of the *Prolegomena*, but Cieszkowski could only formulate his critique by taking a certain distance from the object of his criticism and relying on a number of other reference points. Above all, he drew support from two distinct sources, the German Enlightenment and idealism on the one hand and French utopianism on the other.[4] Thus, the *Prolegomena* appealed to the authority of Schiller and Herder and owed something to Schelling;[5] it contained perhaps the first positive mention of Fourier in German philosophical

---

[1] This is the judgement, for instance, of Guy Planty-Bonjour, *Hegel et la pensée philosophique en Russie, 1830–1917* (The Hague, M. Nijhoff, 1974), p. 160. In my view, he fails to recognize that any criticism of Hegel from within the Hegelian school had to be couched in Hegelian terms both for the sake of coherence and persuasion.

[2] See Shlomo Avineri, *The Social and Political Thought of Karl Marx* (Cambridge University Press, 1968), pp. 124–34. Also Löwith, *From Hegel to Nietzsche*, especially the sections on Feuerbach, Ruge and Bauer, pp. 65–91, 105–10, 294–7.

[3] Avineri, *The Social and Political Thought of Karl Marx*, is particularly valuable in showing Cieszkowski's originality. See also Auguste Cornu, *Karl Marx et Friedrich Engels*, vol. I, *Les années d'enfance et de jeunesse. La gauche hégélienne, 1818/20–1844* (Paris, Presses Universitaires de France, 1955), p. 142, where he writes of the 'revolutionary transformation of the philosophy of Hegel which found its first expression in Cieszkowski'.

[4] The former are partially treated in Benoît Hepner, 'History and the Future: the vision of August Cieszkowski', *Review of Politics*, XV, 3 (1953), pp. 328–50. The latter are exhaustively covered in Andrzej Walicki, 'Francuskie inspiracje myśli filozoficzno-religijnej Augusta Cieszkowskiego', *Archiwum Historii Filozofii i Myśli Społecznej*, XVI (1970), pp. 127–71.

[5] It is perhaps significant that the 'neglected writings of Hegel', the 'Treatise on the relation of natural philosophy to philosophy in general' to which Cieszkowski refers for support in chapter I of the *Prolegomena* has proven to be Schelling's work. See Xavier Tilliette, *Schelling: une philosophie en devenir;* vol. I, *Le système vivant 1794–1821* (Paris, Vrin, 1970), p. 296.

literature.[1] It is the influence of Fichte and Buchez, however, which deserves particular consideration here.[2]

Lukács describes the Young Hegelian movement as a return to Fichte and he cites Cieszkowski as the leading early example of this trend.[3] Actually, certain similarities between Cieszkowski and Fichte are common to the period as a whole: the belief in the religious character of man's destiny; the analysis of the present as a period of transition; the attempts to define historical stages so as to formulate a comprehensive philosophy of history. Nevertheless, other key elements unmistakeably point to a more specific connection. Thus, Cieszkowski follows Fichte in defining the will as a creative faculty directed towards activity and concerned with realizing the Good; indeed, the will becomes the highest category of the spirit.[4] However, even Lukács, who is rather harsh to Cieszkowski, admits that the *Prolegomena* goes further than Fichte in its application of the dialectic to history, its concrete orientation towards the future and its substitution of dialectical proofs for Fichtean exhortation.[5] Consequently, Cieszkowski's relation to Fichte must be seen as one of free inspiration rather than direct dependence.

If the importance of Fichte to the *Prolegomena* is in some measure a reversion to a pre-Hegelian variant of German idealism, the influence of Buchez constitutes an appeal outside German philosophy altogether. Philippe Joseph Buchez's conception of history as a future-oriented science called upon to guide humanity in its free, social activity, his analogies between physical and social laws, his application of organic images to history, are all strikingly similar to Cieszkowski's arguments in the *Prolegomena* – even though Buchez expounded his ideas without any reference to Hegel.[6] Thus, it is not surprising to learn that Cieszkowski had

---

[1] Gans, *Rückblicke*, p. 115, had mentioned Fourier anecdotally. Cornu shows that interest in Fourier was not to develop until the 1840s. See his *Moses Hess et la gauche hégélienne* (Paris, Presses Universitaires de France, 1934), p. 45.

[2] This is not belied by the fact that Fichte and Buchez are mentioned only once in the *Prolegomena*. Although names such as Herder and Montesquieu appear more frequently they do so only in the context of specific sub-arguments whereas the influence of Fichte and Buchez permeate the work as a whole.

[3] G. Lukács, 'Moses Hess und die Probleme der idealistischen Dialektik', *Archiv für die Geschichte des Sozialismus und der Arbeiterbewegung*, XII (1926), pp. 103–55. Translated in *Telos*, 10 (December 1971), pp. 23–35.

[4] See Johann Gottlieb Fichte, *Characteristics of the Present Age*, p. 3, and *The Vocation of Man*, pp. 244–67; both works translated by William Smith (London, The Catholic Series, 1847).

[5] G. Lukács, 'Moses Hess und die Probleme der idealistischen Dialektik', *passim*.

[6] Philippe Joseph Buchez, *Introduction à la science de l'histoire, ou science du développement de l'humanité* (Paris, Paulin, 1833). See also Gaston Castella, *Buchez historien, sa*

read Buchez's recently published *Introduction à la science de l'histoire*;[1] nor is it unusual that their ideas should have subsequently evolved in the same direction.[2]

Apart from Cieszkowski's willingness to draw on such disparate inspiration as Fichte and Buchez even as he sought to remain within the Hegelian framework, the *Prolegomena*'s appeal to the authority of the natural sciences merits mention. Some years later Croce was to scoff at Cieszkowski's attempt to apply the methods and insights of Cuvier and Herbart, as well as Hegel's own philosophy of nature, to history.[3] Ironically, however, it is this very attempt which most attracted and fascinated the first readers of the *Prolegomena*. Indeed, an inquiry into the reception accorded to the work only confirms the persuasiveness of Cieszkowski's arguments, the originality of his theses and the revolutionary potential of the work.

Formal reviews of the *Prolegomena to Historiosophy* seemed to agree on the importance of the work even as they expressed substantive reservations. The anonymous critic of the official Prussian gazette mixed admiration for Cieszkowski's independent philosophical stance with disapproval of the work's 'somewhat bold nature'.[4] Michelet, writing in the principal Hegelian journal, concentrated on demonstrating that Cieszkowski was correct in his conclusions but erred in thinking that he had gone beyond Hegel. According to Michelet, all that Cieszkowski had said was already implicit in Hegel, particularly in the *Philosophy of Right*.[5] This assessment, as well as Michelet's dismissal of what the *Prolegomena* had called 'social life' as simply a Saint-Simonian-sounding name, merely pointed to the fundamental difference between the Old and the Young Hegelians: whereas the former referred to Hegel as an absolute and exclusive

---

théorie du progrès dans la philosophie de l'histoire (Fribourg, Librairie de l'Humanité, 1909).

[1] This information is contained in Cieszkowski's Diaries, two manuscript notebooks (henceforth referred to as *Diaries* I and II) from the 1830s, deposited in the Manuscript Division, University Library, Uniwersytet imienia Adama Mickiewicza, Poznań. The reference to Buchez is in *Diaries* I, p. 4.

[2] Buchez's evolution as a social Catholic is described in Armand Cuvillier, *P. J. B. Buchez et les origines du socialisme chrétien* (Paris, Presses Universitaires de France, 1948). Jean Baptiste Duroselle, *Les débuts du catholicisme social en France 1822–1870*, with preface by B. Mirkine-Gutzevitch and Marcel Prélot (Paris, Presses Universitaires de France, 1951), traces the development of social Catholicism in general.

[3] Benedetto Croce, *Saggio sullo Hegel* (Bari, Laterza, 1913), p. 155.

[4] *Allgemeine Preussische Staatszeitung*, 1838, no. 283, p. 1167.

[5] C.-L. Michelet, review of *Die Prolegomena zur Historiosophie*, *Jahrbücher für wissenschaftliche Kritik*, 99 (1838), pp. 786–92; 100, pp. 794–8.

13

measuring-standard the latter used Hegel as a base for further discovery. As might be expected, the review in what was soon to become the organ of the Hegelian left showed much more understanding for Cieszkowski's position. It fully endorsed the *Prolegomena*'s critique of Hegel but charged the author, quite rightly, with having failed to develop his notion of 'social life' historically and thus leaving it unacceptably vague.[1]

Among all the German Hegelians it was Moses Hess who best understood and absorbed the lessons of the *Prolegomena*.[2] To be sure, Hess approached the work with a favourable prejudice: he had recently published a periodization of history superficially similar to Cieszkowski's.[3] However, Hess's interest went beyond seeing in the *Prolegomena* a more rigorously argued justification for his own historical intuition. In particular, Hess singled out Cieszkowski's notion of *praxis* with its distinction between the unconscious *fact* and the conscious post-theoretical *act*, as well as Cieszkowski's affirmations regarding the social nature of the future and the present need for an effective, concrete reconciliation of contradictions through free and conscious human activity.[4] These very ideas were to constitute the theoretical underpinnings of Hess's philosophical writings throughout the 1840s.[5]

Hess is undoubtedly important in his own right as a German radical publicist and later as a forerunner of Zionism. He is also noteworthy here because it is through Hess's considerable influence on Marx and Engels that the ideas of the *Prolegomena* would have reached the founders of Marxism.[6] To be sure, Engels was personally familiar with the *Prolegomena*, which he was to describe years afterwards in odd terms as a 'naturphilosophisch-botanisches Buch'.[7] Marx's disclaimer that this

---

[1] Julius Frauenstadt, review of *Die Prolegomena zur Historiosophie*, *Hallische Jahrbücher für Deutsche Wissenschaft und Kunst*, 60 (11 March 1839), pp. 476–88.

[2] See Cornu, *Moses Hess et la gauche hégélienne*, especially pp. 31–4.

[3] *Die heilige Geschichte der Menschheit von einem Jünger Spinozas* (Stuttgart, Halberger 1837). Commentators have been unanimously withering in regard to this work. See Cornu, *Moses Hess et la gauche hégélienne*, p. 27, as well as Isaiah Berlin, *The Life and Opinions of Moses Hess* (Cambridge, W. Heffer & Sons, 1959).

[4] Moses Hess, *Die europäische Triarchie* (Leipzig, O. Wigand, 1841), abridged in Horst Lademacher (ed.), *Moses Hess: Ausgewählte Schriften*, (Cologne, S. Melzer, 1962), p. 84.

[5] For further examination of the Hess–Cieszkowski relation see Jan Garewicz, 'August Cieszkowski w oczach niemców w latach trzydziestych i czterdziestych xix-go wieku', *Polskie Spory o Hegla*, edited by Instytut Filozofii i Socjologii Polskiej Akademii Nauk (Warsaw, Państwowe Wydawnictwo Naukowe, 1966), pp. 205–43, especially pp. 226–41.

[6] Hess's intimacy with Marx and Engels dates from 1841 to 1843, during which years he taught his young associates the principles of communism. See Cornu, *Moses Hess et la gauche hégélienne*.

[7] Engels to Marx, letter dated 13 January 1882, *Marx–Engels Werke*, vol. xxxv (Berlin,

'count and...into the bargain doctor of philosophy' had so irritated him that he could never bring himself to read anything the man had written, is too impetuous to be taken at face value.[1] Knowing the voracity with which Marx read philosophy precisely at the time of the *Prolegomena*'s appearance, it is implausible that he could have overlooked this book; nor is it likely that forty years later he would have remembered an author whom he had not read. In any case, whether we are to assume a direct influence or one mediated by Hess, there is a startling similarity between Cieszkowski's notion of *praxis* formulated in 1838 and Marx's understanding of this same concept five years later. Marx chastises Feuerbach's partisans for imagining that they can overcome philosophy by ignoring it, and Bruno Bauer for failing to see that the crucial struggles of the present no longer lie inside philosophy. In short, concludes Marx, 'one cannot transcend philosophy without actualizing it nor can one actualize philosophy without transcending it'.[2]

Cieszkowski's readership was not confined to Germany. In Russia, where Hegelianism had rapidly won numerous adherents, comments about the *Prolegomena to Historiosophy* travelled quickly and excitedly. Stankevich commended the work to Bakunin in spite of numerous critical reservations;[3] certainly, Bakunin was aware of the *Prolegomena* as he moved from a Hegelian philosophy of reconciliation towards a negative dialectic founded upon the free creative deed.[4] Even more significantly, the *Prolegomena* served as Alexander Herzen's introduction to Hegel. Herzen has recorded his enthusiasm upon discovering the essential agreement between Cieszkowski's views and his own, particularly in respect to the periodization of history and the possibility of drawing analogies between

Dietz Verlag, 1973), p. 37. Engels also incorrectly assumes that Cieszkowski had co-operated in the *Deutsche* as well as the *Hallische Jahrbücher*.

[1] Marx to Engels, letter dated 12 January 1882, *ibid.*, p. 35. Marx claims to have received Cieszkowski's visit in Paris during the period of the *Deutsche-Französische Jahrbücher*, i.e. 1843–4. Cieszkowski does not mention Marx either in his diaries or in his published work.

[2] Karl Marx, 'A contribution to the critique of Hegel's "Philosophy of Right": Introduction' in *Critique of Hegel's Philosophy of Right*, edited with an introduction and notes by Joseph O'Malley (Cambridge University Press, 1970), p. 136.

[3] N. V. Stankevich, letter to Bakunin dated 20 May 1840, *Perepiska Nikolaya Vladimirovicha Stankevicha 1830–1840* edited by Aleksei Stankevich (Moscow, 1914), p. 672: 'The division [in the *Prolegomena* – AL] is inexact because it is not founded on the idea of history, but the final idea that science should pass into the deed and disappear in it is right. Now this universal demand is noticeable, that all these scattered categories be tied more tightly with the life of the heart, that philosophy melt so that... it be felt not in the head, but in the blood, body, in the whole being.'

[4] A. A. Kornilov, *Molodye gody Mikhaila Bakunina* (Moscow, 1915).

nature and history.[1] After having read Hegel himself, Herzen was to affirm that 'when science reaches the highest point, it naturally passes beyond itself into "deeds"' and that 'the world is complete only in action...the living unity of theory and practice'.[2] Clearly, both the tone and the theme are reminiscent of the *Prolegomena*.

Elsewhere, unfamiliarity with Hegel or complete lack of interest in philosophy limited the readership of the *Prolegomena*. In France, Edgar Quinet, translator of Herder and a keen observer of German intellectual life, noted Cieszkowski's work as indicative of a new tendency in German philosophy.[3] Apparently upon its author's initiative the *Prolegomena* was reviewed by Hippolyte de Passy at a session of the Académie des Sciences Morales; Passy's judgement, remarks Cieszkowski drily, was flattering but false.[4] In Poland, the *Prolegomena* was to attract attention largely because of the author's close ties to the local intelligentsia. Generally speaking, criticism was harsh partly out of prejudice at a native son who wrote in German but mainly because this criticism came well after Cieszkowski's ideas had been absorbed and radicalized by other Hegelians.[5] Thus, Edward Dembowski (1822–46) denounced Cieszkowski in the name of a philosophy of creativity where the *deed* appeared as a single and partial element, the conscious manifestation of thought.[6] Henryk Kamieński too criticized Cieszkowski's notion of the *deed* as far too vague and, of course, offered his own alternatives.[7] Undoubtedly both would have had to admit that they were continuing in the train of thought of the *Prolegomena*.

[1] Alexander Herzen to A. L. Witberg, letter dated 28 July 1839, in *A. I. Gertsen: polnoe sobranie sochinenii i pisem*, edited by M. K. Lemke, vol. XXII (additions) (Leningrad, 1925), p. 33. See also Raoul Labry, *Alexandre Ivanovič Herzen 1812–1870, essai sur la formation et le développement de ses idées* (Paris, Brossard, 1928).

[2] Quoted by Martin Malia, *Alexander Herzen and the Birth of Russian Socialism 1812–1855* (Cambridge, Mass., Harvard University Press, 1961), p. 247, from Herzen's essay of 1843, 'Buddhism in Science', Lemke, *A. I. Gertsen*, volume III, p. 218.

[3] See Z. L. Zaleski, 'Edgar Quinet et Auguste Cieszkowski', *Mélanges d'histoire littéraire générale et comparée offerts à Fernand Baldensperger*, vol. II (Paris, Champion, 1930), pp. 360.

[4] Cieszkowski, *Diaries* II, p. 13.

[5] See Karol Libelt, *Samowładstwo Rozumu i Objawy Filozofii Słowiańskiej*, 1st edn 1845; edited and introduced by Andrzej Walicki in Biblioteka Klasyków Filozofii (Warsaw, Państwowe Wydawnictwo Naukowe, 1967), p. 268.

[6] Edward Dembowski 'Rys rozwinięcia sie pojęć filozoficznych w Niemczech', originally published in the *Przegląd Naukowy* and reprinted in Edward Dembowski, *Pisma*, edited by A. Sladkowska and M. Zmigroda, in Biblioteka Klasyków Filozofii, volume I (Cracow, Państwowe Wydawnictwo Naukowe, 1955).

[7] Henryk Kamieński, *Filozofia Ekonomii Materialnej Ludzkiego Społeczeństwa*, 1st edn 1843; edited and introduced by Bronisław Baczko, in Biblioteka Klasyków Filozofii (Warsaw, Państwowe Wydawnictwo Naukowe, 1959), p. 139.

Today, the *Prolegomena to Historiosophy* is of interest for various reasons. Many ideas still merit independent attention: the notion of a predictive science of history remains provocative; the socialization of philosophy might be considered realized. Generally speaking, the work is significant as an attempt, indeed the first attempt, to explore the limits of Hegel's system by testing whether his method can in fact be separated from the content of his philosophy, whether his system can be reconciled with or even applied to different purposes and attitudes. Moreover, the *Prolegomena* is historically noteworthy in having suggested an interpretation of philosophy and in having formulated certain notions, particularly that of *praxis*, which were to be a cornerstone of the radical Hegelian programme of the 1840s, not least that of Marx and Engels. To this extent, the work is also a prolegomenon to a historiosophy which is not Cieszkowski's own.

Cieszkowski never abandoned the Hegelian milieu entirely but with time he was to occupy an increasingly isolated position within a Hegelian school which was itself declining.

In 1842, Cieszkowski published his second philosophical work, *Gott und Palingenesie*, a polemical reply to C.-L. Michelet's theses concerning the personality of God and the immortality of the soul.[1] Briefly stated, Cieszkowski accused Michelet of relegating God to the sphere of pure universality, of thus making Him into nothing but an impersonal personality; in terms evoking the *Prolegomena*, of infusing God with a preponderance of thought. This apparently obscure debate carried significant overtones. By 1842 religious views within the Hegelian school were intimately correlated with political positions: the right defended a very literal notion of divine personality and personal immortality; the left, already split into so-called atheists and pantheists, was nevertheless

---

[1] *Gott und Palingenesie: Erster kritischer Teil. Erstes kritisches Sendschreiben an den Herrn Professor Michelet auf Veranlassung seiner Vorlesungen über die Persönlichkeit Gottes und die Unsterblichkeit der Seele* (Berlin, E. H. Schröder, 1842). The second, positive part never appeared although we have some indication as to its possible content in C.-L. Michelet, *Die Epiphanie der ewigen Persönlichkeit des Geistes*, III (Nürnberg, T. Cramor, 1852), pp. 99–135, where Cieszkowski is represented as 'Teleophanes' [Michelet's] Eastern Friend' in a theological debate. This part is translated into Polish in A. Cieszkowski, *Bóg i Palingenezja*, translated by August Cieszkowski junior (Posen, 1912) and reprinted in August Cieszkowski, *Prolegomena do Historiozofii, Bóg i Palingeneza, oraz mniejsze pisma filozoficzne z lat 1838–1842*, introduced by Andrzej Walicki and edited by Jan Garewicz and Andrzej Walicki, Biblioteka Klasyków Filozofii (Warsaw, Państwowe Wydawnictwo Naukowe, 1972), pp. 211–44. See also the unpublished notes to the *Gott und Palingenesie* in Kühne, *Graf August Cieszkowski*, pp. 440–4; 446–54.

unanimous in rejecting both doctrines unconditionally.[1] Michelet's stance constituted a compromise which by means of spiritualizing both controversial doctrines would preserve them in modified form. In fact, if Michelet's centrist position had little chance of reconciling factions who were by now opposed not only religiously but politically, it was clear to Cieszkowski from the outset that his own solution – the notion of God as a concrete–synthetic spirit – was even less acceptable. Translating into political terms, Cieszkowski accused Michelet of defending a *juste-milieu* and compared himself to Lamartine, a progressive conservative who sat on the right of the National Assembly but in fact was much closer to the left.[2] Given the existing polemical conditions Cieszkowski rightly foresaw that the subtleties of this position would pass unnoticed. The accuracy of this judgement makes the *Gott und Palingenesie* the least satisfying of Cieszkowski's works both for its author and its readers.

At the same time, Cieszkowski participated in the last major campaign of the Hegelian school, its defensive battle against Schelling. In 1841, a new Prussian monarch fearful of growing philosophical radicalism invited Schelling to Berlin to counter Hegel's negative teaching with a positive philosophy of revelation. This decision, marking the end of their official protection, profoundly shook all the Hegelians, whatever their internal quarrels.[3] Ironically, however, it was Cieszkowski, receptive to Schelling's ideas to the extent of being accused of crypto-Schellingianism, who took the initiative in organizing resistance to this encroachment.[4] During December 1842 Cieszkowski persuaded a number of colleagues to co-operate in founding a philosophical society and journal where critical

[1] J. E. Erdmann, *A History of Philosophy*, translated by W. S. Hough, 4th edn (New York, Macmillan, 1897), vol. III, p.70.

[2] Cieszkowski, *Gott und Palingenesie*, pp. 8–9.

[3] For the politics of academic philosophy here see Max Lenz, *Geschichte der königlichen Friedrich Wilhelm Universität zu Berlin* (Halle, 1910–18), vol. II, p. 47. Engels gives a vivid account of this event and its impact on the Hegelians in his 'Schelling und die Offenbarung: Kritik der neuesten Reaktionsversuchs gegen die freie Philosophie', *Marx–Engels Werke, Ergänzungsband, Schriften bis 1844; Zweiter Teil: Friedrich Engels*, pp. 173–224.

[4] Cieszkowski to Michelet, letter no. 11, 20 December 1841, in Kühne, *Graf August Cieszkowski*, p. 390, expresses his impatience in awaiting the text of Schelling's first lecture. Cieszkowski prefaced the Polish translation of this lecture in terms much kinder to Schelling than might be expected of virtually any other Hegelian: 'Uwagi na temat mowy Schellinga', *Biblioteka Warszawska*, II, 1 (1842), pp. 424–6 (signed: AC). However, charges of Schellingianism were laid against Cieszkowski by Michelet, who based himself solely on the *Gott und Palingenesie* without any reference to their correspondence. C.-L. Michelet, *Entwicklungsgeschichte der neuesten deutschen Philosophie mit besonderer Rücksicht auf dem gegenwärtigen Kampf Schellings mit der Hegelschen Schule* (Berlin, Duncker und Humblot, 1843), pp. 394–5.

and divisive tendencies would be put aside in favour of a positive and progressive concern for the cardinal questions of knowledge and social life.[1] The result of his efforts was the Philosophische Gesellschaft, which eventually managed to find an appropriate house publication.[2]

The Society survived under various names into the 1890s but it never acquired either the role or the character which Cieszkowski had sought.[3] Even in its original statutes the goal proposed by Cieszkowski and Michelet of 'leading philosophy into life' had given way to the more modest aim of 'all-sided philosophical development'.[4] The revolution of 1848, which dashed the hopes of most liberal Hegelians, left the Society virtually moribund, and even after having revived in the 1850s with new and important members such as Moses Hess and Ferdinand Lassalle, the Society lost its initial purpose to such an extent that by the 1870s it had shed its Hegelian character.[5] Although Cieszkowski continued to support its efforts with generous material assistance, he turned his hopes for the active and social realization of philosophy elsewhere.

As one reflects on Cieszkowski's role within the Hegelian school and his philosophical writings in this period, it becomes clear that although the sense of the work is to free its author of Hegel's attitudes, particularly in respect to the ties among philosophy, political activity and the future, Cieszkowski remains wedded to the notion of reconciliation which constitutes the most central impulse of Hegelian philosophy. As did Hegel, Cieszkowski considers reconciliation between the ideal and the real, between aspirations and attainments, to be both the profoundest human yearning and the ultimate goal of history. Unlike Hegel, however, Cieszkowski affirms that philosophy, even Hegelian philosophy, is unable to satisfy this human need and historical imperative. True reconciliation requires not only intellectual but material, social, political fulfilment. It means not only understanding one's circumstances but shaping them in

---

[1] The foundation and subsequent history of the Philosophische Gesellschaft are described in detail in Kühne, *Graf August Cieszkowski*, pp. 136–247, 320–52.

[2] Having tried various schemes the Society came to an agreement with the *Jahrbücher für spekulative Philosophie und die philosophische Bearbeitung der empirischen Wissenschaften*, familiarly known as *Noacks Jahrbücher*. In 1853 the Society founded its own review, *Der Gedanke*. As might be expected Cieszkowski was to find this title unduly one-sided; Cieszkowski to Michelet, letter no. 27, 1 November 1854, in Kühne, *Graf August Cieszkowski*, pp. 407–8.

[3] The Philosophische Gesellschaft virtually disappeared between 1848 and 1853. In the 1850s it was known first as the Philosophische Mittagsgesellschaft and then as the Philosophische Gesellschaft zu Berlin. See Kühne, *Graf August Cieszkowski*, *passim*.

[4] Michelet, *Wahrheit aus meinem Leben*, p. 190. Michelet's memoirs are an invaluable source for the history of the Society and academic Hegelianism in general.

[5] *Ibid.*, p. 202.

such a way as to abolish physical want and structural conflict. It calls for conscious action, informed by philosophy, willed in virtue, which draws on all the positive tendencies of the epoch. Above all, reconciliation is a programme to cope with the urgencies of an age of transformation. Not surprisingly, the content of this programme is to be found in Cieszkowski's political and social writings, including the *Our Father*, which followed the *Prolegomena* and spelled out its hopes.

III
France: the social question in bourgeois society

Shortly after publishing the *Prolegomena to Historiosophy* and completing his doctoral dissertation,[1] Cieszkowski travelled to France, which was to be the focal point of his activities for the coming decade. To be sure, he was entering an intellectual terrain familiar to him from his readings; for Cieszkowski, as for so many others, Paris was a pilgrimage. Nevertheless, the experience of France under the bourgeois monarchy was to be a considerable revelation. Briefly stated, three aspects of contemporary France attracted Cieszkowski's attention and were to be reflected in his writings: in French socialism Cieszkowski encountered a concrete prefiguration of social life as adumbrated in the *Prolegomena*; in French society as a whole, he discovered not only a vivid example of the inadequacies of *laissez-faire* economics, *juste-milieu* liberalism, and rampant individualism but also a laboratory for the application of his own social and economic schemes; finally, in the underlying spiritual malaise of the period with its bizarre manifestation of redemptive fervour and messianism Cieszkowski found confirmation of his own beliefs concerning the pervasive nature of religious life and the urgent need for religious regeneration.[2]

---

[1] The dissertation, *De philosophiae ionicae, ingenio, vi, loco* has not survived. However, Cieszkowski later published on the same subject in Polish presumably reproducing the same material; 'Rzecz o filozofii jońskiej jako wstęp do historii filozofii', *Biblioteka Warszawska*, I, I (1841), pp. 287–306 and 536–61. Although the article remains unfinished its apparent continuation can be found in Kühne, *Graf August Cieszkowski*, pp. 431–40, where pp. 9–16 of the German manuscript of the dissertation appear.

[2] Literature on this period is abundant. Concerning the French socialists see Maxime Leroy, *Histoire des idées sociales en France*, vol. II: *De Babeuf à Tocqueville*, vol. III: *D'Auguste Comte à P.-J. Proudhon* (Paris, Gallimard, 1962, 1954). For the relation between socialism and other currents see David O. Evans, *Social Romanticism in France, 1830–1848* (Oxford, Clarendon Press, 1951). For the relation between religion and society, see Duroselle, *Les débuts du catholicisme social*, as well as D. G. Charlton, *Secular Religions in France 1815–1870* (London, Oxford University Press, 1963).

The *Diaries* give us an insight into Cieszkowski's activities and impressions during his first year in Paris. He divided his working time among public lectures, readings, discussions with French intellectuals, and observations of various social and industrial novelties. Thus, Cieszkowski assiduously attended sessions of the Académie des Sciences Morales et Politiques, where the concerns of liberal economists predominated but where one could hear critical studies of the working class as well.[1] He continued to read voraciously and encyclopedically, with more emphasis than previously on economics.[2] Above all, he succeeded in meeting a veritable galaxy of notables.

The wide range of Cieszkowski's acquaintances in Paris was quite astounding.[3] Through Louis Wołowski, a Polish emigré economist who was to assume the presidency of the Académie des Sciences Morales et Politiques as well as the editorship of the liberal *Journal des Economistes*[4], Cieszkowski came to know the liberal economic establishment – Auguste Blanqui, Hippolyte de Passy, P. L. E. Rossi[5] – as well as a very important outsider, Pierre-Joseph Proudhon.[6] Moreover, he had easy access to official ideologues – Royer-Collard and Victor Cousin in particular[7] – as

---

[1] *Diaries*, II, pp. 13–14 (November 1838 – February 1839). Cieszkowski particularly noted a series of lectures on Corsica by A. Blanqui, who occupied the chair of political economy in Paris until his death in 1854 and who was a brother of the famous revolutionary. He was also impressed with graphic descriptions of working-class misery by Villermé, author of *Tableau de la situation de la classe ouvrière* (Paris, 1840).

[2] Cieszkowski's readings for November 1838, for instances, include the following: Aristotle, *De caelo*; Wroński, *Rails mobiles ou chemin de fer*; Besson, *Histoire financière de la France. Religion saint-simonienne: recueil des Brochures*; Wołowski, *Régime hypothécaire*; Blackstone, *Commentaires sur les lois anglaises* etc. *Diaries* II, p. 13.

[3] Virtually all Cieszkowski's acquaintances mentioned here are discussed, or at least noted, in Leroy, *Histoire des idées*. For a catalogue of influences of these acquaintances on Cieszkowski's writings both before and after his Paris visit, see Walicki, 'Francuskie inspiracje myśli filozoficzno-religijnej Augusta Cieszkowskiego'. For an exhaustive list, see Cieszkowski's *Diaries*.

[4] See Jules Rambaud, 'Louis Wolowski' in Léon Say and Joseph Chailley, *Nouveau dictionnaire d'économie politique*, vol. II (Paris, Guillaumin, 1892), pp. 1192–4.

[5] P. L. E. Rossi (1787–1848) professor at the Faculty of Law, was later to serve as secretary of state for Pius IX. See Say and Chailley, *Nouveau dictionnaire*, pp. 755–8. Passy (1793–1880) was to play an active political role but at that time was known mainly for his work *De l'aristocratie considérée dans ses rapports avec les progrès de la civilisation* (Paris, 1826).

[6] Cieszkowski's name appears in Proudhon's notebooks with the comment 'l'ami de Wolowski' and reappears occasionally: Pierre-Joseph Proudhon, *Carnets*, edited by P. Haubtmann, vols. I–III (Paris, M. Rivière, 1961–68), vol. I, pp. 177 and 234; vol. II, p. 258; vol. III, p. 80.

[7] *Diaries* II, p. 13 (29 November 1838) mentions a long conversation with Cousin about 'Berlin, Fichte, Göschel, historiosophy'.

well as such eminent figures as Jules Michelet and Edgar Quinet.[1] At the same time, however, Cieszkowski met a number of leading socialists – Lamennais, Pierre Leroux – and he frequented the offices of the Fourierist publication, *La Phalange*, where he became familiar with Louis Blanc and Victor Considérant, the leader of Fourierist reformism.[2] Outside the mainstream of Parisian currents, Cieszkowski noted his meetings with two unorthodox thinkers: Ballanche, whose palingenetic theories Cieszkowski already admired,[3] and Hoene-Wroński, an inventor and self-styled messianist concerned with combining mathematics with mysticism.[4]

Cieszkowski studied his physical and social surroundings as well. He visited prisons and factories, expressed a fascination with trains, pursued his agronomical concerns.[5] To a large extent, these activities were the continuation of previous interests, so one might say that in this, as well as in other respects, Cieszkowski's discovery of France offered him not only novelty but confirmation of earlier ideas and an opportunity to elaborate previously nurtured schemes. For instance, while still in Poland Cieszkowski had referred to the discovery of three new types of manure as a particularly significant omen and wrote – in all seriousness – of sweetening human life by the introduction of sugar beet plantation.[6] Accordingly,

[1] *Diaries* II, p. 14 (23 December 1838) mentions meeting Michelet. Concerning Quinet, see Zaleski, 'Edgar Quinet et Auguste Cieszkowski'.

[2] *Diaries* II, pp. 14–15 (8, 15, 26 December 1838); also January 1839. Cieszkowski also mentions visiting Fourier's grave.

[3] *Diaries* II, p. 12 (3 November 1838), records meeting Ballanche, whom Cieszkowski had already read in Poland and who was cited in chapter I of the *Prolegomena*. Leroy, *Histoire des idées*, vol. II, pp. 126–33, describes Ballanche's doctrine as plebeian mysticism, a marriage of Condorcet and Bossuet. On this important precursor of social Catholicism who influenced the Saint-Simonians and Lamennais see further Charles Huit, *La vie et les oeuvres de Ballanche* (Paris and Lyon, E. Vitte, 1904).

[4] Joseph-Marie Hoene-Wroński (1776–1853) has been relegated to comparative obscurity in large measure because of his eccentricities, personal and intellectual. However, Balzac, apparently fascinated by this figure, incorporated him into his *Recherche de l'Absolu* and *Les martyres ignorés*. For an account of Hoene-Wroński's peculiar philosophy and notion of messianism see *Hoene-Wronski: une philosophie de la création*, edited with a foreword and bibliography by Philippe D'Arcy (Paris, Seghers, 1970).

[5] *Diaries* II, p. 10 (24 August – 14 September 1838). Cieszkowski attaches particular significance to having begun his twenty-fifth year on a train. On that occasion too he describes the 'gorgeous view from the Belgian border, blooming flowers and agriculture, pastures, plantations, orchards and hedges, a choir of cattle'. *Diaries* II, p. 11, 1–16 October 1838, mentions 'visit to Institute for young prisoners'.

[6] *Diaries* II, p. 2 (18 June 1837): 'In almost every event this year some important social purpose is to be seen. We even find it where we least expect it. For example, the discovery this year of three types of fabrication of artificial manure is an extremely important omen. We are approaching a radical reform of the world in which Nature

when abroad he carefully noted the fertility of different soils and sought out developments in the sugar beet industry. All in all, he must have seemed an extremely earnest, even humourless, young man in the eyes of his numerous acquaintances.

In 1839 Cieszkowski published his first economic work, a three-hundred-page treatise which appeared in French as *Du crédit et de la circulation*.[1] In fact, the plan and even a draft of the book were ready much earlier. Notwithstanding the Hegelians' neglect of economics at that time, Cieszkowski had read a number of classical English liberals while still in Poland. Under the influence of a continental tradition which saw economics as a branch of public policy – a tradition exemplified for Cieszkowski in the person of Frederick Skarbek[2] – he adopted a critical posture towards these English doctrines reproaching them for their anti-state and even anti-social bias.[3] This criticism found reinforcement in Cieszkowski's reading of Sismondi, who had abandoned his own early liberalism in favour of a more historically oriented and more compassionate political economy.[4] Although it may be rash to list Cieszkowski among Sismondi's disciples alongside Pecqueur and Villeneuve-Bargemont it should be noted that he read the latter assiduously and sympathetically.[5] Taken together

will also know a rebirth and in which original sin will be not only morally but physically evened out by its results. The earth will be freed of this mighty curse and from now on it will give birth to more than merely shrubs and thorns. For this to happen it will need substantial nourishment of which this manure will be the means'. See also Cieszkowski to Michelet, letter no. 1, 30 June 1836, in Kühne, *Graf August Cieszkowski*, pp. 357–8.

[1] 1st edn (Paris, Treuttel et Wurtz, 1839).

[2] Count Skarbek (1793–1866), author of *Théorie des richesses sociales*, vols. I–II (Paris, 1829); influenced by Say and Sismondi, he is considered a precursor of List. Skarbek's activities in creating a savings bank for the lower classes and in the Warsaw Society of Friends of Knowledge coincide with Cieszkowski's interests. See Wacław Szubert, *Studia o Frederyku Skarbku jako ekonomiście*, Prace z historji myśli społecznej, III (Łódź, 1954).

[3] *Diaries* II, *passim*, comments on Smith, Ricardo and MacCulloch.

[4] Simonde de Sismondi (1773–1842) in the 1826 revised edition of his *Nouveaux principes d'économie politique* (1st edn Paris, 1819), considerably modified his original unconditional liberalism. See 'Sismondi and the origins of the Critical School', in Charles Gide and Charles Rist, *A History of Economic Doctrines*, 2nd edn, translated by R. Richards (Boston, D. C. Heath, 1948). Also Henryk Grossman, *Simonde de Sismondi et ses théories économiques: une nouvelle interprétation de sa pensée* (Warsaw, Bibliotheca Universitatis Liberae Polonae, 1924).

[5] *Diaries* II, p. 3 (December 1837 – January 1838), lists Villeneuve-Bargemont's *Économie politique chrétienne* (volumes I–II, Paris, 1834) among Cieszkowski's readings. For a study of this Catholic critic of industrialism see M. Ring, *Villeneuve-Bargemont: Precursor of Modern Social Catholicism 1784–1850* (Milwaukee, Bruce, 1935); for his influence see Duroselle, *Les débuts du catholicisme social*, *passim*.

with his Hegelian training, it is this background which defined Ciesz-kowski's attitude to economic questions.

Du crédit et de la circulation contains both a particular proposal for the reform of the monetary system and a general inquiry into economic policy. The specific concern of the work is a new type of interest-bearing note based on real values, primarily land, which would both expand a nation's real capital stock and reduce the amount of 'fictitious' fiduciary assets. If consistently applied, this scheme would not only create new capital and guarantee existing assets but would amount to an abolition of money in its present form. The broader theme of the work is the role of the state as economic agent. In this context, Cieszkowski undertakes a critique of both liberalism and protectionism as he searches for a proper principle of demarcation between the public and the private spheres.

The scheme for interest-bearing notes may appear idiosyncratic. In fact, it belongs to a well-defined tradition which reaches back in France to John Law and later the assignats of the French Revolution.[1] Both experiments sought to make the state a creditor rather than a borrower by drawing on land instead of precious metal as a guarantor of value. Although in other countries similar schemes enjoyed various fortunes,[2] in France they failed dismally, discrediting not only themselves but all manner of credit institutions and condemning French banking and finance to extreme underdevelopment. In addition to these historical precedents, Cieszkowski's scheme can be easily situated in the context of the concerns of contemporary French socialists. With a few notable exceptions,[3] they – and later such gallicized Hegelian radicals as Moses Hess[4] – saw the abolition of money as a precondition of any overall social reform.[5] Other, more moderate economists contented themselves with attacking paper

---

[1] See H. Svoboda, *Grund und Boden als Wahrungsunterlage* (Nürnberg, 1928).

[2] G. R. Bark, *Boden als Geld: ein Beitrag zur Geschichte des Papiergelds* (Berlin, E. Ebering, 1930), lists experiments ranging from eighteenth-century Silesia to the Massachusetts Bay Colony.

[3] Neither the Fourierists nor Saint-Simonians advocated abolishing money and indeed the latter extolled the banking system. See Henri Louvancour, *De Henri de Saint-Simon à Charles Fourier. Etude sur le socialisme romantique français de 1830* (Chartres, Durand, 1913). Also J. B. Vergeot, *Le crédit comme stimulant et régulateur de l'industrie; la conception Saint-Simonienne* (Paris, 1918).

[4] See Hess's article 'Uber das Geldwesen' first published in *Rheinische Jahrbücher zur Gesellschaftlichen Reform*, 1 (1845), reprinted in *Moses Hess. Socialistische Aufsätze 1841–1847*, ed. Theodor Zlocisti (Berlin, Welt Verlag, 1921), and discussed in Edmund Silberner, *Moses Hess: Geschichte seines Lebens* (Leiden, Brill, 1966), pp. 184–92.

[5] See Leszek Kołakowski's essay on the yearning for a world without money, 'Dlaczego potrzeba nam pieniędzy?' *Aneks*, 5 (Spring 1974), pp. 10–30.

money and seeking more authentic standards of value.[1] Thus, virtually all social reformers in France about 1840 could have been expected to sympathize with Cieszkowski's scheme – although most would have probably found it timid, inadequate or ineffective.

Both Cieszkowski himself and his contemporaries considered the plan for interest-bearing notes to be the essence of *Du crédit et de la circulation*. In the context of this study, however, it is Cieszkowski's perspective on the state as economic agent which is particularly illuminating, for it both reveals an original attempt to apply philosophy to economics and demonstrates the continuity connecting Cieszkowski's seemingly disparate concerns. Basically, Cieszkowski proposes a common-sense principle: the state can best encourage economic progress by co-ordinating public and private activities in such a way as to assume functions connected with the general well-being and abstain from intervention whenever the pursuit of private interest does not collide with public well-being. Significantly, however, Cieszkowski attains this principle by a dialectical reasoning which presents the stultifying prohibitive system as thesis, anarchic and individualistic liberalism as antithesis and his own principle as synthesis. However schematic it may seem, this reasoning and Cieszkowski's defence of both his overall economic notions and his monetary proposals in terms of dialectics proved convincing for his own generation. Indeed, virtually all the French readers of *Du crédit et de la circulation* commented admiringly on the solid philosophical grounding of the work.[2] Similarly, Cieszkowski's extended organic analogy which defined an economic body with essential organs and reproductive and circulatory systems seemed persuasive to his audience.[3] Today, it is primarily of interest as a

---

[1] Valentin Wagner, *Geschichte der Kredittheorien. Eine dogmenkritische Darstellung* (Vienna, J. Springer, 1937). Also Marc Aucuy, *Systèmes socialistes d'échange* (Paris, F. Alcan, 1907).

[2] Michel Chevalier (1806–1879), former Saint-Simonian and later liberal minister under the second empire, wrote in a review article of *Du crédit et de la circulation*, published in the *Journal des Débats*, 22 August 1840: 'we are intentionally joining the title of doctor to Monsieur Cieszkowski's name... nothing could give us a better idea of the spirit of this excellent work or of the special merit which distinguishes it. The philosophical capacity of M. Cieszkowski deserves a title in our eyes... M. Cieszkowski's book shows what results one can hope to attain regarding public and private credit, banks, loans, the monetary system, all with the help of a good philosophical method, a tight logic and a sharp metaphysic... It proves that philosophy does not force those who cultivate it to isolate themselves in a distant cloud. One can remain philosopher and yet, when necessary, descend from the sublime to touch, measure and weigh the interest of the earth'.

[3] It may be noted, for instance, that in 'Über das Geldwesen' Hess resorts to a similar organic analogy to describe the evils wrought by money. See Silberner, *Moses Hess: Geschichte seines Lebens*, p. 197.

reminder of the similar organic analogies in the *Prolegomena* and thus as an indication of the pervasiveness of this image in Cieszkowski's thought.

The success of *Du crédit et de la circulation* remains difficult to evaluate. Certainly, it was Cieszkowski's most widely read work, going through three separate editions in his own lifetime.[1] Thus, its success was more durable than that of the *Prolegomena*, which after its initial reception was virtually forgotten, only to be rediscovered in this century. Moreover, *Du crédit et de la circulation* attracted attention not only in France but throughout Europe. In Russia, the work was invoked as evidence at the trial of the first Russian socialist group, the Fourierist Petrashevskiĭ Circle.[2] The British economist, H. Macleod, polemicized against the work, drawing the author's rebuttals in the book's later editions.[3] Elsewhere too, references to the work were frequent.[4]

Above all, *Du crédit et de la circulation* impressed and influenced Pierre-Joseph Proudhon, who considered credit reform the very crux of his social programme and for whom Hegelian philosophy held a peculiar fascination.[5] Proudhon's tribute to Cieszkowski in the *Système des contradictions économiques* bears full citation:

The problem of credit is to find a combination where the circulating agent would

[1] 1839; 1847; 1884.

[2] Wiktoria Sliwowska, *Sprawa Pietraszewców* (Warsaw, Wydawnictwo Naukowe, 1964), pp. 203–6.

[3] See Henry Dunning Macleod's (1821–1902) influential *Dictionary of Political Economy: Biographical, Bibliographical, Historical and Practical*, vol. I, A–C (London, Longman, Green, Roberts, 1863), pp. 431–2.

[4] *Ibid.*: 'Under ordinary circumstances we should have passed over this work without notice, merely lamenting that the author had wasted so much ingenious labor in bringing forward as new, the doctrines of John Law, which have seduced so many persons. But when we find that several of the ablest economists on the continent have approved of Count Cieszkowski's doctrines, the matter assumes a very different aspect indeed, and is calculated to inspire some alarm, that these pernicious follies should become more popular. To our inexpressible amazement, economists so well known as M. Joseph Garnier, M. Baudrillart, the associate of M. Chevalier at the Collège de France, and Professor Boccardo, the author of the great Italian Dictionary of Political Economy, have all adopted the doctrines of Cieszkowski.' The reference is to G. Boccardo, *Dizionario della economica politica e del commercio*, vol. I (Turin, Franco, 1857), pp. 518–19. Clément-Joseph Garnier (1813–1881) was a founding member of the liberal Société d'Economie Politique as well as the *Journal des Economistes*.

[5] Referring to his forthcoming *Contradictions économiques*, Proudhon wrote: 'It will be a general criticism of political economy from the point of view of social antinomies. At the end I hope to teach the French public what the dialectic is... I have never read Hegel but I am certain that it is his logic which I shall use in my next work'. Letter to Bergmann, 19 January 1845, *Correspondance de Proudhon*, vol. II (Paris, Lacroix, 1875), pp. 175–6.

be, at the same time, and in an equal degree, both a perfect guarantee – like money – and a perfect sign of credit – like a banknote. Moreover, it should be productive like the earth and capital, hence incapable of lying around uselessly. This combination exists, M. Cieszkowski tells us, and he proves it to us in the most beautiful philosophical language and with the most perfect experience. This double quality should certainly make him almost unintelligible to both economists and philosophers.

. . .

Will M. Cieszkowski's system be put into practice? If we are to rely on the economic movement which is sweeping society, we can certainly believe that it will be. All ideas in France revolve about mortgage reform and the organization of land credit, two things which in a more or less acknowledged form necessarily imply the application of this system. M. Cieszkowski, like a true artist, has traced the idea of this project. He has described the economic law to which all further reforms of society are subject. The different ways in which it will be applied and changes in detail are not important; the idea is his in his capacity as theoretician and even, in the case of realization, in his capacity as prophet.[1]

Unfortunately for both Proudhon and Cieszkowski, the *Système des contradictions économiques* is best remembered by Marx's scathing attack on it which appeared as *Misère de la Philosophie*; in fact, it was Proudhon's pretensions to Hegelian scientificity which drew Marx's best-aimed barbs.[2] Engels' later unkind words about *Du crédit et de la circulation* can also be understood in the light of this polemic.[3]

Even apart from the Marx–Proudhon feud, however, *Du crédit et de la circulation* incurred heavy, if contradictory, criticism as both excessively and inadequately utopian as well as technically imperfect. Predictably, a German reviewer scoffed at it as another system promising universal happiness and important only to the extent that it was a sign of the times.[4] Ironically, the Fourierist *La Phalange* also saw the work as evidence of a

[1] Pierre-Joseph Proudhon, *Système des contradictions économiques, ou Philosophie de la misère*, vol. II, in *Oeuvres complètes*, edited by C. Bouglé and H. Moysett (Paris, M. Rivière, 1923), pp. 110–11.

[2] Karl Marx, *The Poverty of Philosophy*, being a translation of the *Misère de la philosophie* (a reply to *La Philosophie de la misère* of M. Proudhon) with a preface by F. Engels, translated by H. Quelch (Chicago, Kern, 1910), chapter II, part 7: 'M. Proudhon flatters himself on having given a critique of both political economy and communism. In fact, he is beneath them both...He wants to be the synthesis; he is a compound error. He wishes to play the man of science, standing above both bourgeois and proletarians: he is but a petit bourgeois thrown about between labour and capital'.

[3] F. Engels, letter to Bernstein, 25–31 January 1882, *Marx–Engels Werke*, vol. XXXV, p. 267: 'Bürkli's [a Swiss Fourierist – AL] mortgage note which bears interest and represents money is even much older than the arch-confused old Hegelian Polak [*der urkonfuse, althegelsche Polacke*] Cieszkowski.'

[4] E. Baumstark, review of *Du crédit et de la circulation*, in *Jahrbücher für wissenschaftliche Kritik*, 119 (June 1842), pp. 944–59.

'profound instinct' but rejected it for failing to understand that the root causes of human misery lay not in the monetary but in the distributive system.[1] Finally, Cieszkowski's compatriot and later political colleague, Karol Libelt, posed a number of incisive questions: how was it possible for the same capital to produce a separate profit for its owner and another for the holder of the interest-bearing note without making one a deduction from the other? who would actually benefit from the scheme, particularly since the truly destitute would have no access to the notes at all?[2] In short, Cieszkowski's unwillingness to commit himself to a specific ideological camp once again deprived him of the sympathetic audience which his work deserved.

The decade following the publication of *Du crédit et de la circulation* was a period of apprenticeship for Cieszkowski as he followed his own call to make philosophy practical and to give concrete form to the social life of the future. Most of his writings in this period were occasional pieces connected with very specific issues but they merit consideration as efforts to apply the theoretical principles of the *Prolegomena*, *Du crédit et de la circulation*, and the emerging *Our Father*.

Cieszkowski's attempts to translate *Du crédit et de la circulation* into operational terms led him into involvement with the incipient French land-credit movement and publication of an article entitled 'Du crédit immobilier'.[3] In fact, the article originated as a report of the agricultural credit committee at the Central Congress of Agriculture where Cieszkowski participated as delegate and rapporteur.[4] The Congress is significant primarily as a milestone toward the formation of a land-credit bank in France[5] and the article itself is of interest for the strong role which it assigns to the state in regulating and encouraging credit reform. Above all, this phase of Cieszkowski's activities indicates the sort of institutional and reformist measure through which he hoped to realize his plans.

[1] E. B., 'Des banques administratives', *La Phalange*, vol. IV (1846), p. 476.

[2] Karol Libelt, 'Du crédit et de la circulation', *Pisma Krytyczne*, vol. V (Posen, 1851), pp. 17ff.

[3] First published as 'Du crédit foncier', *Journal des Economistes*, XVII (May 1847), pp. 263ff.; annexed to the third edition of *Du crédit et de la circulation* (Paris, Guillaumin, 1884), and reprinted as a separate pamphlet *Du crédit immobilier; rapport fait au congrès central d'agriculture* (Paris, 1847).

[4] Regarding the Congress see the 'Chronique', *Journal des Economistes*, XVII (16 March 1847).

[5] The Crédit Foncier bank was established in 1852 with Wołowski as head of its Paris branch. See Wołowski's article on *crédit foncier* in Charles Coquelin and Urbain Guillaumin, *Dictionnaire de l'économie politique*, vol. I (Paris, Guillaumin, 1854), pp. 497–508.

Most of Cieszkowski's articles of the 1840s reaffirm his critical view of *laissez-faire* liberalism,[1] but their principal concern is the phenomenon of pauperism and its remedies. The very definition of the problem points to a limitation in Cieszkowski's perspective: by 1840 the use of the term pauperism was an anachronism inasmuch as it denoted a pre-industrial poverty unrelated to the structural unemployment and enforced misery of the new working class.[2] In fact, however, Cieszkowski was aware of both the novelty of the problem and the inadequacy of traditional palliatives. Like many of his contemporaries he sought solutions in the power of association – which he understood as the systematic organization of philanthropy.[3] Thus, in a seminal article, 'On village shelters', Cieszkowski urged the establishment of a system of moral and practical education at the local level which would relieve parents of part of the burden of child-rearing even as it trained conscientious and qualified future workers.[4] In spite of the breadth of the reform advocated and the progressive, Pestalozzian character of the schooling proposed it is the paternalism of these suggestions which strikes today's reader most forcefully. Cieszkowski's plans for assuring villagers both purpose and security, eventually from cradle to grave, show that association as he interpreted it was not necessarily a synonym but often a substitute for principles of self-help.

This sort of limitation applies in a lesser degree to Cieszkowski's most notable article of the period, 'On the improvement of the condition of rural workers'.[5] First delivered as an address before the assembly of a Provincial Agricultural Union, more or less a German counterpart to the French Agricultural Congress, the article seeks to refute some of the

---

[1] See Kühne, *Graf August Cieszkowski*, pp. 237–45 for Cieszkowski's comments on a paper concerning differential tariffs given at the Philosophische Gesellschaft. Also Cieszkowski's 'Organizacya handlu drzewem i przemysłu leśnego' ('Organization of the wood trade and forest industry'), *Biblioteka Warszawska*, I (1843), pp. 112–43.

[2] See W. Conze, 'Vom "Pöbel" zum "Proletariat". Sozialgeschichtliche Voraussetzungen für den Sozialismus'. *Vierteljahrschrift für Sozial- und Wirtschaftsgeschichte*, LI (1954), pp. 333–64.

[3] See Hans Stein, 'Pauperismus und Assoziation', *International Review for Social History*, I (1936).

[4] Cieszkowski, 'O ochronach wiejskich', *Biblioteka Warszawska*, II, part 2 (1842), pp. 367–411. Appeared as a separate pamphlet in German, *Antrag zu Gunsten der Klein-Kinder-Bewahranstalten als Grundlage der Volks-Erziehung* (Berlin, 1855).

[5] *Zur Verbesserung der Lage der Arbeiter auf dem Lande. Ein Vortrag gehalten an der zweiten General Sammlung des landwirtschaftlichen Provinzial-Vereins für die Mark Brandenburg und die Niederlausitz, am 17 mai 1845* (Berlin, Schröder, 1846). A French translation appeared in the *Journal des Economistes*, XII (October 1845) as well as a separate brochure, *Sur les moyens d'améliorer le sort de la population des campagnes* (Batignolles, De Hennuyer, 1846).

Assembly's least enlightened positions.[1] Above all, however, it contains a concrete proposition for profit-sharing among all the workers on an estate – a proposition, Cieszkowski tells his listeners, already tested and successfully applied on his own lands. The very cautious tone of this address can be explained by its context: the assembled German landlords were more interested in economic efficiency than social experiments. In spite of this apparent moderation, it is clear that Cieszkowski is defending a goal which amounts to no less than a universalization of property. The actual feasibility and implication of making everyone a co-owner of capital leave much room for speculation. It may be noted, however, that in spite of the subsequent evolution of socialist thought this conception fully conforms to the thinking of early socialists such as Saint-Simon and Fourier who were prepared to generalize proprietorship if this would further their ultimate goal of human happiness.[2]

Beyond these occasional and largely circumstantial articles, in 1844 Cieszkowski also published *De la pairie et de l'aristocratie moderne*.[3] Briefly stated, this short work is a legislative reform project concerned with revitalizing the largely ineffective and illegitimate French Upper House. In Cieszkowski's view, the problem is one of finding a principle of selection to reflect adequately the Upper House's proper role as representative of universal interests. Election would simply reproduce the particularisms of the Lower Chamber, whereas hereditary selection, whatever its advantages, would clash with the spirit of the age. Only if the most meritorious members can be co-opted from every walk of life and the means provided to ensure their material independence[4] will we see the emergence of a 'popular patriciate' adequate to its intended role and to the requirements of the times.

This variant on a familiar meritocratic theme draws its force from the critique of bourgeois society on which it rests. As he reflected on France under the July monarchy, Cieszkowski was appalled by the pervasiveness of a rapacious individualism which was destroying the nation's social and

---

[1] The *Landwirtschaftliche Vereine* must also be understood as an aspect of associationism. See W. Conze (ed.), *Staat und Gesellschaft im deutschen Vormärz 1815–1848* (Stuttgart, E. Klett, 1962).

[2] See Louvancour, *De Henri de Saint-Simon à Charles Fourier*, as well as George Lichtheim, *The Origins of Socialism* (New York and Washington, Praeger, 1969), chapter II.

[3] Paris, Amyot, 1844; 164 pages.

[4] Cieszkowski realistically assumes that most peers will be men of means, but in order to prevent property ownership from opening or barring entry into the peerage he advocates a system of honoraria (*ibid.*, p. 74).

political cohesion.[1] Egoism and opportunism were running rampant, undermining even such institutions as the Chamber of Deputies which should have been bulwarks against the vitiation of democracy. On the basis of this experience Cieszkowski argued that each democracy requires a corresponding aristocracy, and thus the broad purpose of *De la pairie et de l'aristocratie moderne* could be defined as that of developing an appropriate and acceptable theory of elites for the modern state.

In reading this work one cannot help comparing its ideas to those of such more familiar nineteenth-century thinkers as Saint-Simon, Hegel and Tocqueville. Apart from Cieszkowski's overall indebtedness to Saint-Simon's vision of social relations in industrial society, it is clear that *De la pairie et de l'aristocratie moderne* owes much to Saint-Simon's *Organisateur*, which proposes a tri-cameral parliament composed of engineers, artists and *industriels* to replace the present holders of legislative power.[2] Hegel's influence is more diffuse but the core of this work – the plan to create a body or class which stands above civil society and represents universal interests – is directly related to the central preoccupations of the Hegelian polity.[3] It is Tocqueville's presence, however,

---

[1] The spirit of the work might be conveyed by citing Cieszkowski's indictment of individualism which introduces the chapter entitled 'On the necessity of a substantial power in the State': 'There exists an immense sore which threatens to invade contemporary society; in general terms this sore is called individualism: it is the progressive isolation of individuals, localities, specialities; it is the perpetual play of egoism which shakes all authority, all substantial ties. Whereas society evidently gravitates towards an ever more normal organization individuals become isolated in their tendencies, their opinions and in their acts. A petty and exclusive spirit has taken hold of the dominating mass of the nation, above all these *middle classes* which today alone constitute the *pays légal*' (*ibid.*, pp. 83–4).

[2] See C.-H. de Saint-Simon, *L'Organisateur*, November 1819–February 1820, in *Oeuvres de Saint-Simon publiées par les membres du conseil institué par Enfantin*, vol. IV (Paris, E. Dentu, 1869); reprinted as *Oeuvres de Claude-Henri de Saint-Simon*, vol. II (Paris, Anthropos, 1966). Cieszkowski's overall debt to Saint-Simon is well documented both in his *Diaries* and his published works, and has been discussed by Walicki, 'Francuskie inspiracje' as well as by Hepner, 'History and the Future'. Significantly, the Fourierist *Phalange* in reviewing *De la pairie et de l'aristocratie moderne* accused its author of propagating 'industrial feudalism', much the same criticism which it levelled at Saint-Simon himself. I. R., *La Phalange*, IV, pp. 174–8.

[3] Cieszkowski's recourse to Hegelian terms and concepts is so marked as to be almost instinctive. Thus, he describes the functions of the Upper House as those of representing the 'permanent interests, the universal element and the substantial tendencies of the state', (*De la pairie*, p. 22). To be sure, the qualities which Cieszkowski attributes to the Upper House correspond not to those of the Hegelian legislature (Hegel, *Philosophy of Right*, paragraphs 298–301) but to those of the universal class of civil servants (*ibid.*, paragraph 303). Nevertheless, the Hegelian flavour of the work is strong enough to have been noted by the Philosophische Gesellschaft. See *Noacks Jahrbücher für spekulative Philosophie*, I (1846) p. 180.

which is most keenly felt not merely because Cieszkowski appeals to Tocqueville's authority or because he proceeds in the manner of a sociological inquiry similar to that of *De la démocratie en Amérique*.[1] Above all, Cieszkowski shares Tocqueville's concern with the evolution of democracy towards petty and vulgar mediocrity. In some contrast to Tocqueville but with characteristic optimism Cieszkowski refuses to acknowledge this tendency as inevitable. His attempts to counter the trend as expressed in *De la pairie et de l'aristocratie moderne* demonstrate that even though Cieszkowski understood both the currents and needs of the emerging liberal industrial society he underestimated the strength of the very forces which he had himself identified.

From the perspective of the entire corpus of Cieszkowski's writings and activities, his experience of France can be seen as a logical consequence of the concerns expressed in the *Prolegomena to Historiosophy*. Both the grand schemes of *Du crédit et de la circulation* or *De la pairie et de l'aristocratie moderne* and the more modest proposals contained in the various articles on credit, education or rural welfare are elements of an apprenticeship for the heavier responsibilites which Cieszkowski was to assume after 1848 and for the slowly gestating *Our Father*. These years of apprenticeship confirmed Cieszkowski's earlier intuition that henceforth philosophy would have to be practically applied and that its most pressing task lay in the resolution of what was globally known as 'the social question'. At the same time, Cieszkowski's experience in the 1840s tempered plans, not in their intensity but in their scope and schedule. It became clear that the overall reform which he and so many others sought and which Cieszkowski visualized so clearly would have to be founded on a number of partial and intermediate reforms. When confronted with the choice between eschatology and compromise Cieszkowski did not waver, for unlike many of his contemporaries he did not find the two incompatible.

IV

Poland: messianism or reform

The 1840s were also years when Cieszkowski was attempting to define his attitude to his native land.[2] His protracted sojourns abroad were to some

---

[1] Cieszkowski's *Diaries* indicate that he both read and met Tocqueville. See *De la pairie*, pp. 70, 95 and 144.

[2] Perhaps the best insight into Cieszkowski's attitudes and state of thought in this period can be gleaned from the letters of his bosom friend, the Polish poet Zygmunt Krasiński (1812–1859), *Listy Zygmunta Krasińskiego do Augusta Cieszkowskiego*, vol. I–II, ed. J. Kallenbach, introduced by A. Żółtowski (Cracow, Gebethner, 1912).

extent an escape from the intellectually claustrophobic and politically desperate conditions of Tsarist Poland. At the same time, in spite of this self-imposed exile and his familiarity with leading Polish emigrés, Cieszkowski rigorously abstained from emigré politics under any form or banner.[1]

Cieszkowski's aloofness from the activities of his exiled compatriots can be understood in the light of the evolution of the Polish emigration: not only did it split into right and left factions but its dominant ethos turned towards an increasingly mystical messianism.[2] In essence, messianism as expounded by the Polish romantics was a philosophy of history which attributed redemptive qualities to Poland's sufferings; Poland was the Christ of nations crucified to save mankind as a whole.[3] To be sure, Cieszkowski was sympathetic to this vision even to the extent of echoing it in a modified and more universal form as early as the *Prolegomena to Historiosophy*. In the conditions of exile, however, these messianic ideas increased in fervour, millenarian imagery and apocalyptic violence, eventually degenerating into an obsessive national cult.[4] Obviously, Cieszkowski could not identify himself with this deviation and he kept ostensibly silent even as he continued to work on the significantly different interpretation of history, both past and future,

---

[1] Cieszkowski, *Diaries* II, p. 14, January 1839, records an evening at the house of Prince Cz[artoryski–AL], the leader of the right wing of the Polish emigration. Cieszkowski was also a frequent visitor at the Paris home of the great Polish bard, Adam Mickiewicz. See Władysław Mickiewicz, *Pamiętniki*, vol. I (Warsaw, Gebethner Wolff, 1926), p. 68.

[2] For the standard reference work on the Polish emigration see Ludomir Gadoń, *Emigracya polska; pierwsze lata po upadku powstania listopadowego* (Cracow, Spółka Wydawnicza Polska, 1902). More specifically, J. Ujejski, 'Allgemeiner Uberblick der religiös-sozialen Strömmungen unter der Polnischen Emigranten nach dem Jahr 1831', *Bulletin de l'Académie des Sciences de Cracovie* (1915), pp. 11–28.

[3] For a study in English of nineteenth-century messianism which looks briefly at the Polish variant see J. L. Talmon, *Political Messianism: The Romantic Phase* (New York, Praeger, 1960), especially pp. 265ff. For an interesting effort to theorize nineteenth-century messianism see Henri Desroche, 'Messianismes et utopies: note sur les origines du socialisme occidentale', *Archives de Sociologie des Religions*, VIII, 2 (1959), pp. 131–46.

[4] The most vivid manifestation of this degeneration is the hold which one Towiański exerted on the literary leader of the emigration, Mickiewicz. This mysterious seer accentuated Mickiewicz's anti-rationalist bias to the point of reducing the bard to madness. See J. Kallenbach, *Towiański na tle historycznym* (Cracow, Nakład Przeglądu Powszechnego, 1926). Even earlier, however, Mickiewicz's praise of Cieszkowski's *Gott und Palingenesie* betrayed such utter lack of sympathy with philosophy as a whole that it could only have been embarrassing to Cieszkowski. See Adam Mickiewicz, *Cours de littérature slave professé au Collège de France* (Paris, Martinet, 1860), lecture of 6 June 1843, no. XXII.

which was to become the *Our Father*.[1] Indeed, when seen against the backdrop of the prevalent mood and conceptions of the Polish emigration, the *Our Father* is not so much another version of messianism as an alternative to messianism.

Even while Cieszkowski continued to work primarily in France he attempted to exploit the possibilities for activity in Poland. In 1841 he co-operated in founding the *Biblioteka Warszawska*, an enlightened general periodical which was to be blessed with extraordinary longevity and was soon to become the herald of Polish positivism.[2] Here, apart from his material and organizational contributions, Cieszkowski published a number of articles, travel sketches and topical accounts. However, the limits to any intellectual enterprise in Russian Poland were so narrow that Cieszkowski chose to move to Posen, thus joining a number of like-minded compatriots drawn to this German province of Poland by the existence of a relatively liberal regime.[3] Within a few years Cieszkowski had integrated himself fully into this new environment and after 1848 Posen was to be the base for most of his activities as well as his most permanent home.

The values and attitudes brought to Posen by Cieszkowski and others fused with pre-existing tendencies to form what came to be known as 'organicism'. Perhaps best understood in contrast to the revolutionary messianism of the emigration and the feudalistic ethos of eastern Poland, organicism declared that national regeneration could only be brought about by hard labour, good husbandry, and useful industry. In short, the key to Poland's restoration lay in economic and intellectual development. It is not surprising that this doctrine of salvation through modernization should have flourished in one of Poland's most developed provinces where there was a possibility of co-operation between a strong bourgeoisie and a pragmatic gentry. Nor is it surprising that organicism should have found a more solid foundation in positivism than in the theories on which Cieszkowski drew. Nevertheless, Cieszkowski threw himself whole-heartedly into the organicist enterprise and remained closely identified with its fortunes.[4]

[1] Cieszkowski's keen concern and detailed monitoring of the spread of Towiański's 'Cause' is recorded in Krasiński, *Listy do Augusta Cieszkowskiego, passim.*

[2] For studies of this review see Henryk Lewestam, *Obraz najnowszego ruchu literackiego w Polsce* (Warsaw, S. Orgelbrand, 1859) as well as Antonina Kloskowska, 'Socjo-logiczne i filozoficzne koncepcje "Biblioteki Warszawskiej" w pierwszym dziesięcioleciu pisma 1841–1850', *Przegląd nauk Historycznych i Społecznych*, VII (1956), pp. 160–74.

[3] See Witold Jakóbczyk, *Studia nad dziejami Wielkopolski w XIX wieku. Dzieje pracy organicznej* I 1815–1850 (Poznań, Poznańskie Towarzystwo Przyjaciół Nauk, 1951).

[4] The best treatment of organicist ideology is Barbara Skarga, 'Praca organiczna a

Cieszkowski's article 'On the co-ordination of intellectual aims and works in the Grand Duchy of Posen' is both a personal manifesto marking his espousal of organicism and a warning that organicism must not become simply one faction among others.[1] Here as elsewhere, Cieszkowski reaffirms his conviction that the era of negation has ended; indeed, following Saint-Simon he consistently uses 'organic' to signify the opposite of negative.[2] Moreover, Cieszkowski insists that organicism can only succeed if it is founded on the power of association. In this case, association would mean the creation of a Society of Friends of Progress in Posen which should co-ordinate, even fuse, all the efforts currently invested in individual pursuits or, even worse, wasted in factional bickering.

To some degree, the proposition of creating nothing more adventurous or forceful than a Society of Friends of Progress could be seen as a tactical concession. Freedom from censorship was a recent and fragile acquisition; indeed, when censorship was restored soon afterwards the journal in which Cieszkowski's article appeared, Rok, was its first victim.[3] One may thus assume that Cieszkowski intended his projected Society to be the nucleus of a more political body just as in the past similar voluntary organizations in Posen had evolved into political forces.[4] At the same time, Cieszkowski's later concerns demonstrated that he certainly considered such a society as valuable in its own right. The Posen Society of Friends of Learning which Cieszkowski founded in 1857 was to be a partial adoption of the project sketched in 1843.[5] Thus, to the extent that the Rok article was truly non- or supra-political its ideas were eventually realized. However, insofar as the article was a call upon all parties to form a common and constructive platform it fell upon deaf ears.

filozofia narodowa i konserwatywna katolicka przed 1864 rokiem', *Archiwum Historii Filozofii i Myśli Społecznej*, VIII (1962), pp. 171–213. For Cieszkowski's place in organicism see Jakóbczyk, *Studia*.

[1] 'O skojarzeniu dążeń i prac umysłowych we Wielkim Księstwie Poznańskim', *Rok pod względem oświaty, przemysłu i wydarzeń czasowych* ('The Year: its enlightenment, industry and events'), I (1843), pp. 132–43.

[2] See C.-H. de Saint-Simon, *Introduction aux travaux scientifiques du XIXième siècle*, in *Oeuvres*, vol. VI.

[3] M. Laubert, 'Presse und Zensur in neupreussischer Zeit 1815–1847', *Studien zur Geschichte der Provinz Posen in der ersten Hälfte des neunzehnten Jahrhunderts* (Posen, Sonderöffentlichungen der historischen Gesellschaft für die Provinz Posen, 1908). *Rok* was similar in scope and character to the *Biblioteka Warszawska* but more consistently progressive than the latter. It was, for instance, the first Polish review to discuss Engels' *The Condition of the Working Class in England*; *Rok*, IV (1846).

[4] See Jakóbczyk, *Studia nad dziejami Wielkopolski*, p. 115.

[5] Andrzej Wojtkowski, 'Stulecie Poznańskiego Towarzystwa Przyjaciół Nauk', *Roczniki Historyczne*, IX (1957), pp. 310–31.

The events of 1848 proved a test for Cieszkowski's many plans and expectations. Retrospectively, 1848 was to mark the final expiration of Hegelian hegemony in philosophy, the defeat of liberal hopes in central Europe, and a bloody demonstration of the incompatibility between labour and capital.[1] In short, it signified an end to Cieszkowski's own epoch and its hopes. Ironically, however, 1848 also marked the beginning of Cieszkowski's active political career, which was to be his chief concern into the 1860s.

Cieszkowski's rise to political prominence was favoured by the unusual circumstance that amid a general European conflagration the Poles had broken with their insurrectionary tradition and were confining themselves to pacific means of furthering their national cause. In perfect consistency with his principles, Cieszkowski responded eagerly to a call upon his patriotism which dictated peaceful participation in organizational activity and co-operation among various groups. Thus, after having taken part in the last assembly of Posen's provincial estates in April 1848, Cieszkowski travelled to Breslau, where a congress had been convoked for the purpose of uniting all emigré and home factions and of eventually setting up a single Polish government.[2] As a member of the short-lived correspondence bureau established there, Cieszkowski soon realized the unattainability of any truly political unity and responded by lobbying energetically, though unsuccessfully, for the creation of an organized pressure group modelled on the British Corn League which might exploit the legal opportunities for the defence of Polish interests offered by the new Austrian and German constitutions.[3] From Breslau Cieszkowski hastened back to Posen to be elected to the newly formed Prussian National Assembly. In the meantime, unable to attend the Pan-Slavic Congress in Prague which was attempting to find common ground among the aspirations of the Slavs of three empires, Cieszkowski despatched a brochure to be published at the congress on his behalf by the Polish delegates.[4]

The brochure which appeared anonymously as 'Prophetic words of a Pole',[5] as well as the Breslau address 'To the Representatives of Free

---

[1] For a concise account of the events of 1848 see L. Namier, *1848: Revolution of the Intellectuals* (Oxford University Press, 1944).

[2] Marian Tyrowicz, *Polski kongres polityczny we Wrocławiu 1848 roku* (Cracow, 1946).

[3] The project is described in Władysław Wisłocki, *Jerzy Lubomirski 1817–1872* (Lvov, 1928).

[4] For the Prague Congress see Benoît Hepner, *Bakounine et le panslavisme révolutionnaire: cinq essais sur l'histoire des idées en Russie et en Europe* (Paris, M. Rivière, 1950), p. 265.

[5] *Słowa wieszcze Polaka wyrzeczone roku MDCCCXLVI* (Prague, Haase, 1848). It is

Peoples',[1] are undoubtedly Cieszkowski's most messianic pronouncements. Nevertheless, even in these texts written under the enthusiasm of the 'Spring of Nations' and on behalf of such nationalistic bodies as the Breslau and Prague congresses, Cieszkowski's messianism is characterized above all by its universalism. The Breslau address is an indictment of the bankruptcy of the existing international system and an appeal for a new order based on 'the free and universal development of all social elements and all nations'. More concretely, the goals of the new order must be universal disarmament and the replacement of traditional diplomacy with peoples' congresses and a 'jury of nations' or international court. 'Prophetic Words of a Pole' is a panegyric to all the Slavs, not only the Poles. Here, in spite of Cieszkowski's concessions to the myth of a primeval Slavonic innocence, his arguments are strictly dialectical much in the manner of the *Prolegomena to Historiosophy*: the Slavs will be bearers of future freedom because today they are so completely unfree. Thus, even here Cieszkowski does not yield to the more popular and less coherent versions of Polish messianism.

The abortive attempts towards Polish and Slavonic unity at Breslau and Prague confirmed Cieszkowski in his conviction that Polish goals could be best advanced by working within the constitutional framework created through the revolution. Consequently, Cieszkowski focused his hopes and energies on his role as deputy from Posen to the first Prussian National Assembly which sat in Berlin from May to December 1848.[2] Here, his activity on behalf of the Poles made him a consistent ally of the German left, for whom the restoration of Polish national rights was a litmus test of German democracy.[3] To the horror of some, Cieszkowski supported radical measures for the abolition of aristocratic titles and privileges[4] and joined such improbable allies as Bakunin on the editorial

not clear whether this was actually written in 1846 or whether the date is simply a literary device. The text constitutes part of the *Our Father*, vol. I, published anonymously in Paris in 1848. In the complete edition of the *Our Father*, vols. I–III (Poznań, Fiszer i Majewski, 1922–3), vol. I, pp. 142–70.

[1] 'Memorjal do reprezentantów ludów wolnych', published in *Gazeta Polska*, 93 (14 July 1848), and reprinted in Wisłocki, *Jerzy Lubomirski*, pp. 46–53.

[2] W. Bleck, 'Die Posener Frage auf dem Nationalversammlung im Jahr 1848 und 1849', *Zeitschrift der historischen Gesellschaft für die Provinz Posen*, XXIX (1914), pp. 1–82.

[3] Marx and Engels summarized the position of the German left: 'The establishment of a democratic Poland is the first condition for the establishment of a democratic Germany', *Neue Rheinische Zeitung*, 81 (20 August 1848), in *Marx–Engels Werke*, vol. V, p. 331.

[4] Krasiński in particular showered his friend with abuse and accusations of Machiavellianism for his stand in the debate on the nobility. See *Listy do Augusta Cieszkowskiego*, vol. II, pp. 34–67, 76–7.

board of a leading democratic organ, *Die Reform*.[1] Indeed, the German left considered Cieszkowski so much one of its members that it chose him as a secretary of the Assembly.[2]

Even as Cieszkowski was pursuing tactical alliances in Berlin, he intensified his efforts to establish a Polish National League.[3] The failure of the Breslau congress condemned the project – originally proposed at Breslau as an inter-zonal Polish lobby – to application in Posen alone. Here, the League was founded as a mass pressure group modelled on Cobden's Corn League in its strategy, organization and openness.[4] It was to act on behalf of the Polish national cause by legal means alone, primarily by influencing public opinion, and it was to stand above all political factions.[5] In fact, the scope of the League's activities was much larger. Not only did it defend Polish rights in the most general sense but it also furthered public education by establishing schools and libraries and contributed to material welfare with savings banks, insurances and subsidies. Thus, the League actually became a more nationalistically conceived variant of the Society of Friends of Progress which Cieszkowski had advocated years earlier. Eventually, however, the success and breadth of the League's activities transformed it into something of a 'state within a state' with its executive as a crypto-government and Cieszkowski, the head of its external section, as a sort of foreign minister. Not surprisingly, the League was dissolved by the Prussian government in 1850.[6]

Meanwhile, Cieszkowski had been returned to the Prussian Lower House where he was to sit from 1849 to 1855 and 1859 to 1866. The heady days of 1848 were clearly over and the fortunes of both the left and

---

[1] Jakóbczyk, *Studia nad dziejami Wielkopolski*, p. 105.

[2] Krasiński could not understand why, as he put it, Cieszkowski wanted 'to play the secretary in Berlin and ruin his lungs for the sake of German ears'; *Listy do Augusta Cieszkowskiego*, vol. II, p. 34.

[3] The League was founded on 25 June 1848 and its first general assembly was held in January 1849. For a detailed account of the League and particularly Cieszkowski's role see Witold Jakóbczyk, 'Cieszkowski i Liga Polska', *Przegląd Historyczny*, XXXVIII (1948), pp. 137–68.

[4] For an account of the Corn League's successful mobilization of public opinion through skilful propaganda and agitation see Archibald Prentice, *History of the Anti-Corn Law League* (London, Cash, 1853). Jakóbczyk, *Studia nad dziejami Wielkopolski*, p. 108, points out that Cieszkowski's idea was actually closer in aim to Daniel O'Connell's Irish Repeal Association.

[5] See the relevant parts of the statutes of the Polish National League reprinted in Jakóbczyk, 'Cieszkowski i Liga Polska', p. 152.

[6] *Ibid.*; apparently at its height the League numbered 20,000–30,000 members and 246 local chapters.

the Poles declined steadily.[1] Thus, Cieszkowski's activities centred on defending whatever legal guarantees remained for the Polish minority and in maintaining the cohesion of the group of Polish deputies in Berlin.[2] Since the group was torn between a left and a right wing, this task consisted primarily of mediation and Cieszkowski's election to the vice-presidency and presidency of the caucus may be taken as an indication of his success in reconciling divergent views.[3] With respect to the recurrent question of the position which the Polish faction should take on purely German matters Cieszkowski tended to solve the problem on a pragmatic and *ad hoc* basis, but the logic of the situation systematically led him into opposition to the Prussian government.[4] Indeed, as Cieszkowski himself put it: 'Let us, as long as the Germans have lost their conscience, be the guardians of a just conscience and let us present a shade of opposition'.[5]

Cieszkowski's withdrawal from active politics was motivated largely by family reasons. During his last three decades he lived quietly but hardly inactively, as he continued to pursue his many interests and projects. He founded a short-lived agricultural college,[6] led the Posen Society of Friends of Learning,[7] carried out historical research in Venice[8] and

---

[1] See Z. Grot, 'Koło polskie w Berlinie w dobie Wiosny Ludów', *Przegląd Zachodni*, VIII, 9 (1952), pp. 126–72.

[2] To affirm Polish legal rights to autonomy in Posen Cieszkowski published the *Zusammenstellung von Staats- und Völkerrechtlichen Urkunden, welche das Verhältnis des Grossherzogtums Posen zur preussischen Krone betreffen* (Berlin, Unger, 1849). He also campaigned actively but unsuccessfully for the creation of a Polish university in Posen. *Zwei Anträge des Abgeordneten August Cieszkowski die Posener Universitäts und Unterrichtsfrage betreffen* (Berlin, 1853).

[3] The published minutes of the Polish caucus's deliberations provide valuable insight into this aspect of Cieszkowski's activities. See Z. Grot (ed.), *Protokoły posiedzeń koła polskiego w Berlinie*, vol. I, 1849–1851 (Poznań, Państwowe Wydawnictwo Naukowe, 1956), and also Z. Grot, *Rok 1863 w zaborze pruskim* (Poznań, Wydawnictwo Poznańskie, 1963) for examples of Cieszkowski's quiet intercession on behalf of his compatriots.

[4] Ferdinand Lassalle wrote to Cieszkowski, whom he addressed as a personal friend and philosophical colleague (from the Philosophische Gesellschaft), that the 'only democratic words which the House [i.e. the Prussian Lower House] has heard in recent years have fallen from Polish lips'. W. Kühne, 'Neue Einblicke ins Leben und Werke Cieszkowskis: aus unveröffentlichem Nachlass', *Jahrbücher für die Kultur und die Geschichte der Slaven*, VII, 1 (1931), p. 24.

[5] Grot, *Protokoły*, p. 17.

[6] N. Urbanowski, 'Wspomnienia o wyższej szkole rolniczej imienia Haliny w Żabikowie', *Roczniki Poznańskiego Towarzystwa Przyjaciół Nauk*, XX (1894), pp. 267–82. The college was closed by government order after eight years of existence.

[7] A. Wojtkowski, 'Stulecie Poznańskiego Towarzystwa Przyjaciół Nauk'. Cieszkowski was the first president in 1857 and also 1861–1868 and 1885–1894.

[8] 'August Cieszkowski i akta polskie w Wenecji', *Kronika Miasta Poznań*, X, 4 (1932),

concerned himself with public hygiene.[1] It is revealing that Cieszkowski travelled to the Vatican Council to lobby against the intractable positions eventually adopted there.[2] Well into his seventies he continued to attend international scientific congresses and, in spite of dwindling funds, he remained ever ready to subsidize intellectual activity of any sort.[3] Nowhere did he show any bitterness at the disappointment of his plans for national regeneration nor at the incomprehension of a younger generation for the social hopes and philosophical attitudes which had preceded 1848.[4]

During these years Cieszkowski also continued writing the *Our Father*, a work conceived in the 1830s and still unfinished at his death in 1894. Ever inclined to search for the mystical and supernatural, Cieszkowski's son maintains that the inspiration for the *Our Father* came in a vision during a thanksgiving mass offered upon completion of the *Prolegomena* in 1832![5] However implausible this account, Cieszkowski's *Diaries* do prove that the central theme of the *Our Father* – the Lord's Prayer as a prophetic insight into a third, post-Christian era – dates back to the 1830s;[6] indeed, the earliest dated part of the manuscript, the 'Amen',

pp. 389–401. The publication which resulted was *Fontes rerum polonicarum e tabulario reipublicae Venetae* (Posen, 1890–1902).

[1] F. Chłapowski, 'O stosunku ś.p. Augusta Cieszkowskiego do nauk przyrodniczych', *Roczniki Poznańskiego Towarzystwa Przyjaciół Nauk*, XXI (1895), pp. 335–55.

[2] A. Żółtowski, 'August Cieszkowski' in S. Chlebowski et alii (eds.), *Sto lat filozofii polskiej: wiek XIX*, vol. V (Cracow, 1909), pp. 421–37.

[3] See H. Barycz, 'Stosunki Augusta Cieszkowskiego z uniwersytetem Jagiellońskim', *Sprawozdania Polskiej Akademii Umiejętności*, XLIII (1938), pp. 287–8. Cieszkowski offered stipends in statistics, administration and cameral studies for students who knew only Polish (!). He also endowed a prize for the history of the Polish economy and 'the least studied of classes', the peasantry.

[4] Indeed, invoking a familiarly organic image, Cieszkowski went so far as to call the torpor which reigned in Poland after 1863 beneficial: 'Sleep is a necessary condition of maintaining the human organism, strengthening it and making it grow. It is not in vain that Providence has made Poland leave the community of living nations in this century when merchantdom and material strength dominate spiritual law…If we sleep through this century we alone shall preserve what other nations will lose: the spiritual heritage of our fathers, the purity of intentions and a faith in the future…Let us only maintain the normal functions of the body organism; as a man breathes in his sleep so we shall work economically and culturally in our political sleep'. Cited in L. Dębicki, *Portrety i Sylwetki z XIX-go wieku*, series 2, vol. I (Cracow, Spółka Wydawnicza Polska, 1905), p. 159.

[5] Kühne, *Graf August Cieszkowski*, p. 55, who records this account, is also more than sceptical in the light of internal evidence within the *Prolegomena* and such sources as the Cieszkowski–Michelet correspondence.

[6] For instance, Cieszkowski writes of 'the daily bread which we ask for in the prayer and with which the future epoch is to endow us' (*Diaries* I, p. 15); muses about replacing in the future 'today's banal greetings' with the address 'Forgive us our trespasses' (*Diaries* II, p. 35); in an entry dated about 1837–8 lists 'explicatory additions and new

which also happens to be the final section, is dated 1836.[1] Inasmuch as the work was not written in sequence, however, it is extremely difficult to establish periodization. Thus, the first volume was published anonymously in 1848.[2] There is evidence that Cieszkowski was working on what was to be the third volume of the first edition in the 1870s and even in the 1890s.[3] Volume II of the first edition may well antedate volume I.[4] Above all, the unequal lengths of the various parts seem to indicate that the work developed in an agglutinative fashion: once the structure had been erected the author kept on adding elements for an indefinable period which stretched over most of his life.

The problem of reconstructing the composition of the *Our Father* is further complicated by the secrecy which surrounded this work. It is plausible, as some contemporaries claimed, that Cieszkowski refrained from publishing or even acknowledging this manuscript for fear of scandal and heresy.[5] He is reputed to have stated on his deathbed that the times were not yet ripe for the work,[6] and his fears turned out to be well founded, as the posthumous edition of the *Our Father* was soundly denounced by Catholic theologians.[7] In addition to prudence, however, the secrecy about the work was dictated by the intensely personal nature of the *Our Father*. Although Cieszkowski's purpose was to verbalize a personal intuition so as to give it a rational and objective form,[8] the work remained to some extent a dialogue of the author with himself, an attempt to verbalize his hopes and allay his fears through an appeal to the authority

arguments for the Commentary' (*Diaries* II, p. 11) which almost certainly refer to the *Our Father*.

[1] *Ojcze Nasz*, vol. III, 2nd edn (Poznań, Fiszer i Majewski, 1922), p. 286.

[2] *Ojcze Nasz*, vol. I (Paris, Maulde et Renou, 1848). Some information on the writing of this work can be gleaned from Krasiński, *Listy do Augusta Cieszkowskiego*. The identity of the author seems to have quickly become common knowledge.

[3] Kühne, 'Neue Einblicke', quotes an 1876 letter from Cieszkowski to F. Benary which corresponds to a discussion in *Ojcze Nasz*, vol. III, 1st edn (Posen, Leitgeber, 1903), p. 25. See also Wojtkowski in Jakóbczyk, *Wielkopolanie*, who states (p. 173) that a note on alcoholism dates from the 1890s.

[4] Editor's note, *Ojcze Nasz*, vol. II, 1st edn (Posen, Leitgeber, 1899).

[5] Bronisław Trentowski, *Panteon Wiedzy ludzkiej* (Posen, 1874), p. 222.

[6] August Cieszkowski junior, editor's note to *Ojcze Nasz*, vol. III, 1st edn, p. 1 (unnumbered).

[7] R. Koppens, review of *Ojcze Nasz*, vol. II, in *Przegląd Powszechny*, LXVII (1900), pp. 242–53; T. Gapczyński, 'Cieszkowskiego Ojcze Nasz (tom III), wobec nauki kościoła katolickiego', *Przegląd Kościelny*, IV (1903), pp. 367–84, and 'Królestwo Boże wedle Cieszkowskiego', *Przegląd Kościelny*, XII (1907), pp. 267–81.

[8] This is the point of 'O drogach Ducha' ('The Ways of the Spirit'), which appeared in the *Roczniki Poznańskiego Towarzystwa Przyjaciół Nauk*, II (1863), pp. 735–76, and was subsequently reprinted as an introduction to the posthumous editions of the *Our Father* (1st and 2nd).

of history and of Scripture. Cieszkowski's reluctance to submit the results of this exercise to outside scrutiny may be an indication that he was not entirely convinced of his own success.

The only person whom Cieszkowski exposed to the *Our Father* as it was being written was the Polish romantic poet, Zygmunt Krasiński.[1] In spite of their intimate friendship nurtured by a similar search for a Christian philosophy of history, a mutual suspicion of messianic tendencies among their exiled compatriots and a common revulsion against bourgeois culture, Krasiński's apocalyptic pessimism and aristocratic nostalgia were the very antitheses of Cieszkowski's hopeful and reforming zeal.[2] Reading Krasiński's letters to Cieszkowski with their constant inveighings against social radicalism and religious innovation, there can be no doubt of the direction in which Krasiński influenced the *Our Father*.[3] Although it was Krasiński who saved the work by dissuading its author from burning the entire manuscript and prevailed upon him to publish the first volume in 1848,[4] Krasiński's intervention clearly tempered the élan of the original manuscript by forcing its author to take account of a thoroughly conservative outlook which equated democracy with barbarism and progress with degeneration.

In somewhat summary terms, the *Our Father* is a monumental exercise in the construction of a world-view. Formally, it is based on the notion that the Lord's Prayer is a prophetic statement regarding a coming third era. In other words, the Prayer's truths are fully relevant not to the Christian past but to a future which they esoterically describe.[5] Substantively, the *Our Father* rests on the attempt to join Christian millenarianism with a Hegelian-inspired philosophy of history which culminates in a highly socialized modern utopia. Whether one accepts Cieszkowski's exegesis of the Lord's Prayer at face value or sees it as an elaborate metaphor obscuring what is, in fact, a thoroughgoing secularization of

[1] For studies of Krasiński see Juliusz Kleiner, *Krasiński* (Lublin, Lames, 1948) and Maryan Zdziechowski, *Wizja Krasińkiego. Ze studiów nad literaturą polską* (Cracow, S. A. Krzyżanowski, 1912). In English, N. O. Lossky, *Three Polish Messianists* (*Krasiński, Cieszkowski, Lutosławski*) (Prague, J. Rokyta, 1938).

[2] For an interesting analysis which moderates the traditional image of Krasiński as a die-hard reactionary by emphasizing his dialectical and tragic historicism see Maria Janion, 'Romantyczna wizja rewolucji' in *Problemy polskiego romantyzmu*, ed. Maria Żmigrodzka and Zofia Lewin (Wrocław, Ossolineum, 1971), pp. 159–207.

[3] For Krasiński's and Cieszkowski's specific influences on each other see A. Żółtowski's Introduction to their correspondence, *Listy do Augusta Cieszkowskiego*, as well as Bolesław Gawecki, *Polscy myśliciele romantyczni* (Warsaw, Pax, 1972), pp. 69–87.

[4] Krasiński, *Listy do Augusta Cieszkowskiego*, vol. II, letter dated 7 February 1847, p. 231.

[5] *Ojcze Nasz*, vol. I, part I, 2nd edn, pp. 1–28.

eschatology,[1] there can be no doubt that the object of the work is wider than its formal framework. Indeed, it is only by examining the different currents and traditions on which Cieszkowski draws that one can grasp the real reference points of this work.

The religious sources of the *Our Father* lie somewhat outside the Christian mainstream. To be sure, the work invites comparison with Augustine's *Civitas Dei* as an attempt to explain the ways of God to men. Notwithstanding Cieszkowski's admiration for Augustine's achievement,[2] however, any such comparison can be only superficial since Cieszkowski's optimism and intense this-worldliness are the very opposite of Augustine's teachings. Cieszkowski actually stands closest to the chiliastic tradition exemplified by the thirteenth-century monk, Joachim di Fiore, who established a concordance between the Old and New Testaments in order to prove the imminence of the third era of the Holy Spirit.[3] Certainly, the undogmatic and eclectic nature of Cieszkowski's appeal to Christian tradition is confirmed by the unorthodox theology of the *Our Father*. which posits God's dependence on His own creatures,[4] effectively denies the doctrine of original sin[5] and substitutes earthly palingenesis for heavenly rewards.[6]

The philosophical underpinnings of the *Our Father* must also be sought

---

[1] Professor Wiktor Weintraub has drawn my attention to the anti-religious implications of Cieszkowski's evocation of Jules Michelet's slogan 'the age of grace has ended, the age of merit has begun', which was first formulated as an atheistic response to Quinet's interpretation of the French Revolution as an outburst of Christianity. See the introduction to Michelet's *Histoire de la révolution française*.

[2] *Ojcze Nasz*, vol. III, 2nd edn, pp. 40–2. See E. Gilson, *Les métamorphoses de la cité de Dieu* (Paris, Vrin, 1952), especially chapter 9.

[3] Marjorie Reeves, *The Influence of Prophecy in the Later Middle Ages* (London, Oxford University Press, 1969), gives a straightforward account of Joachim's teachings. The importance of Joachimism as a sub-current in modern philosophy of history is brought out forcefully and most relevantly to this context in Karl Löwith, *Meaning in History* (Chicago and London, University of Chicago Press, 1949), which devotes a chapter to Joachim and an appendix to modern transfigurations of Joachimism, pp. 145–59 and 208–13. An interpretation of political thought in general which insists somewhat eccentrically on Joachim's significance is Eric Vögelin, *The New Science of Politics* (Chicago, University of Chicago Press, 1952), especially the chapter entitled 'Gnosticism: the nature of modernity', pp. 107–32.

[4] In his *Diaries* I, p. 11, Cieszkowski writes: 'God suffers, we cause God pain just as our heart, head, etc. causes us pain', and the same idea appears in *Ojcze Nasz*, vol. III, 2nd edn, p. 190, where Cieszkowski writes of God's health and happiness.

[5] See the short chapter 'Lead us not into temptation', *Ojcze Nasz*, vol. III, 2nd edn, pp. 243–55.

[6] See *Ojcze Nasz*, vol. I, 2nd edn, part IV ('This-worldly and other-worldly under the category of time'), pp. 172–206, where Cieszkowski appeals to the authority of Kant and Fontenelle.

in certain recurrent but rarely dominant undercurrents of thought. Admittedly, Hegel's powerful presence defines the method, tone and even the structure of the *Our Father* just as it shapes Cieszkowski's other work. However, inasmuch as the *Our Father* draws on a rather marginal aspect of Hegel, what might be called Hegel's illuminism[1] or even Schellingianism,[2] Cieszkowski demonstrates once again that his relation to Hegel's system is creative rather than derivative. In fact, the most obvious philosophical inspiration of the *Our Father* is to be sought in a work of the German Enlightenment which preceded and influenced Hegel himself: Lessing's *Education of the Human Race*.[3] Here, human history is seen in terms of growth from childhood to maturity, which culminates in recognition of the identity between the truths of revelation and the precepts of reason. Not only does Cieszkowski adopt Lessing's organic metaphor – as others, including Hegel, were to do – but he makes essentially the same claims on behalf of the Lord's Prayer as Lessing does for Scripture as a whole.[4] It is not surprising, therefore, that the *Our Father* should follow Lessing too in affirming that Joachim di Fiore's expectation of a third era, when the Holy Spirit will have enlightened mankind with a final and eternally valid revelation, is not mistaken but premature.

It is the historical context of the *Our Father* which distinguishes Cieszkowski from either Lessing or Joachimism. Like so many other nineteenth-century thinkers, Cieszkowski writes under the shadow of the French Revolution[5] and therefore cannot avoid inquiring into the significance and consequences of an event which may have effectively ended the Christian era even if it did not yet inaugurate a succeeding, third era. Consequently, one might anticipate Cieszkowski's repeated references to

[1] For this aspect of Hegel see Jacques d'Hondt, *Hegel secret: recherches sur les sources cachées de la pensée de Hegel* (Paris, Presses Universitaires de France, 1968).

[2] Tilliette, *Schelling: une philosophie en devenir*, vol. I, pp. 295–302, discusses the Schelling–Hegel relationship. See also his article 'Schelling contre Hegel', *Archives de Philosophie*, XVIII, 1 (1966), pp. 89–108.

[3] Concerning Gotthold Ephraim Lessing (1729–1781) and his *Erziehung des Menschengeschlechts* (Berlin, 1780) see most recently, Henry E. Allison, *Lessing and the Enlightenment: His Philosophy of Religion and its Relation to Eighteenth-Century Thought* (Ann Arbor, University of Michigan Press, 1966). It is interesting to note that the work was translated into French by a leading Saint-Simonian, Eugène Rodrigues, *Lettres sur la réligion et la politique, 1829; suivies de l'Education du genre humain, traduit de l'allemand de Lessing* (Paris, A. Messier, 1831).

[4] G. E. Lessing, *The Education of the Human Race*, translated by F. W. Robertson, 4th (revised) edn, (London, Kegan & Paul, 1896), especially pp. 3–16. See also Löwith, *Meaning in History*, p. 208.

[5] For an illuminating discussion of the impact of the French Revolution on political thought and its connection with nineteenth-century romantic despair see Judith N. Shklar, *After Utopia: The Decline of Political Faith* (Princeton University Press, 1957).

contemporaries who addressed themselves to the same question although one can hardly help expressing surprise at his ability to integrate so many diverse answers within his own vision. Thus, Cieszkowski appeals not only to the curiously dynamic traditionalism epitomized by de Maistre's call for a 'new explosion of Christianity'[1] but also to Saint-Simon's anti-traditional formulation of novel principles of order and authority which culminates in the 'New Christianity'[2] – perhaps showing that at a certain level the contradiction between the two can be sublimated. Similarly, Cieszkowski's reliance on the French utopian socialist tradition – primarily Fourier[3] but also Cabet or Lamennais – can be understood in the context of his demonstration that all reforms aiming at either carrying the Revolution through to its ultimate consequences or overcoming its negative, anti-social effects are compatible with the revelation hidden for so long in the Lord's Prayer.

From another standpoint, Cieszkowski appears to have broken an important utopian convention. Most utopian writers, and particularly those of the last century, have sought to mark the distance between themselves and their utopias by resorting to a variety of literary devices – a dream, a parable, a tale told by a sailor from afar. In each case the purpose has been to certify for the reader the author's detachment from his own creation and thus to establish a complicity of fantasy between author and reader. All of this is absent in Cieszkowski. Whether Cieszkowski did or did not believe in a literal sense in his construct, nowhere within his work does he allow himself any detachment from his production. Lacking both humour and fantasy, an author who takes his own utopia seriously and perhaps even believes in it is unlikely to find understanding with the modern reader.

The *Our Father* might be somewhat fancifully compared to a quarry which needs to be excavated rather than contemplated. Thus, working through the text, one encounters a number of obstacles which modify the initially harmonious impression. For instance, one might note the tension

---

[1] The phrase appears in *Ojcze Nasz*, vol. I, 2nd edn, p. 26 and is repeated several times throughout the work. See Joseph de Maistre, *Les soirées de St. Petersburg: entretiens sur le gouvernement temporel de la providence*.

[2] H. de Saint-Simon, *Nouveau christianisme: dialogues entre un conservateur et un novateur*, in *Oeuvres*, vol. II; also Rodrigues, *Lettres sur la réligion et la politique*.

[3] Curiously, Fourier's name is consistently misspelled in the *Ojcze Nasz* as 'Fourrier' although the name is correctly written in the *Prolegomena*. The French sources of the *Our Father* are quite comprehensively covered in Walicki's 'Francuskie inspiracje', where emphasis is laid on Cieszkowski's Saint-Simonian rather than Fourierist inspiration and special attention is paid to Ballanche.

between the mysticism implicit in Cieszkowski's project and his rationalist preoccupation with uncovering and explaining truths previously hidden.[1] At some points, it would seem that Cieszkowski himself questions the final character of the third era which he is announcing as he speculates, quite seriously, on a possibly angelic future for mankind and suggests that the filial bonds between man and God might be replaced by a marital relation.[2] Elsewhere, Cieszkowski abandons his scrupulously even-handed critique of both 'Reds' and 'Blacks' to denounce the present in terms so harsh as to suggest that any change, however violent, would be preferable to the perpetuation of the injustices and aimlessness of the present.[3]

Such tensions are built into the very structure of the *Our Father*. Indeed, they impart a dynamic and undogmatic quality to the work which distinguishes it from other utopian projects without impinging on its fundamental theses. Moreover, the limitations imposed on the *Our Father* by its peculiar exegetical form do not obstruct the formulation of a coherent social philosophy. For instance, Cieszkowski's exposition of freedom as perfect socialization claims to be derived from the social message of the Lord's Prayer but it could just as well be deduced from Hegel's notion of ethical life and from Fourier's ideas of universal attraction. Similarly, Cieszkowski's emphasis on labour as the key to the third era is supposedly founded upon the venerable Christian precept *orare et laborare*; in fact, it rejoins in all respects contemporary formulations referring to the dignity or even the sanctification of labour.[4] Finally, the call for fusion of religion and politics in a world Church and a universal priesthood, a call which Cieszkowski sees as the essential meaning of the invocation 'Thy Kingdom come', lies at the very heart of his age. It is both a nostalgic and a revolutionary cry uttered by all those unable to accept the finality of a sundered social whole where men are haunted by political and spiritual homelessness.

Cieszkowski is said to have compared his *Our Father* to a tree trunk

---

[1] Compare, for instance, the rationalism of 'The Ways of the Spirit', which introduces the work, with the mystical invocation preceding the analysis of the first entreaty 'Hallowed be Thy Name'; *Ojcze Nasz*, vol. III, 1st edn, pp. 1–7.

[2] *Ojcze Nasz*, vol. II, 1st edn, pp. 407–26. 'Passage from the name of God revealed by Christ to his still *hidden* but *augured* and presaged name, i.e. from the invocation, "Our Father, who art in Heaven", to the first entreaty: "Hallowed be Thy Name"' (description by editor of the 1st edition).

[3] *Ibid.*, pp. 174–326, the section on 'Our', referring to social solidarity, which contains an 'Address to those who neglect the truth as well as those who abuse false conclusions and prepare an awful crisis for the world' (description by editor of the 1st edition).

[4] K. Zieliński, 'Problem pracy u Cieszkowskiego', *Zet*, I, 7 (1932), pp. 3–6.

of which all his other writings are but branches.[1] Certainly, the *Our Father* is Cieszkowski's lengthiest as well as broadest work and it fulfils a unique function in making explicit the philosophical underpinnings of certain other writings. It is also his most intimate work and as such can even be seen as a formal and literary continuation of his early *Diaries*. Most notably, however, the *Our Father* imparts an object to the notion of *praxis* which Cieszkowski had enunciated in the *Prolegomena to Historiosophy* – *praxis* turns out to be the construction of that social harmony referred to as the 'Kingdom of God'. Similarly, the *Our Father* vindicates the notion of merit advocated in the *De la pairie et de l'aristocratie moderne* by postulating a universal priesthood of the third era which generalizes the principle of meritocracy.[2] On the other hand, the *Our Father*'s vagueness concerning the economic structures of the Kingdom of God makes it difficult to relate this work to *Du crédit et de la circulation* although Cieszkowski's emphasis on participation in the future creates an obvious link with his economic articles.[3]

Although the *Our Father* is an achievement of towering proportions and a paradigmatic attempt to synthesize religious and secular thought one cannot judge Cieszkowski primarily by this work. The *Our Father* attains something of a tour de force in building an entire system of thought on the framework of the Dominical Prayer and in evoking layers of meaning from a familiar text. Otherwise, however, the work does not so much invent as reflect themes found among Cieszkowski's contemporaries as well as in his own lesser writings. Indeed, Cieszkowski's argument in the *Our Father* is precisely that he is not inventing but engaging in a 'revelation of revelation'[4] – unveiling the recondite meaning of what had been previously known and stated. Consequently, any claim to originality on behalf of Cieszkowski should be based not simply on the *Our Father* but rather on the relation between Cieszkowski's goals expounded in the *Our Father* and the means of achieving them as presented in his other writings and his own activities. The central question which ensues concerns the adequacy for these goals of the means proposed.[5] One might

[1] August Cieszkowski junior, in the Introduction to *Ojcze Nasz*, vol. I, 1st edn.
[2] The notion of universal priesthood already appears with references to Tertullian in *Diaries* II, p. 29. It reappears specifically in *Ojcze Nasz*, vol. III, 1st edn, pp. 290–3.
[3] *Ojcze Nasz*, vol. III, 2nd edn, especially the passages concerning the idea of the Kingdom of God on earth and the conditions and material means for its realization.
[4] *Ojcze Nasz*, vol. III, 1st edn, especially p. 233. 'Passage from reasoning to acting, from the thought to the deed' (description by editor of the 1st edition).
[5] Cieszkowski himself poses the question indirectly at several points in the *Our Father* and directly in the invocation preceding the first entreaty 'Hallowed be Thy Name', *Ojcze Nasz*, vol. III, 1st edn, pp. 3–7.

suggest that Cieszkowski's refusal to publish the statement of his goals which is the *Our Father* constitutes a tacit acknowledgement that all the means required to achieve these goals have not yet been found.

V
Conclusion

Cieszkowski's work as a whole may be summarized as an attempt to enlist Providence as history in the service of reform. This explains how Cieszkowski can be seen as both a social thinker of prosaic and partial innovation and an exalted prophetic figure of grand proportions. Indeed, an understanding of the nature of this attempt puts into perspective, as much as contextual and historical analyses, the apparent contradictions discussed in the opening pages of this essay – that between the utopian form and the programmatic content of Cieszkowski's writings, that between his nostalgic religiosity and his apparent modernity, that between ideology and utopia.

At the same time, to understand Cieszkowski is not to validate his conclusions. For example, the incongruence between the aims portrayed in Cieszkowski's writings and the means proposed to attain them undermines in a very fundamental way the acceptability of his construction. One cannot help feeling that if the means proposed are inadequate, they are irrelevant; if the Kingdom of God is to come through non-human intervention then *praxis* is superfluous. In other words, the tension between what Lukács has so perceptively called the fatalism of pure laws and the ethics of pure intention is not resolved here any more than it is elsewhere.[1]

Whatever judgement one is to make on the ultimate coherence of Cieszkowski's system and the value of his contribution to both theory and politics in his time, one is led to conclude that his thought and place in history do not allow of a unique formulation or explanation. Rather, they require a careful unravelling of threads, distinguishing the original from the typical elements, the formal from the substantial. The complexity of Cieszkowski's writings does not facilitate this task. One suspects, however, that if it were any easier Cieszkowski would already have become a far better known figure.

[1] G. Lukács, *History and Class Consciousness*, translated by Rodney Livingstone (Cambridge, Mass., MIT Press, 1971), p. 39.

Prolegomena to historiosophy (1838)

Chapter I
THE ORGANISM OF UNIVERSAL HISTORY

Mankind has finally reached that stage of self-consciousness where it no longer considers the laws of its normal progress and development simply as concoctions of zealous and self-deceiving scholars but rather as faithful portrayals of the absolute thought of God, as manifestations of objective reason in universal history. The very affirmation and partial realization of this principle is already a significant attainment worthily conforming to the character and needs of our epoch. Although we are only beginning to find our way in the labyrinth of history we have already come to know many fundamental principles which explain the necessity of its phases and we have unriddled numerous abstract as well as particular relations. In general, however, we must admit that these results have been attained only formally and potentially. In spite of the many treasures which philosophy has prepared for us we are still far from a solution of the problem of history as a whole which would cover its entire content, its completion and its realization. In other words, although mankind has seized conceptually the speculative necessity and regularity of historical progress it has not yet accomplished this progress in accordance with the concept.

Even the hero of the newest philosophy who worked out the most intricate metamorphoses of thought in their pure element and in their worldly manifestations was not able to apply the essence of his dialectic – so successfully pursued in regard to the particularities of history – to the general and organic course of its idea. Regardless of his great merit in the field of the philosophy of history it is as if he had intentionally wanted to abandon his own method, standpoint and discoveries in so vital a question for humanity. In masterful fashion he describes a number of passages from one sphere to another, the succession of epochs and peoples as well as their reciprocal interconnection. When we come to consider the structure as a whole, however, we find only a series of ingenious exposi-tions or admittedly brilliant general perspectives. Nowhere do we find the total, rigorously speculative development executed with such great dialectical skill in other fields. The laws of logic which he was the first to reveal are not adequately reflected in his philosophy of history. In short, Hegel has not attained the concept of the organic and ideal totality of history in its speculative articulation and its architectonic perfection.

We must begin here with the question of form and method and pass on from there to the substantial aspect of the problem. It will turn out, however, that in considering the merely formal we shall soon be con-fronted with the substantial.

Hegel divided the entire course of history unto our day into four principal periods which he calls the *Oriental, Greek, Roman,* and *Christian-Germanic* worlds. To be sure, he sought to submit the course of history to a trichotomous architectonic pattern and to retain only three main epochs: the *Oriental,* the *Classical* (Greece and Rome) and the still-existing *Christian* world. He soon recognized, however, that Greece's essence was so distinct from Rome's that it would be impossible to join the two and that as proportionally great a difference existed between these two spheres as between the Orient and Greece. A still greater objection to retaining these three epochs, however, would have been the instant reproach that we have not reached the end of history and that therefore we cannot close history in such a way, denying any place for possible further developments. Indeed, we could sooner suppose the opposite, as *Herbart* does, that history to date is only a beginning – although this proposition too is inadmissible.

The above observation alone might suffice to destroy a framework of this sort. However, the most important argument which could be invoked for this particular Hegelian division would be the rule of *tetrachotomy* in nature and in the external world generally where the second moment again splits imparting a quadripartite character to the whole. Here the answer is very simple: universal history is certainly not a stage of nature and this highest process of the spirit can in no way share the fate of the external world . . .

Finally, some who perceive the speculative unsuitability of the quadri-partite division take refuge in another excuse in order to make a virtue out of the master's vice. They say that it is in this very peculiarity that the strength of his spirit is brilliantly revealed, for he refuses to tie himself down to any schema or to set up any forced aprioristic construction. Rather, he knows how to respect the free course of reality and does not force the content of universal history into the prefabricated forms of a pedantic schematism.

To this we must reply: either the laws of dialectics are universal and inviolable and should thus find their real manifestations in history; or else they are weak, partial and inadequate, in which case they should not be proclaimed in other spheres of knowledge and their deduction must everywhere be deprived of all necessity. It is because these laws carry in themselves the criterion of their necessity that history, this touchstone of all speculation, must reveal them to us *sub specie aeternitatis* in the sphere of *deeds*. As long as these laws have not found their very strictest realization in history they are robbed of their surest supports. Thus, if philosophy does not confirm them in history it commits either suicide or infanticide, destroying either itself or its corollaries. In this case, the intention of avoiding a pedantic schematism and thus maintaining an alleged freedom is merely a self-deception or a weak excuse.

Anyone who establishes a principle is obliged by the same token to acknowledge its most extreme consequences regardless of whether these are drawn out by him or someone else. Woe to him if the principle is overturned but glory, eternal glory, if the result which he himself was perhaps not able to attain later confirms the new discovery! This is precisely Hegel's lot as well as the fate of all those whom we can call in any way great. Admittedly, Hegel himself was not able to draw out all the consequences of his standpoint, but this does not detract from his merit, and whoever remedies an acknowledged deficiency in his system or even simply develops the system normally by progressing beyond Hegel's point of view will doubtlessly render a far greater tribute to Hegel's genius than someone who sets out to preserve an untouchable tradition. After all, could Hegel, who deduced the laws of development so forcefully and demonstrated them in the genesis of ideas, repudiate his own discoveries?

The totality of universal history is thus to be grasped integrally and absolutely as a speculative trichotomy, but if we are to avoid prejudicing the freedom of its development it is history in its totality and not simply a *part* of history such as the past which we must seize speculatively and organically. The totality of history must consist of the past and of the future, of the road already travelled as well as of the road yet to be travelled, and hence our first task is the cognition of the essence of the *future* through speculation.

Science too is not exempt from prejudices which have the unfortunate quality of sprouting roots in the strongest spirits and naturally crippling further progress. How often have such theoretical prejudices stifled living elements, thus robbing mankind of what it is on the point of discovering! If anyone could be free of such prejudices it would undoubtedly have been Hegel's speculative spirit but on this very point he gave way to this sort of anomaly. To be sure, Hegel could not establish all the consequences of his discoveries and left much to be done without anywhere prejudicing the *possibility* of a further progress, so that his mistakes were almost always *privative* and not absolutely *negative*. In the philosophy of history, however, he gave way to a negative prejudice which however natural and valid it may seem was no less an obstacle to proper comprehension. In his work he did not mention the *future* by name at all and he was even of the *opinion* that in exploring history philosophy can be only valid retroactively and that the future should be completely excluded from the sphere of speculation.

The position which we, on the other hand, affirm in advance is that without the *knowability of the future*, unless one conceives of the future as an integral part of history where the destiny of mankind is realized, it is impossible to know the organic, ideal totality and the apodictic process of world history. For this reason the establishment of the knowability of the future is an essential *precondition* for the organic structure of history. Indeed, the unknowability of the future in Hegel presents the same problem as the unattainability of the absolute in general in Kant, the only difference being that in Kant the problem is a necessary result of his critical standpoint and system whereas in Hegel the problem is brought in from the outside and thus destroys the entire order. Just as later philosophy dared to transgress Kant's limits in the field of pure speculation so it is now the vocation of the philosophy of history to overcome this analogous prejudice of Hegel. Just as we could never have attained absolute knowledge in philosophy without this first breakthrough so we can never attain absolute knowledge in the philosophy of history without the second, and should our challenge appear presumptuous and paradoxical it is in fact no more so than the challenge which triumphed over critical philosophy. Indeed, if it is possible for reason to seize the essence of God, freedom and immortality why should it not be able to seize the *essence* of the future?

We emphasize that our concern here, and particularly in this case, is with the *essence* because only the *essence* can be the object of philosophy. The necessary essence can manifest itself in an endless number of *existential contingencies* which must always remain arbitrary and hence cannot be foreseen in their particularities but must always appear as receptacles of the inner and the universal, suitable and adequate for the essence. It is precisely here that lies the advantage of the past in regard to the philosophical investigation of facts: we see what already lies behind us as laws in all their particulars and so we can admire the accuracy with which the depth and universality found in them reveals itself and the appropriateness with which the existing expresses its being. In regard to the future, however, we can only probe the *essence* of progress in general. There the possibility of realization is so rich, the freedom and fullness of the spirit so great that we may always incur the danger of being out-distanced or even deluded by a particular reality.

In this question, as in every logical investigation, we must distinguish accurately the sphere of universality and necessity from that of particularity and contingency so as to grasp true, concrete–synthetic freedom in the course of the spirit. Every essence must appear but just as it is unique and necessary in itself so its mode of manifestation is multiple and arbitrary and if it does not appear in *one* form and way it will appear in *another*. This is the distinction which explains the gulf between speculative *knowledge of the future* and these individual prophecies which can only be a deciphering of the future (*praesagium*) and in no way a foreknowledge (*praescientia*). We are not trying to divine this or that particularity or to predict a specific hero or event. We are seeking rather to investigate the true nature of mankind, to define the laws of its progress and to discern rationally their manifestations in history as well as to evaluate in itself and in relation to the future the road already covered. Finally, we are seeking to establish the periods of this continuing self-formation defining specific types where elements *virtually* impressed upon humanity have already been effectively realized. It is precisely this which is the true concern of philosophy.

The following remarks may serve to confirm the knowability of the future as a possibility. We all know that Cuvier required only a single tooth to investigate the whole organism of an antediluvian animal. No one objects to so paradoxical an affirmation; even the natural sciences, which usually deride all aprioristic speculations and choose to believe only the empirical, have not taxed him with arrogance. Instead, they have transformed his affirmation into an axiom acknowledging that this affirmation was founded upon the deepest concept of nature. But what makes this affirmation so irrefutable? – nothing other than recognition of the nature of an *organism* in general, namely the insight that in every organic totality each member must correspond completely to all others, that all members are mutually interdependent and condition each other. Why then do we not recognize a similar organic structure in history as well? Why do we

53

not consider past deeds as our fossils, the antediluvian fragments out of which we must erect the general structure of the life of mankind? Why do we not construct, out of that part of the complete historical process which we have already covered, the ideal totality of history in general and in particular the future part which we still lack, which must correspond to the past, and which together with the past can establish the true idea of humanity?

Having ascertained the possibility of the future being knowable let us turn to the reality of the proposition and demonstrate how consciousness comes to appropriate this knowledge unto itself.

Generally speaking, the future can be determined in three ways: through feeling, through thought and through the will. The *first* mode of determination is immediate, natural, blind and contingent. Consequently, it generally seizes only the particularities of being, individual facts; it becomes *pre-sentiment* and produces *seers* and *prophets*. Hence Saint Paul's profound words: 'Our knowledge is imperfect.' (1 Cor. 13.8 etc.). The *second* mode of determination is reflected, cogitated, theoretical, conscious, necessary; for the most part, it seizes thought in its generality, laws, the essential: it engenders *philosophers of history*. This is no longer imperfect knowledge, *we no longer see in a mirror dimly but face to face* (1 Cor. 13.12). Finally, the *third* mode of determination is truly and effectively practical, applied, complete, spontaneous, voluntary and free. Thus, it embraces the whole sphere of the deed, facts and their meaning, theory and praxis, the concept and its reality; it produces the *executors of history*.

Let us now inquire into the criteria of these three modes of determination. The criterion of the first lies outside itself in the external fulfilling of promises; that of the second lies within itself in the apodicticity of the laws of thought; the third criterion, however, lies both within and outside itself in the objective realization of a subjective, conscious teleology. The first is proper to Antiquity where thought was not yet as developed and where mankind lived more instinctively; this presentiment produced what we could call *historiopneustia* or *historomance*. The second is proper to our times for since the appearance of Christianity we have had no more prophets. We do, however, have *thinking* spirits because truth came into the world through Christianity whereas Antiquity attained only beauty in its different variations. Thus we now come to *historiosophy* and through this philosophy of history the *sealed books of Daniel* will be opened *because they are to remain closed only until the pre-determined time when many seekers shall come upon them and knowledge shall increase* (Daniel 12.4).

Finally, the third determination belongs to the future. It will be the objective, effective realization of known truth and it is precisely this which is the *Good*, i.e. the practical already containing the theoretical within itself.

Some may object that, contrary to what we have affirmed, consciousness does not outpace but usually follows events thus explaining and trans-figuring them. This is undoubtedly true *as soon as* we have made an extremely important distinction between facts (*facta*) and deeds properly speaking. Although apparently synonymous they are completely hetero-geneous in character and their differentiation is of the utmost importance. Facts (*facta*) are those passive events existing without our concurrence and consciousness which we, so to speak, stumble upon and in relation to which we remain completely indifferent. Obviously, our consciousness must step up to these in order to assimilate them and to discover the inner essence in their externality. The deed (*actum*) is something completely different. It is no longer an immediate result to be received and reflected. It is *already* reflected, already mediated, already cogitated, *intended and then accomplished*. It is an active event which is entirely ours, no longer foreign but already conscious before being realized. One can thus say that facts are *natural* events whereas deeds are *artificial*. The *praxis* formed by facts is unconscious and thus *pre-theoretical* whereas that formed by deeds is conscious and thus *post-theoretical*. Theory enters in the middle between the two practices revealing post-theoretical praxis as the true synthesis of the theoretical and of the immediately practical, of the sub-jective and the objective, insofar as *doing* in general is the true substantial synthesis of being and thinking.[1] [2]

We have thus long outgrown the sphere of presentiment which must precede consciousness and we are already in the sphere of knowledge, indeed at the point where consciousness through *historiosophy* becomes completely adequate to pre-theoretical praxis. Now a return into the opposite element is inevitable: consciousness outpaces the facts and after having advanced beyond them engenders the true *deed*, namely the post-theoretical praxis which properly belongs to the future. With the maturity of consciousness we have reached a *turning point in events*: consciousness can as easily look forwards as backwards in order to think through the totality of universal history. Facts are transformed into deeds and this is precisely what historiosophy is doing today.

[1] This is why Ballanche and others have noted the priority of 'opinions' over 'mores'.
[2] We shall return to this in more detail in chapter III.

We thus see that history does indeed traverse the three instances of *feeling, consciousness, deed,* and only thanks to this do we understand why the past has been so opaque, why the present is bright with the light of truth, and why a resolutely conscious future will develop *by its own might.* If the past seemed natural and almost haphazard in revealing the dispensations of Providence only *post factum,* mankind, having now attained its true self-consciousness, should henceforth accomplish deeds which are truly in conformity with the dictates of art and the idea. This does not mean that Providence must step out of history and leave the latter to its own fate but only that mankind itself has attained the degree of maturity where its own decisions are completely identical with the divine plans of Providence. World historical individuals, those heroes who represent nations in such a way that their own biographies can conveniently pass for universal history, should no longer be *blind instruments* of contingency but *conscious artisans* of their own freedom. Only then can God's will be done on earth as it is in heaven, i.e. with love, consciousness, freedom, whereas until now it has been realized through divine omnipotence without the self-conscious and self-determined co-operation of humanity.

Having shown the abstract possibility and the reality of the know-ability of the future (its precise and properly substantial demonstration can only come after the effective exposition of the material of history) we finally pass on to the *necessity* of this knowledge, whence we first grasp the higher principle of the organism of history. The principle of the know-ability of the future is only a special case of this higher principle of the organism from which we shall be able to develop the substantial categories of world history and then its true teleological process.

The destiny of mankind is to realize that its concept and history is precisely the execution of this process of realization. The fruit of this development, however, can only be attained at the end, and earlier stages are merely *preparations* and *premisses* which in their totality make up the great syllogism of the universal spirit. This process is thus a definite whole and if progress were a purely formal question then insofar as we possess the consciousness of so many centuries we could establish the remaining elements of this progress with mathematical certainty. However, the process of universal history is not limited to an abstract, formal and – as it were – quantitative development; it continuously develops qualitatively substantial rules, and consequently mathematical inductions cannot suffice here even though they must always constitute the base of the process. Accordingly, it will be the task of historiosophy to investigate the past *substantially*, to analyse profoundly all the already developed elements of the life of mankind *in their content*, to recognize their one-sided and exclusive nature, their struggle and reciprocal preponderance.

Historiosophy must define the particular sections of the general historical fabric so that we may know in which of these sections we already are, which ones we have already traversed, and which ones still remain for us to traverse in order to attain the highest peak of development of the universal spirit. Thus, wherever we find only a *definite one-sided* element in the past we must shift its precisely *opposite moment* into the future; *wherever we find already developed conflicts and contradictions in the past – as we generally do – we must ascribe their synthesis to the future.* Thus, we shall construct speculative syntheses out of the chaos of these already developed antitheses. These specific syntheses converge still further and must attain unity in a universal synthesis (*synthesis syntheseon*) which will be the truly highest and ripest fruit of the historical tree. Thus, *the wants of the past form the satisfactions of the future.* The *privative* image of the past will itself be the *positive* image of the future, and only thus will we necessarily come to know that the past and the future, commonly conditioning each other, form the *fully explicit organism* of universal history.

In this way the principle of the knowability of the future, or specifically its internal concept, leads us into the totality of the process of universal history to its *organism* and next to its true division according to the speculative–rational laws which alone produce the apodictic division of history. This division is nothing but trichotomic or – to put it more precisely – its first period is thetic, its second period is antithetic, and its third period is *synthetic* and perfectly *concrete*. These main forms of the universal spirit must be completed successively on the universal road of history but without excluding their *juxtaposition* and reciprocal interdependence.

To give the reader a general insight into our position – and a prolegomenon must be confined to general insights – let us only mention that the universal spirit is presently *entering the third, synthetic period* whose *first* or *thetic* period consists of all Antiquity and whose *second* or *antithetic* period, radically opposed to the first, is the Christian–Germanic world. Accordingly, in our view, Hegel's first three main periods are only three moments of the *first* overall period which makes up the ancient world. Hegel's *fourth* period is our *second* period and consists of the modern world. Finally, our third period is the *future* whose proper definition can be gleaned from the one-sided opposition of the two preceding ones.

Before Christianity externality and immediate objectivity reigned in history. Subjective spirit stood at its first stage, that of sensation, and objective spirit too assumed its most immediate form, that of *abstract right*. In contrast, Christ brought the element of internality, reflection and subjectivity into the world, lifting sensation to the level of internal consciousnesss and raising right to the level of morality. Consequently, Christ is the midpoint of the past because it is He who brought about the radical reform of humanity and turned the great page of world history. At the same time as this new principle appeared equally new peoples inundated what had hitherto been the field of history and rejuvenated an already ossified and grey ancient race with new blood. It is thus at this point of universal history that we find both a physical and a moral rebirth of humanity.

The universal spirit has thus hitherto traversed *two* great spheres of its development: the ancient world which lasted until the migration of nations and the Christian–Germanic world as such which has continued unto our day. Whatever the importance of the reforms beginning in the fifteenth century they do not express as sharp an opposition, as radical a turnover in all vital relations as the two periods contrasted. History has not yet developed all the elements inherent in its concept precisely because *there is a future standing before us* which we have to come to know according to the premisses of past times. We must therefore say that none of the exclusive and one-sided elements which have unfolded until now can suffice mankind precisely because of their one-sidedness, exclusivity and disjointedness. Instead, these elements rush out of their disjointedness into a higher concreteness which will be the true standpoint as well as the crown of all past determinations raising their *mechanical* relations and *chemical* oppositions to an organic concurrence and consensus. . .

In short, it is the task of the absolute will to realize what has been felt and known, for this is the new direction of the future. To realize the idea of *beauty* and *truth* in practical life, in the already conscious world of objectivity, to grasp and regroup in lively co-operation all one-sided and apparently detached elements in the life of mankind, finally to realize the idea of the *absolute Good* and of absolute teleology in this world – such is the great task of the future.

In order to fulfil this task, in order to open this new period through a great physical and anthropological event, a *migration of peoples* is again necessary. But the inversion of relations gives this necessity a completely opposite character, i.e. the new migration of nations must be a reaction against the earlier one and originate with *civilized peoples* to submerge still *barbarian tribes*. In the first migration of nations the raw force of nature triumphed over a still undeveloped spiritual force, but *ironically* this victory only served to *regenerate* the spirit itself. Now, however, spiritual force will assail a disintegrating and upwardly aspiring natural force and the triumph of the spirit will itself serve the *regeneration of nature*. Conversely too, the lifting of natural peoples to the spiritual level which we have already attained will be an uplifting and renovation of our own degenerate nature. This revenge of the universal spirit, i.e. the second, inverted migration of nations, will be an inescapable transition to the third period.

It is truly remarkable that no one has previously come upon this trichotomic division of the organism of universal history, for Christ has so often been seen as the true midpoint of universal history. In fact, as we shall see below, the coming of Christ is so important a turning point and has created such a sharp contradiction between the preceding and following periods that we must acknowledge a definite opposition between the two periods in all specific elements of the life of humanity.

Among Hegel's neglected writings we find several noteworthy passages which seem to have been overlooked both by Hegel's readers and by Hegel himself even though they would have led directly to the conception of history formulated here. In the 'Treatise on the relation of natural philosophy to philosophy in general' the opposition between the ancient and the modern world is stated in absolute terms. The only element missing here from a complete and speculative comprehension of the organism of universal history is the principle of the knowability of the future, i.e. the conception of the future as an integral part of the whole.

In fact, Hegel's proximity to our position is an eloquent guarantee of its accordance with the concept and the times, for in the normal course of development of the spirit no new direction can be followed and no new standpoint established unless it has been legitimized in the past through clear indications attesting to the presentiment of its need. Was not Hegel's method the yearning of centuries? When we read someone like Giordano Bruno do we not have the impression that we are at a point of inauguration of this method? From Giordano Bruno to Solger we see a continuous unveiling of the method, a constant search until finally Hegel completes the discovery and thus identifies himself with this important stage of the spirit.

Thus, one after another, the one-sided traits of the ancient and modern world appear in history leaving the resolution of their opposition to the third, synthetic period *which belongs to the future*. In this way, we dispose the content of universal history according to the true speculative trichotomy without injuring either the past or the future even as we open to the latter a field both vast and rich and yet describable in advance. Thus, we satisfy two opposite demands: to include the totality of universal history ideally and not to *exclude* the possibility of further development. Any other solution to the dilemma posed by these conflicting demands would condemn it to flounder on the Scylla of an unspeculative periodization of universal history hit upon in purely immediate fashion – such as Hegel's quadripartite division – or to crash on the Charybdis which consists of forcing the fabric of history into an aprioristic mould. Hegel quite rightly preferred to fall on the Scylla, for one can extricate oneself from it more *integrally*. Had he applied his attempted trichotomic division the ensuing shipwreck on the Charybdis of empty schematism would have been more dangerous for his honour. At present however, it is certainly honour enough for him to have brought the flagship of philosophy so successfully into port...

It should be clear from this first chapter why we have called our conception of the philosophy of history *historiosophy*. First, we have indicated its phenomenological derivation by opposing it to *historiopneustia* and thus putting it in the middle between the presentiment and the completion of history, at the turning point where facts are converted into deeds; this turning point is the theory, the absolute knowledge of history or, to put it objectively, *the wisdom of universal history*. Second, by erecting the concept of a historical organism we have further justified the term 'historiosophy'. This concept exposes earlier philosophies of history as nothing but preliminary systems and deductions from ingenious *philosophical assertions*. In no way can they be called a rigorously speculative development of universal history in its organic ideality at all comparable to the development which Hegel accomplished for philosophy as such. If we might say that from *Pythagoras* to *Hegel* we had only *philosophia* whereas with Hegel we attained *sophia*, in a methodologically analogous fashion we could say that here we have treated the passage from a philosophy of history to *historiosophy*. We shall continue and broaden our exposition in the following chapter.

Chapter II
THE CATEGORIES OF UNIVERSAL HISTORY

How all things live and work
and ever blending,
Weave one vast whole from

Being's ample range,
How powers celestial, rising
and descending,
Their golden buckets ceaseless
interchange,
Their flight on rapture-
breathing pinions winging,
From heaven to earth their
genial influence bringing,
Through the wide sphere their
chimes melodious ringing.

Goethe

Although the first chapter has established the universality, particularity and individuality of the historical organism it has done so only unilaterally insofar as it emphasized merely the *formal* side of the development of the universal spirit; generally speaking, the question of *how*. All these considerations are to be understood as dealing with *universality* and we now want to pass over to their particularity, namely to the definite elements of content which must come together in the concrete development of the life of mankind. Thus, the abstract *how* must now define itself as a specific *what*; for since we know how development takes place we must learn precisely what it is that develops so that afterwards we may finally ask about the *why*, i.e. about the absolute teleology of universal history in general. In Hegel's lofty and concrete elaboration of philosophy as such we find a great many elements that will be applied to universal history in a manner fully appropriate to their concept. Once again, however, he fails to lead these elements systematically through the material of history, i.e. through the content-full organism of the categories of history. The second main point of our investigation will be precisely to accomplish this.

The consciousness of the analogy reigning in all spheres of the universe and culminating in the identity of thought and being has already expressed itself definitively in Spinoza's statement 'Ordo et connexio idearum idem est ac ordo et connexio rerum', and the latest realizations of science have brought this to the fore as the truly great discovery of most recent philosophy. All is reflected in all since one fundamental thought traverses the essence of all. From the immediate viewpoint of universal identity we must see universal history as a *microcosm* where all spheres of being, thought, and action should preserve their specific resonance and their own manifestation. However, further investigation shows that universal history constitutes the field of *real action* in general and, as we have earlier remarked, the truly substantial identity of thought and being is the deed (which will be explained somewhat more minutely in chapter III). Thus, the whole essence of being and thought must appear on the stage of universal history in the form of *deeds*. But the universal spirit forms the highest peak of the development of the spirit, namely the *immediate unity of the subjective and objective spirit*. Thus, we must designate universal history not as microcosm but rather spiritual *macrocosm* in general absorbing all lower determinations in itself and thus grounding them in itself. Thus, universal history shows itself to us as the peak and the goal not merely of the spirit but of the whole universe in general. It follows from this consideration that all possible abstract and real determinations which philosophy has to develop must reveal themselves in the last instance in the universal spirit in order to soar from there to their loftiest manifestations...

. . . .

...The categories of the spirit are not merely symbolical types *analogous* in some way to historical phases or, like physical categories, only their passive and material foundations. They are also not merely abstract conceptual descriptions, general ideal *foundations* of facts like logical categories. Rather, they are *active* and *concrete* self-manifestations of the spirit which constitute immediate specific elements of history whereas the previous ones were only mediate moments. Just as we have considered physical categories in general as only analogous to the development of the universal spirit and recognized only a few as truly *co-determining*, with spiritual categories it is precisely the reverse; in general, they constitute real and specific means of manifestation of the spirit and only a few are simply *analogous* reflections. Among the latter one could cite the comparison of the course of history with the ages of man and things of this sort, and even this becomes immediate reality as soon as we individualize all mankind as customarily happens in the expression *universal spirit*. What we call individualizing all mankind as universal spirit we already know more thoroughly as the universal course of development of history. Although it may appear to us here as a synthetic *ascension* if we take the individual spirit as point of departure it is in itself according to its logical meaning only the abstract universal.

At this point arises the new challenge of developing the whole range of determinations of the spirit no longer in their secluded meaning as they are in and for themselves but of grasping them in their meaning *for history*. At this higher level, that of universal history, we must simultaneously negate them and show that it is in history that they first acquire their highest meaning and truth and come to participate in its foundations, that the importance which they had until now, though certainly *concrete in itself*, was completely *abstract* in relation to the universal spirit. For this reason too the determinations of the spirit, already real and concrete in and for themselves, must serve for history only as categories. Thus, all anthropological and psychological moments of development will be applied to the *whole of mankind*, to *specific peoples* and to *particular individuals*. In all these spheres they become both *simultaneous* and hence timeless and then in a real sense momentary and hence timely inasmuch as they constitute the specific *movimentum* of *this very moment*. Thus, these moments always appear in part *real* and in part *typical* according to their position and representation. This is the way to consider, for example, the anthropological determinations of age and temperament. Age does not simply impinge immediately and powerfully upon the life of historical individuals but, as Herder already established, a life-cycle inheres in mankind itself. We must add that particular peoples demonstrate particular levels and different stages of life so that the whole life-cycle does not manifest itself simply *extensively* in the total course of history but also unfolds all its integrating moments *intensively* at its particular stages in simultaneous development. So too temperaments distinguish not only individuals but also peoples and indeed affirm these differences in the general progress of history. For the life of mankind itself submits to an alteration of temperament. Determinations still most markedly stamped with the imprint of nature, e.g. the alteration of years and days, sleeping and waking, must be taken account of in history. Naturally this customarily happens automatically, but for that very reason they are deprived of the necessity and the dialectical deduction which we demand for them here...

These remarks are only intended to promote the rehabilitation of elements eliminated by a reactive effect. Both in the spiritual and in the logical spheres we must now revive what was effaced and subsequently rejected as unusable and desiccated, grant rights anew to it and ground it more firmly in its proper place. To be sure, this element should not penetrate into the essential part of the laws nor appear determinant where it can be only subordinate...Further and ever higher moments of the spirit will finally constitute the true and most important elements of history. Religion, language, art, science, law, the state, etc. – these are the proper productions of history because they are at the same time the highest determinations of the spirit. Very appreciable contributions have already been made to the process of deducing these elements in universal history, i.e. to their apprehension not in their proper *meaning* but as *integral* moments of the universal spirit. It thus remains the task of historiosophy to vindicate for our standpoint all these elements which are already partially organized but mostly still to be organized and to deduce them in conformity to this standpoint.

From this perspective all moments of the philosophical system appear to us *in their special relation and application to the history of mankind*. This is because history, as has been said earlier, occupies the highest and most concrete position in the development of the spirit and constitutes the macrocosm to which all lower determinations must converge. Thus, universal history is the *sensorium commune* of the universe. Only one thing stands above universal history, that is the absolute spirit, God. Consequently, just as everything in the world is subordinated to history, the latter in its turn is subordinated only to God. Just as world history is the tribunal of the world, so too God is the judge of world history; precisely God's rule in world history even as history itself rules over everything is both our first and at the same time our final result. Now as always it will be the alpha and the omega. It is for this reason too that the two founders of the philosophical presentation of history, St Augustine and Bossuet, have established divine rule as the principle of universal history; for this reason too the latest labourers of this field will attain the same result since divine rule is as much a principle as a result. This rule has hitherto been asserted; now we are to ordain it in its threefold mode of revelation:

1. immediately in the past through the fulfilment of divine promises in the particular *springs* of history;

2. mediately in the present through the discovery of divine reason in the general *flow* of history;

3. mediated according to a goal in the future through the attainment of the final divine end of happiness in the definitively completed teleological *outflow* of history.

The *first* manner of revelation will be manifested *factually* in the empirical part of historiosophy; it forms the specific element of *belief*. The *second* will be deduced abstractly and genetically in the speculative part where the categories which have only been cursorily schematized constitute the determinate moments of development; these, on the other hand, form the specific element of *wisdom*. The *third*, however, should be developed concrete, free and *really* according to the teleology of the spirit in the synthetic part, and this constitutes the specific element of the highest *cult*, for the *active* elevation of mankind to God is certainly superior to its elevation in feeling or in thought. Thus, this powerful penetration of divinity into history, this admitted rational providence, in no way remains an empty thought; rather, in conformity to the concept and in a determinate manner it forms a pillar of light which mankind is to follow in the name of the Father, the Son and the Holy Ghost.

Chapter III
THE TELEOLOGY OF UNIVERSAL HISTORY

> The spirit aids; from anxious scruples freed
> I write: in the *end* will be the deed!
>
> Goethe[1]

After the hollow theory of perfectibility had proven inadequate for a philosophical comprehension of universal history, the first fundamentally teleological view appeared; precisely because it was the first it also had to be the most immediate and the lowest in the development of the idea. For the teleology of universal history too must undergo an evolution and must fix each of the individual stages of the idea in its proper order. Here we must again seek to recognize the organic structure of these stages, i.e. the completely speculative development of teleology.

The idea in its immediacy – in its first external and natural shape – is the idea of the *beautiful* and of *art*. Hegel grasped this perfectly well in his teaching about the absolute spirit although he did not deduce it logically with equal clarity. Immediacy remains the true position of the *beautiful* and of *art* even if someone like *Weisse* tries to assign them a different position or, conversely, if others choose to look at the idea of beauty as the speculative unity of the idea of the true and the good, hence as the synthesis of the theoretical and the practical. The former error, arising from the wish to vindicate the priority of thinking, insists that beauty must have truth as its prerequisite. In fact, the situation is quite the opposite, for even though truth stands in contradiction to the initially encountered determination it is higher and broader, as Hegel rightly showed, in the transition from art to philosophy. The latter error doubtlessly arises from a misunderstanding of Hegel's statements in the *Aesthetics*. There he describes the beautiful as the union of both *finite* intelligence and *finite* will, which is admittedly true, but the point is that the beautiful is only this and in no way the unity of the absolutely true and good. In other words, this conception is correct in attributing such unity to the beautiful

[1] Cieszkowski is paraphrasing what originally read: 'in the beginning was the deed!' – AL.

65

with the reservation that this unity is immediate and undeveloped, hence thetic but in no way synthetic and absolutely mediated, that it only constitutes a natural indifference, a unity in itself which has not yet undergone the process of differentiation.

It lay within the idea's very essence that the idea of the beautiful should constitute the first stage of the teleological process of universal history. To describe this idea more specifically from the point of view of universal history one could speak of *culture, humanity, the aesthetic education of mankind*. Indeed, the first thinker who established the teleological view of history brought these concepts forward without hesitation, and even though the idea of culture had been advanced before *Herder* by *Iselin* the latter did so in such an indeterminate way that in presenting the development of historical teleology he merits no more than an honourable mention. What *Iselin* vaguely, abstractly and, so to speak, instinctively *brought into* universal history, Herder *brought through* the empirical matter of universal history precisely, concretely and consciously until finally *Schiller brought* it *out* and in doing so *brought* it *forward* to a higher and broader position.

· · · ·

Schiller asks of nations what Herder had asked of individuals. Moreover, he raises the artistic view to a higher level of generality, saying, 'Wholeness of character must therefore be present in a people' (Schiller, *Aesthetic Education*, letter 4). As we look at the artistic formation of a nation we find that the call to preserve natural differences among nations represents a demand that the same artistic criterion be applied to the universal spirit as the one which *Hirt* affirmed in regard to art in general and which, formally and abstractly speaking, is correct. However, Schiller does not stop there but reaches right into the content of artistic formation where he foresees the reconciliation of universal antagonisms through art; it is here that we see him coincide with Schelling.

· · · ·

In ancient Greece the beautiful and artistically fitting character of the universal spirit was a *natural state*. In no way did subjectivity act to generate or preserve it since subjectivity had itself not yet developed. Precisely because it was a purely objective state it was limited to *being* and consequently as soon as it began to be *thought* it had to disintegrate internally. Now, *thought itself has thought itself through*. It has reconciled itself with being for it tends towards being not as a *condition* but as a

66

process of formation called upon to bring forward an art which has already passed through thought and is therefore mediated. Thus, the artistic life of the past stands in relation to the future as *fact* is related to *deed* (*factum* to *actum*; see the first chapter of these *Prolegomena*). A. W. Schlegel aptly calls Greek culture a perfectly natural education. After its decay an *artificial* education must be set up – a *factual*, artistic formation must be replaced by an *active* one. This is the supreme end which Schiller seeks to attain and it would truly be supreme *if art as such could be the highest end*.

In this way, Herder and Schiller have laid the foundations of the true *aesthetics of universal history*. At this stage the life of mankind is an artistic formation, states and individuals are works of art, great men are political artists. As we proceed to the second stage, we first encounter the true philosophy of universal history. At this stage the life of mankind is a cultivation of consciousness, states are ideas, great men – and we do not say this ironically – are political philosophers. Here, therefore, *aesthetic* formation must give way to *philosophical* formation.

. . . .

When beauty is comprehended as no longer sufficient because it is only the *lowest stage of the highest ends* it must be dialectically converted into its opposite. The conversion occurs only by bringing into prominence beauty's essential element and since this proves inadequate then its opposite must appear as adequate. The essential element in beauty and art is precisely immediacy, natural and artificial exteriority, within which the highest ends come into existence *spontaneously* but not *self-spontaneously* (i.e. wholly spontaneously in the sense of *generatio spontanea*, but not *sua sponte*). Thence arises the need for the opposite which is *reflection-for-itself*, supra-sensible interiority where the highest ends are henceforth to develop in the form of *thought* and *consciousness*. Thus, beauty truly becomes a transition whose situation Hegel very correctly describes (*Lectures on Aesthetics*) by saying that the work of art stands in the middle between immediate sensibility and ideal Thought. Hegel was the first who could clearly express the consciousness of the preceding stage; that is why he recognized in artistic beauty 'one of the mediations which dissolved and led back to unity the opposition and contradiction between spirit abstractly resting on itself and nature' (*ibid.*).

Like Schiller, Hegel does not remain standing at this retrospective recognition but marches forward to the subsequent mediation which will appear to us again later as the true *mediation of mediations*. Here 'the form which is higher *in relation* to sensually concrete representation, i.e.

thought is admittedly abstract *in a relative sense* but must be concrete rather than one-sided in order to be true and rational thought' (*ibid.*).

This is precisely the point we wanted to reach here; for our purposes it forms the foundation of the true *philosophy of history* in opposition to the preceding *aesthetics of history*. Just as the first teleological viewpoint apprehended history only according to its individual and natural shape so now history is apprehended according to its objective generality. Beauty has ceded to truth, the artistic life of mankind has been absorbed by its philosophical idea; instead of humanity and the cultivation of beauty the 'final cause of the world at large we allege to be the consciousness of its freedom on the part of spirit' (*Lectures on the Philosophy of History*).

This *second*, truly philosophical stage of the teleology of history, which was first exposed with the most thorough clarity by Hegel, must be *recognized* in its opposition to the first aesthetic stage and *acknowledged* in its truth in order afterwards to be itself again *overcome* and dissolved in a higher *third* stage. We can deal with the essence of this viewpoint quite summarily since it is precisely this which constitutes the present scientific position; moreover, the first two chapters of this study should be seen as contributions to its perfection and completion (after this achievement nothing remains but that it dissolve itself and make way for a higher viewpoint). We need only take into consideration Hegel's definition of universal history as given in his *Lectures on the Philosophy of History* in order to apprehend this whole standpoint with the utmost clarity. It reads: 'The history of the world is none other than the progress in the consciousness of freedom, a progress whose development according to the necessity of its nature it is our business to investigate' (*ibid.*).

· · · ·

Hegel's freedom is thus a true and real freedom which is nevertheless encumbered with a *preponderance* of necessity based, as we shall soon see, on the principle of absolute idealism. It is thus abstractly opposed to Schiller's freedom which is encumbered by immediate contingency. The whole basis of the familiar polemic against Hegelian freedom may be reduced to this point which is false inasmuch as it is not the outcome but the principle which should be assailed; a freedom based in thought must be thoroughly incapable of not being. That Hegel's freedom is still encumbered with necessity and hence in spite of its concreteness remains partially one-sided is so well-known, recognized and misunderstood a fact that we do not need to dwell on it any longer.

Thus, at this stage, thought is the highest form of the spirit. Reason is the conductor and the objective truth of history and, finally, consciousness of this is the highest aim and need of humanity. Connected with this is what could initially be seen as coincidental, that the development of the universal spirit in history is apprehended as the corollary of the phenomenological development of consciousness and that the development of the universal spirit links itself from the beginning quite naturally with the critique of consciousness. Indeed, consciousness in Hegel is the alpha and the omega; *from this* he deduces the whole system of his philosophy in general, *to this* we see him lead the whole process of universal history. Moreover, it is this which accounts for the great importance of the *Phenomenology* in the history of philosophy: with this work, with this genesis of consciousness, the spirit developing in the form of thought itself attains *consciousness par excellence*, i.e. Hegel's position itself has assumed that position in the history of philosophy in general which consciousness as such assumes in the system of philosophy itself. This is why consciousness is the specific core of Hegelian philosophy and although its development accompanies the whole process of history *in extenso* only with Hegel does it *coincide intensively with itself*. For this reason, consciousness here is consciousness *par excellence*. To be sure, this coincidence may split but the result of the completed coincidence has already been attained; the split will no longer be a *falling out and apart* but a *stepping out of itself*, i.e. a split which maintains its identity with itself. Here we find the kernel of this position's dissolution and we understand why *at this very moment* we find ourselves at the turning point of universal history where facts are converted into deeds. This is to say that since consciousness occupies a determinate place in the true system of philosophy the universe does not end with it. According to thought what precedes it is unconscious, i.e. fact; what succeeds it, however, must develop consciously and this is the *deed*.

Through the absolute conquest of consciousness the spirit will unfold from now on along its further road with a completely different determinateness and henceforth will find itself at home in its objective and absolute metamorphoses.

At the previous stage of historical teleology we were not satisfied with a *presupposed* view; rather we recognized it as posited within self-developing reality under the form of beauty in the ancient, primarily Greek world. We must do the same for this stage although according to what we have just said it will be clear that what corresponds to this stage is precisely the unfolding of the modern spirit. Indeed, for philosophy in general this sphere already had its beginnings, but nothing more than its beginnings, in Aristotelian *thought of thought*. Only Christian philosophy, the philosophy of thought, was able to broaden and develop this sphere absolutely in its true *inner* element, an accomplishment which has recently been fully completed by the second Aristotle of our times. Just as classical Antiquity, and particularly Greece, was the world of art and of immediate beauty so too the Christian modern epoch is the world of thought, of consciousness and of philosophy. This world which Aristotle opened with the *thought of thought* was closed more concretely by Hegel with the *thought of the identity of thought and being*; from Hegel's standpoint this is the highest definition of philosophy.[1] But this world which is itself abstract and diametrically opposed to the preceding one must itself dissolve and find its formal transition in the postulate of a *third* world. The content of this transition lies in the recognition that consciousness is not the supreme end but must itself advance over and outside itself and, even better, *out of itself*. The transition appears as the demand for a *substantial* unity of thought and being which is not simply in and for itself but must also generate a substratum *out of itself*.

Because of this transition we must put aside specific considerations on historiosophy for a more general and more comprehensive examination.

When Aristotle affirmed that 'theory is the noblest' he dealt art its death blow. Admittedly, this was stated in a completely different context, nonetheless its absolute spiritual meaning was its mortal effect on art and the enthronement of philosophy in place of art which followed. When art lost its supremacy in the spirit of mankind this supremacy fell to inner thought, theory, in a word, to philosophy.[2]

The supremacy of philosophy has maintained itself unto our day where the era of intelligence has reached its apogee. This is perceived even by those who can give no clear account of the essential task which remains

[1] Even if not stated literally it is *nonetheless* truly Hegel's. Moreover, the definition given that 'philosophy is the science of reason insofar as the latter is conscious of itself as all being' accords perfectly with the preceding one.

[2] One cannot speak of religion here; a true comprehension of religion, as Hegel understands it in paragraph 554 of the third edition of the *Encyclopedia* and as Richter has brought out very clearly more recently in his *Lehre der letzten Dingen*, encompasses the whole absolute sphere of the spirit in which art, philosophy, etc. are only particular stages. Religion is thus in no way assimilated or subordinated to them; it is precisely the highest substantiality of the whole sphere and it governs these stages absolutely, reflecting itself constantly in them and not *separating* itself from them as something *different*, as Hegel and his school normally assume. If we say that in Antiquity art was supreme we mean religion as art, just as the later opposition of philosophy to art expresses itself also in the form of religion since the Christian religion appears vis-a-vis that of Antiquity as philosophical, meditated, believed and conscious.

for philosophy after the discovery of the absolute method. The attainment of the absolute method is the essential core of philosophy; thus it would be truly underestimating Hegel's greatness and historical significance not to see in him at least – to borrow Weisse's use of Talleyrand's *bon mot* – the *beginning of the end* of philosophy, just as in Aristotle we see if not its beginning properly speaking, at least the *end of the beginning*. Yes, with Hegel thought has solved its essential task and even though its course of development has in no way ended, it will nevertheless retreat from its peak and yield before the ascent of another star. Just as art, having attained its classical form, rose above itself to dissolve in romanticism even as it ceded its universal hegemony to philosophy, in the same way at this very moment philosophy stands at such a classical point where it must surpass itself and in doing so yield effective universal domination to another. From this perspective we recognize as correct both those who promise a great many transformations and advances in philosophy and those who, conscious of the importance of the position attained, demand absolute self-sufficiency for it. Transformations in philosophy, even very important ones, are certainly still to be expected, but the most important are behind us and the more philosophy progresses the more will it become alien to and distant from its classical position. Nevertheless, this will be a progress of the spirit just as romanticism in relation to the art of Antiquity was actually an advance in the idea of beauty.

· · · ·

To resolve the contradiction between art and philosophy, to eradicate the preponderance of being and thought in identity, to develop a substantial identity out of a formal one, finally, to *synthesize* the highest synthesis *itself* and to raise it to its *third*, true power – this is the new challenge which we must lay down.

Art is a matter of representing the internal, i.e. of *objectivizing meaning*, whereas philosophy, conversely, deals with the *meaning of objectivity*. Thus art as well as philosophy is the identity of thought and being, the internal and the external, subject and object. In art this identity is still inadequate precisely because it is the first and is, consequently, a sensibly natural identity. In philosophy, on the other hand, this identity has been completed a second time and thus is deficient too because it forms only the reflected antithesis of the first standpoint and is one-sided in its supra-sensibility. The sharp contradiction existing between art and philosophy could not be emphasized until now, both because the second element of the opposition, i.e. philosophy, had not yet attained its *classical ripeness* and thus could not be put upon the same relative height as already developed art, and because the more concrete and the higher an opposition the less glaring is its manifestation. This is why the contradiction now reigning between art and philosophy is not as visibly pronounced as that seen at lower levels, for in the poorest and most immediate designations the elements of opposition are furthest from each other. The higher we rise, however, the weightier and the more complex these elements become. At the same time, they deviate less from each other so that, at the absolute level, they attain their highest meaning as well as their infinitely smallest divergence; consequently, from the standpoint of the understanding, they coincide in abstract, immediate and natural unity. (This is why we may also say that for the understanding there is nothing contradictory in God; for speculation, however, contradictions are to be stimulated to the utmost and precisely through this dissolved in the highest unity without having rejected their power of differentiation. Accordingly, speculation may say that God abounds with contradictions inasmuch as God is the highest unity and the foundation of all contradictions.) Thus, if the contradiction reigning between art and philosophy is *less apparent* than other lower contradictions it is still *more important* because it absorbs such high interests of the spirit and because contradictions are only lowest where they *only appear* most. For this reason too the quiet inner strife of the sentiments and inner psychic contradictions are so intense and hard because they appear least and are almost inexistent for the *crowd* which sees everything externally. The contradiction between art and philosophy is of such immense importance that it alone could express the huge chasm which separates the ancient from the modern world. To solve this contradiction and to bridge this chasm is the supreme destiny of practical, *social life* which itself will revitalize both a decadent art and a somewhat degenerate philosophy.

To bridge this chasm we must ask: what has philosophy decisively negated in art? Where is the turning point of one-sidedness? The task of further progress is to negate this negation itself and integrate earlier one-sidedness. The immediate sensibility of art has passed into the suprasensibility of thought and thought has revenged itself in philosophy at the cost of being for art's earlier encroachments. To solve this contradiction and overcome one-sidedness a reversal to the first standpoint is necessary, but a reversal no longer burdened by contradictions and preponderance, a reversal which is a harmonious identification of both elements and must itself develop further not only formally as neutral indifference but also *substantially* as *an affirmative new formation.* Thus, absolute thought must return to absolute being without alienating itself. This re-begotten being, unlike the first, will not be passively present; it will be the created, consciously begotten being which is the absolute *deed*. Here, it is no longer a question of a mere identity of thought and being; this identity expresses itself as a substratum in a new affirmation which is, for the first time, the true and real identity. Just as supremacy passed from immediate artistic practice to theory as such so now theory cedes before self-begetting, synthetic, post-theoretical praxis whose unprecedented vocation is to be the basis and truth of art as well as of philosophy. Henceforth, absolutely practical, social action and political life (not to be confused with *finite* activities and practices) will be determinant whereas art and philosophy, hitherto considered the highest identities, will be reduced to the significance of abstract premises of political life. *Being* and thought must dissolve in action—*art* and *philosophy in social life* in order to re-emerge anew and truly bloom for the first time in conformity to their final destiny.

. . . .

. . . Although reason may reveal itself in Hegel as the most objective and absolute it still remains *only* reason – it is supreme for philosophy but not for absolute spirit as such. *Now it is the absolute will which should be raised to the heights of speculation which reason has already known.* There are already very perceptive hints of this in the elder Fichte, but for all their importance they remain only hints analogous to the truly speculative hints which emerge with Kant and whose true and complete discovery we owe to Hegel. We have already remarked in the first chapter that in philosophy as in life no new direction emerges and no important discovery is completed without having been foreshadowed by some sort of meteor. This also applies to the new direction which the spirit must now take as philosophy leaves its own proper position and rises above itself into a domain which is alien but which nevertheless thoroughly conditions its further development, i.e. into the *absolutely practical* sphere of the *will*. We shall see that this sphere is one which has often been announced by more recent philosophers and that its meaning for the process of development of philosophy corresponds to romanticism's meaning for art. Truth, the idea, reason – these are the proper elements of philosophy in general and to the extent to which philosophy has attained its absolute, classical form it now goes beyond and above them. One could say that this constitutes a fall from the heights for philosophy itself but for the spirit it means a colossal upward soaring.

73

Hegel has led the spirit only to the *in-* and *for-itself*. The *in-* and *for-itself*, however, only find their full truth in the *out-of-itself*, not to be confused with the *outside-itself* which is very immediate and abstract in comparison to this lofty and concrete category. The *out-of-itself* comprehends bringing forth without self-alienation, thus in no way does it leave itself or even remain outside itself. This is why the *out-of-itself* first occurs as the result of the *in-itself* and the *for-itself*, as the substantial and steady unity of these premisses which themselves are abstractions in relation to the *out-of-itself* but are in no way excluded or abstracted by it. To be sure, the *out-of-itself* is also reflected as the third sphere in the normal course of thought itself. Consequently, speculative reason in its character *as a third sphere* is not merely thought in- and for-itself but thought out-of-itself as such. Precisely in this way thought becomes truly *active* and self-active. The spirit is only spirit when it is itself and this selfness is the specificity of the spirit as *otherness* is the specificity of nature. Thus, the principal forms of the spirit are:

    a. self-being;

    b. self-thinking;

    c. self-acting.

a. In-itself the spirit is *self-being*, i.e. ideal, living individuality which for the first time has sundered itself from nature and has its centre *in itself*; this is the first natural stage of the spirit, its *sense certainty*.

b. For-itself the spirit is self-thinking, i.e. *consciousness*, which is the level of reflection of the spirit in general.

c. Out-of-itself, however, the spirit is *self-acting*, i.e. *free activity* as such, which is the most concrete evolution of the spirit.

Nature, on the other hand, can only attain *in-*, *for-* and *out-of otherness*. Since its being is alien it is a *means*, its thought is the consciousness *which others have* of it, finally its activity is fixed from outside. This is why nature is subordinate to physical laws. This is why no miracle can arise in nature. Only the *spirit* is capable of miracles because only it is *autonomous*. This autonomy of self-acting is the highest element that can be designated as absolute.

Consequently, the spirit is not *only* activity but indeed activity in general. Since thought in its purest element is the *logical* as such and being's own element is the *physical*, the element proper to the spiritual is action and the spirit is activity *par excellence*. As has been stated, the spirit first reveals that side of itself which is being, *sense certainty in itself*; then, it presents that aspect which is thought, *consciousness for itself*; finally, the spirit is free activity and this is its third, *most proper* destiny. Thus, Hegel

is perfectly correct when he says that the spirit is initially one and immediate and that it doubles when it *becomes for itself* through consciousness.
One need only add that its further destiny is to *triple* as *it must reproduce
consciousness and translate thought into being practically and out of itself.*
This reproduction and translation in no way constitute a mere moment of
consciousness comparable to the relation of the practical to the theoretical
but, precisely to the contrary, make up a specific stage higher than consciousness. This is the stage into which consciousness flows and to which
the spirit must rise in order to satisfy its destiny for the first time in a way
in which theory as such could not. I realize perfectly well that I am
diminishing the meaning of theory itself and that I could be accused of
falling back into an already historically surpassed opposition between
theory and praxis. However, the present extension of the meaning of
theory is an anomaly which could only persist as long as theory itself was
most eminent and *passed for* universally dominant and applicable, i.e. as
long as the highest synthesis had developed only *in the form of thought.* As
for any eventual opposition, one should be careful not to confuse *identity*
with *indifference.* Spinoza's important statement, 'Voluntas et intellectus
unum et idem sunt', is certainly to be understood in the former and not
in the latter sense and the difference between these two meanings must be
posited as nothing but the difference between *stages of development*; accordingly, praxis is related to theory as speculative to reflected thought. Hegel,
who himself was so profoundly aware of the essence of the practical (for
example in the introductory paragraphs of the *Philosophy of Right*), has
nevertheless contributed most among the moderns to this misunderstanding which in fact cannot be properly called a misunderstanding but
only a *not yet apprehended understanding.* In Hegel the *practical* is *still
absorbed* by the *theoretical* and has not yet distinguished itself from it; one
could say that here the practical is still a *tributary* of the theoretical. The
true and proper destiny of the practical, however is to be a *separate,
specific,* indeed the *highest* stage of the spirit. The question of which stage
is higher or lower has already been resolved in advance by distinguishing a
pre- and *post-theoretical* (i.e. an unconscious and conscious) *praxis.* This
distinction allows us to see that both views on the matter of relative height
are well founded and the question is only to define which praxis we are
speaking of: the immediate, where theory is still a future element *outside
itself,* or the absolutely mediated, which has already penetrated theory and
thus comprehends theory *within itself.* According to Hegel the only goal of
all spiritual activity is to become conscious of the unity of the subjective
and the objective (*Lectures on the Philosophy of History*). Taken abstractly

75

this is true but phenomenologically it would be much more correct to *invert* the relationship completely and to say that the only goal of all spiritual consciousness is to *realize this unity actively out of itself.* The phenomenologically perfectly correct statement: 'Nihil est in intellectu quod non fuerit in sensu' will now be *pushed one step of the spirit higher* to read: 'Nihil est in voluntate et actu quod prius non fuerit in intellectu.'[1]

Thus, the real identity of knowledge and the will is established without any detriment to their difference. Consciousness in all its activity – to repeat, activity is the principal attribute of the spirit and must thus reveal itself at each of the spirit's stages – is not yet *pure* activity and still remains encumbered with passivity. Thus, its activity is still a *passive activity* which hopefully will not be seen as any more of a contradiction than *necessary freedom. Active activity* (which according to what we have said is no pleonasm but expresses activity *par excellence* burdened by no foreign influences) will first develop in the future:

a. *subjectively* by the adequate perfecting of the will;
b. *objectively* by the adequate development of political life;
c. *absolutely* by the attainment of the substantial and highest identity of being and thought which is absolute *action.*

The will must thus undergo its phenomenological process as reason has already done. Political life must, in its turn, affirm its universal hegemony as art and philosophy have successively. Finally, absolute action must attest to its teleological character *par excellence* as it is essentially process, continually carries struggle in itself, persistently traverses obstacles, and constantly attains victory. Thus, both the *struggling* and the *still* synthesis pass over into the *creative* one. That the synthesis of art was insufficient and only strife-ridden is factually demonstrated by its demise. As for philosophy, we believe that we have shown *theoretically* that this synthesis is just as defective by bringing out its one-sidedness and abstraction even while recognizing its *relative concreteness.* To make this relation more visible we may compare this second, philosophical synthesis to the magnet, where the two poles may well be recognized as identical but where the north pole is nevertheless considered – completely one-sidedly – more important than the south pole and is the only *indicative pole.* In the Hegelian identity, *thought is the indicative pole*; moreover, his method is the *compass* where the north pole enjoys greater recognition although everyone

---

[1] We use the term 'phenomenological' intentionally here because, as Hegel shows from another point of view, the inverse is also true. Phenomenologically considered, however, Locke's formulation is correct. Our statement too can be thus translated for nothing can be generated in thought which we do not *want* to think. In the normal development of the spirit, however, thought must precede conscious realization.

knows that the south pole has equal rights. However, just as in the more advanced electro-magnetic process the north pole is deprived of the dominant authority which it still possesses in the compass and is *dynamically* recognized as equal in rights to the south pole, so in the future development of philosophy thought will be divested of its dominant polarity and will be integrated normally in the process of *action*.

．．．．

We thus announce a new era for philosophy as such which will amount to a progress of the spirit even though philosophy will have abandoned the element and standpoint most proper to it. On the other hand, just as art, which, as soon as it had outgrown itself, and although raised to a higher level, still had to cede before the rising sun of thought and philosophy and had to exchange its absolute importance for a readiness to serve the interiority of thought, so in the future philosophy must agree to become principally *applied*. Just as the poetry of art passes over into the prose of thought so must philosophy descend from the height of theory into the field of praxis. The future fate of philosophy in general is to be practical philosophy or, to put it better, the *philosophy of praxis*, whose most concrete effect on life and social relations is the development of *truth in concrete activity*. One should not consider this an unworthy position for philosophy any more than is art's subordination to the interiority of thought in romanticism. It cannot be denied, however, that this is a displacement of its proper being and a partial *abdication* whose cause has already been sufficiently indicated in the non-attainability of the highest level of identity through thought. Just as thought and reflection surpassed fine arts so the *deed* and social activity will now outstrip *true* philosophy. Consequently, at this very moment consciousness hastens to penetrate everything and, hardly having attained itself, now seeks to precipitate the deed. This phenomenological circumstance is the reason why it is precisely in this very epoch that suddenly, as if in a flash of lightning, both the future and the past become clear. Consciousness has come to maturity; it has opened the eyes of its Janus-like head.

One may object that instead of dying out philosophy seems, on the very contrary, to be now establishing its hegemony and flowering. This would be as incorrect as if one wanted to consider the sun's zenith as its dawn. When Greece rejoiced in the work of a Phidias the hour of art was already near; Hegel is the Phidias of philosophy. He has thought through the universe and, without affirming that nothing more remains to be investigated in the field of speculation, we must grant that the essential has already been discovered. The discovery of the method is truly the long-yearned-for discovery of the *stone of wisdom*. Now it is a question of *producing the miracles* which lie in the power of this stone. To be sure, philosophy will still discover a great deal, but *it has already discovered itself* and precisely for this reason it is outliving itself at this moment. No prejudice has been done to the era of philosophy, for it has been celebrating its flowering from Aristotle to Hegel. Thus, if thought has now reached its culminating point and has solved its essential task, progress itself calls for thought to *step back*, i.e. to pass over out of its purity into a foreign element. We must not be shy of saying that from now on philosophy will begin to be *applied*. It will still remain an end in itself, like art, but when it ceases to pass as the centre of the spirit it begins to enter into a relative servitude. Its next fate is to popularize itself, to transform its esoteric character into an exoteric one. In a word, if we may be allowed to speak antinomically, philosophy must *become shallow in the depths*; for all are called to it and everyone who *wants* to think is *chosen*. Thus, it is now that its normal influence on the social relations of humanity will begin so that absolutely objective truth is developed not only in merely passive but also in self-created reality. On the basis of this one can grasp the rage for building social systems and constructing society *a priori*, which has attained monomanic proportions in our era and which otherwise would be only a dull pre-sentiment of a requirement of the times whose consciousness has not yet fully ripened. Is this abnormal? In its content, certainly; in its form, not at all. Formally, consciousness now feels itself entitled to guide true deeds and no longer merely to acknowledge reality as present but to determine it as *known* and *willed*. Since consciousness *only felt* this and finding itself merely on the level of feeling and perception could not yet attain its *true content*, the content is still anomalous. But now as consciousness steps *out of itself* it will follow its path into the rich field of the objective spirit and its discoveries along this new road will be precisely the results of the future orientation of philosophy. On the other hand, it would be a great mistake to underestimate the normality of today's generally *practical* universal tendency out of love for philosophy.

.   .   .   .

If today the *rational* has managed to resolve its internal contradictions, the *same victory* must be celebrated in *reality*. Just as in the course of development of the spirit there is only *one* philosophy which is destined finally to come unto itself and seize itself organically, so too in reality there is but *one* normal unfolding of *social life* which can only set foot on its *true* course with the ripeness of thought. Thus, the real *objective dialectic of life* approaches its highest mediated standpoint and the contradictions of the times only come into prominence so glaringly because they are ripening unto their overturn and solution. I draw the attention of speculative thinkers to *Fourier*'s system, not that I should misjudge the essential deficiencies which make of this system still a *utopia* but in order to show that a significant step has been taken in the development of organic truth in reality. To be sure, this organic structure still stands on the *level of a mechanism* but it is already an organism. This is not realized by those who perceive not the living nucleus but only the still dead husk. As *immediate* reconciliation of *Plato*'s principle with *Rousseau*'s this utopia certainly has immense significance *for the future*. I say *nothing more* than *immediate* reconciliation, for if it were already the highest reconciliation of these two opposed principles of universal history which are *prototypical* of two epochs and if, moreover, it allowed the organic kernel still to develop *organically* it would cease to be a utopia. Consequently, one can say that Fourier is the greatest but also the last utopian. In general, the main defect of utopia is not to unfold with reality but *to want to step into* reality. It can never do this as long as it is utopia, and thus an unbridgeable gap arises between utopia and reality. Otherwise, if the unfolding of the principle were not utopian, then – as has been said – the rational would have to coincide with reality at once. Certainly, since consciousness now has to outpace the deed one need not be too anxious about such attempts at constructing social relations; precisely what utopias lack is not that they are too rational for reality but inversely that they are *not rational enough*. Utopia even as it means to come closest to reality strays furthest from it. One can never be ideal enough in order to develop a truth, for the true good is always its other side. Thus, Fourier's system is a utopia because it capitulates too readily before a *preconceived* reality. Nevertheless, it is the most speculative statement that has been made concerning contemporary relations of life, though not all in a speculative form and without speculative consciousness. Anyone will see this who is capable of recognizing the speculative even when it is only instinctively brought up to the surface in the ocean of contingencies. Thus the future does not belong to Fourier's system as he supposed, but rather the system itself belongs to the future, i.e. it is a significant *moment* in the development of *true* reality but only a moment and in a very *limited* sphere at that. As nothing new comes into the world at a single stroke no utopia can be realized at once. Thus, if the rational is separated from the real, the two must gravitate toward each other and come closer through imperfect reconciliations until finally they coincide organically. Any one-sided retrieval is unthinkable.

.　.　.　.

The system of institutions is for the idea of universal history what the system of particular arts is for the idea of beauty in general. The different orientations of the universal spirit which often formed contradictions here attain their organic *unification* and each abstract element of the life of mankind finds in it the field appropriate to itself in objectivity where it can move *autonomously*; here this autonomy is synthetic, no longer apprehended in oppositions and consequently already including heteronomy in itself. This system of institutions, positive and organic in itself, is the first real concrete freedom; inversely, it is not in the least like that abstract, hollow, unilaterally subjectively originating thing which we still today honour with the name of freedom. Where there is no positive foundation, no determined being, indeed one could say, no reality limited by the concept – for all reality is limited – there is no speculative freedom either. For freedom in general is synthetic and *liberum arbitrium* is in no way its general principle but only one of its principles. Thus, when Leibnitz dares to say, 'Ex mero Dei arbitrio nihil omnino proficisci potest', why should we wish to draw the good 'ex mero hominis arbitrio'? As *concrete* freedom is the *highest* good, so too abstract freedom is the highest evil, the true social original sin which will be redeemed through humanity's organic condition for mankind as it is already for the reborn individual.

The objectivity of freedom has unfolded gradually through the whole process of history, but as hitherto we have traversed only two main stages of the spirit we are thus effectively in possession of two *classes of institutions*, the *juridical* and the *moral*. The first already experienced its completely mature formation in Rome even before Christianity; thus the Roman juridical system is and remains the most perfect in its *abstractness* and cannot be led any further beyond this point of maturity. The inner morality which awoke with Christianity and penetrated the whole Christian–Germanic period has also already developed absolutely; the moral principle which is general but which in fact has only made itself felt in private relations and hence has remained abstract in its mere interiority has nothing higher to develop than what has already been revealed in the universal spirit. But ethical life, the third, concrete sphere which must emerge in the two preceding abstract spheres without finding a place for itself there, is now destined for the first time to begin its true development and to appear in as adequate a form as right and morality already have.

Admittedly, relations of family, civil society, the state were all present at each stage of the universal spirit but they were always burdened with the one-sidedness and the insufficiency of the respective premisses in which they appeared so that their real and absolute consequence still remains to be drawn out. We already see that this is the real demand of the times in the instinctual turmoil marking the most important spiritual and material interests of humanity. This tumult can be called nothing but a real elementary process of life announcing itself by fermentation and even partially by putrefaction.

Thus *man* emerges out of this abstraction and becomes the social individual *par excellence*. The *naked I* abandons its universality and *defines* itself as the concrete *person rich in relations*. The state too abandons its abstract separateness and itself becomes a *member* of *mankind* and of the concrete *family of nations*. Peoples pass from their natural to their social condition and international law, until now still very new, develops ever more richly into international morality and ethical life.

Finally, *mankind*, whose universality was scarcely able to exist in consciousness and in thought, apprehends itself concretely and vitally to become an *organic humanity* which can certainly be called a *church* in the highest sense. Thus the universal spirit organically unites the activization of beauty, truth, the good and develops concretely out of itself into an articulated totality of real institutions.

The total character of the universal spirit will produce the active application:

a. of the beautiful, in feeling – *love*;

b. of the true, in knowledge – *wisdom*;

c. of the good, in will – *the strength and omnipotence of life*.

Thus, the life of mankind is destined to participate in these three highest principles and it is precisely this which will constitute the highest transfiguration of the universal spirit.

. . . .

Of credit and circulation (1839)

Chapter I
OF THE NATURE AND PROGRESSIVE
DEVELOPMENT OF CREDIT

Credit has spread both so many blessings and so many afflictions on modern societies that it is high time for us to demand an exact account of its existence, its inner nature, its resources and abuses, in short, what it has already produced and what it could produce. Notwithstanding the multitude of various books, pamphlets and studies which for so many years have undertaken to explore this land of good hope, notwithstanding the sustained attention which the parliaments and press of various nations are constantly obliged to accord it under the dominion of contemporary facts, one cannot help recognizing that credit has remained one of the most obscure parts of political economy.

·   ·   ·   ·

The most striking proof of credit's still infant state is the absence of a thorough knowledge of its nature and destination. Not to be conscious of oneself or to misjudge one's own significance is characteristic only of a very young or very imperfect institution. Since the advantages of credit greatly prevail over its disadvantages it is therefore credit's underdevelopment and not its abuse which must be blamed above all.

First, we must rectify an error, capital in theory and of no less palpable importance. Inquiries into the true nature of credit have led in the last instance to the conception that credit is but an anticipation of the future; an admissible definition relatively speaking and in a very restricted sphere but, as we shall soon see, eminently false if regarded as supreme and absolute. In adopting this definition consistent economists have found themselves obliged to deny all productive power to credit by accusing it of being a *chrematistic* deception which merely displaced capital while seeming to create new capital and which discounted future resources by accumulating them at present to the detriment of posterity. Truly, if this opinion were not erroneous it would constitute a terrible accusation against all those who preach the advantages of credit or who excuse such flagrant spoliation, which is all the more odious in that it operates with full security and spills all burdens on as yet unborn generations unable to protest against such a misdeed. Fortunately, however, the evil is not nearly as great as this opinion could make us presume, for the anticipation of the future is but *one* partial and very subordinate aspect of the question of credit; we shall soon see in which circumstances this definition is admissible but as a general thesis it is false and dangerous.

Credit is the metamorphosis of stable and engaged capital into circulating or disengaged capital, i.e. the means which make *available* and *circulable* capital which was not so and thus allow it to be applied wherever the need is felt. This fundamental definition suffices as a *point of departure* for establishing our ideas. The definition will be developed and completed after we have undertaken an analysis of the nature and needs of circulation (*currency*) which we shall soon recognize as but the obverse of the medal of credit. Accordingly, if credit is and should be but the *putting into circulation* of existing capital, circulation in its turn is and should be but *the development of the general credit of a nation*.

. . . .

It is productive circulation, or if you will, reproductive consumption which affects the progress of wealth to the greatest extent. Its agent *par excellence* is *circulating capital* just as *fixed capital* is the principal agent of direct production properly speaking. All other circumstances being equal, i.e. given the absolute and proportional share of fixed and circulating capital in a given enterprise, it is incontestably true that *circulating* capital's return is superior to *fixed* capital's. Fixed capital engenders only *interest* while circulating capital engenders *profits*; moreover, it increases in surprising proportion the revenue which fixed capital was capable of yielding before circulating capital had sufficiently fertilized it. Yes, all fixed capital needs to be properly fructified by circulating capital and only under this condition can capital be truly fertile. This is a very elementary truth, well known in theory and yet quite unknown in practice where often the most important fixed capital of a nation, land property for example, is completely bereft of circulating capital. It is thus eminently important for the well-being of societies to increase the mass of capital *in the state of circulation* as much as possible and it is supremely important for them that this circulating capital be true capital and not fiction, signs, or purely nominal values.

Were there but an instrument capable, so to speak, of *disengaging* genuine *engaged* capital without obliging it to lose its fixed and productively stable character, i.e. without obliging its owners to relinquish it, even though according to Adam Smith and Malthus the difference between circulating and fixed capital lies precisely in this obligation; in other words, if fixed capital could simultaneously function as *working* capital and thus redouble in order to tackle these two functions simultaneously, this instrument would be the greatest motor of wealth accumulation and would introduce an enormous force for the development of all industry. As it happens, this instrument is credit in its normal and general conception.

. . . .

Here we have reached the point of being able to formulate the two radical evils of the present organization of credit and, at the same time, to point to its reform. These evils, each the exact reverse of the other, are:

1. the lack of a *real guarantee* of circulation assets.
2. the lack of *circulability* of real assets.

This is to say that whereas assets put into circulation are bereft of capital funds, capital funds on the contrary are deprived of *mobilization*. A double *disadvantage* results which might appear contradictory if it did not in fact exist; there is both a *dearth* and an *excess* of circulating assets but a dearth of real assets and an excess of fictitious assets. This is why exuberant circulation is often accompanied by a veritable lethargy. We run after the future and abandon the present; we *anticipate* what does not yet exist and neglect *provisions already made*.

. . . .

It is thus not only a question of disengaging engaged capital, one must also organize its issue in such a way as to assure it complete and permanent circulability without redemption. This cannot really exist except to the extent that the assets put into circulation properly speaking will not be mere signs but circulating warranties as well. Hitherto, only specie has enjoyed this double character, as we shall argue in the second chapter. Nevertheless, the progress of credit already realized and the considerations which we shall invoke regarding the effects of circulation will suffice to show not only that specie does not have the exclusive monopoly of this double character but also that it is only too vulnerable to the inconveniences which paralyse most of its advantages. Now, if titles of real deposit, engaged mortgages, indeed, *actual* securities of all sorts were issued for circulation in a general form by a universal institution of credit – in place of bank-notes which, apart from their other defects, are but a sign – would not the issue of such certificates or securities satisfy from this particular point of view the two conditions enunciated?

.   .   .   .

In effect, an institution destined to *mobilize engaged funds* would evidently be a deposit bank, in the most general use of the term. At the same time, through its issue of circulating securities which would play the role of a legal tender based on these funds, this institution would share in the nature of circulation banks. Through its intervention only *actually existing funds* and in no way future benefits would become discountable. Credit would merely *disengage* and not effect unsecured advances; it would only issue *circulating warranties* and in no way promises. In short, these would be non-redeemable securities since they emanate from an already effected redemption; they would be securities without expiry date because they will have already expired, so to speak, before they appear. Consequently, far from being anticipatory they would be accumulation assets; this is how these warrants would represent hitherto inert assets which would find themselves put into activity and endowed with the faculty of movement, or, on the contrary, hitherto floating and vaguely mobile assets would find themselves endowed with a sufficient foundation and, as it were, provided with substance. It is evident that in such a combination, the security of deposit banks would find itself combined with the advantages of circulation banks.

.   .   .   .

In this case, what would be the organization of real credit in its most general expression? It would be the following:[1] all effective and material funds, represented either by a mortgage certificate for immovables or by an insurance policy for movables or, finally, constituting a deposit in kind, would flow toward a central and general institution to participate in a disengagement of credit. That is to say, they would be redoubled and reflected in circulation, as has just been shown, by means of the issue of credit titles which would uniformly represent the circulable values of these funds as evaluated, to be sure, within their market value. These funds would thus

[1] What we shall present will be somewhat analogous to the organization of a new credit establishment called the *Omnium*, whose conception is certainly the most advanced of all those which have hitherto emerged concerning credit.

be monetized and would then spread in circulation in the form of circulating and unitary *warrants*, not redeemable but bearing interest and valid as specie. As for these *warrants* they would not be redeemable otherwise than through their further transmission; since they share in the nature of specie they should continuously exercise its functions; since specie is in no way exchangeable by right against anything else but simply acceptable as payment in any sort of transaction, these warrants, being themselves a *real standard of value*, will only be legal tender at a permanent rate but will not be redeemable.

. . . .

Chapter II
OF THE NATURE AND DEVELOPMENT OF INSTRUMENTS OF CIRCULATION

In order to arrive at this end one must create a new kind of monetary instrument which could replace cash and public bonds at the same time; since it would thus share in the hitherto exclusive characteristics of its premises, it could spontaneously substitute itself for them. To satisfy these conditions let us suppose new notes, issued on a determined mortgage and guaranteed by the state as *legal tender*, consequently valid at all administrative pay-desks in discharging tax obligations, circulable in transactions according to their legal rate (which it is important never to confuse with a forced rate). Finally, let us join to their character as a general intermediary of circulation, the property particular to public bonds of bearing interest at a fixed rate, payable every semester but, for the sake of transmission, calculated and indicated day by day. Consequently, such a *revenue-note* would unite the two sorts of function which hitherto seemed irreconcilable; whether kept invested or cast into speculation, it would always and in every way be useful and advantageous.

The immediate and specific property of such a paper would be not to permit the smallest capital to remain inactive and unproductive for a single moment. During the entire period between acceptance of the note and its further transmission, interest, far from being lost for the temporary possessor as is the case with liquid cash, would grow continuously. Thus one would earn every time one took such a note in payment, since before returning to circulation it would already have undergone an increase in value to the profit of its temporary holder.

. . . .

In reflecting on the nature of this operation we perceive at once that its definitive and spontaneous result will be to *transform revenue into capital*. . . Thus, introducing [such revenue-bearing notes] into circulation would become a powerful lever of accumulation by organizing in a normal and spontaneous manner one of the most important nerves of any growth of social wealth, *saving*. Moreover, this would be done without either sterile hoarding or auxiliary institutions but by the sole intervention of these new instruments of circulation.

Indeed, any saving, any portion of revenue which we reserve in cash is still far from being capital in spite of the usage which attributes this term to any sort of sum. It does not acquire this character otherwise than through productive employment, for the sole criterion of all capital is that it produce a revenue. Thus, to convert the fruit of one's savings and one's revenue into capital, one must necessarily render it apt to yield something; without this it will always remain a mass of sterile coin. It must either be employed in some operation or placed in a savings bank. If, on the contrary, the revenue which one collects from one's funds, instead of arriving in the form of sterile cash, comes directly as revenue-notes, it is clear that this revenue is spontaneously *converted into capital* without any delay or displacement so that the simple possession of these notes is equivalent to a payment into a savings bank.

· · · ·

Chapter III
OF THE ORGANIZATION OF CREDIT AND CIRCULATION

To this day, the question of the organization of credit and circulation has oscillated between two contradictory opinions: on the one hand, the *monopoly of a central bank*; on the other, the *free competition of private banks*. We can affirm from the very outset that both these opinions are equally faulty and that nevertheless both conceal an element of truth. It is evident that this question corresponds to the great controversy regarding commercial freedom which is approaching its maturity – albeit still very slowly. In practice as well as in theory, a continuous counter-balancing operates between the restrictive system on one side and the system of absolute liberty on the other. Nevertheless, these contradictory doctrines are reciprocally false and their falseness consists precisely in what is *exclusive* to them. When then shall we come to understand the following? It is never this or that immediate and absolute affirmation, nor its pure and simple negation, i.e. its equally exclusive and vicious counterpart, which can prevail and constitute the normal state of a question. When the two contradictory elements of a question find themselves already developed, truth resides in their reciprocal combination or, to speak more rigorously, in their *synthetic organization* alone. Let us also remark that this organization, which presents itself as the consequence of exclusive premises, is never a middle term of *accommodation* incapable of completely satisfying either of the contrary opinions and consequently running the risk of being equally rejected by both. This is not an ambiguous and impotent *compromise* which could effectively only *compromise* instead of reconciling opposed interests. On the contrary, this is the intermediate term of an *absorbing* and *superior* organization, i.e. a consequence which does not remain only *in the middle* but places itself *above* extremes joining their reciprocal advantages and their contradictory characters to make them *integrating elements* of its superior nature even while itself enjoying a specific character. Thus, the question of systems of commerce will not really be settled until we have abandoned the track of present reasoning to take up the concept of *organizing institutions* which would join a positively protective influence rather than today's negatively restrictive influence to the advantages of free competition; in other words, it will be settled when we have abandoned the exclusive arguments of the prohibitive system on the one hand and the negative reasonings of *laissez-faire* and *laissez-passer* on the other to take up a positive and organic system whose formula would be: *aid and develop.*

. . . .

In short, the age of *laissez-faire* and *laissez-passer* has just as surely passed as the age of the prohibitive system. Henceforth, the principles of science should be *aid, develop, organize.* They are organic principles since they imply the normal and positive concurrence of public and private action, institutions and individuals, of the collective interest and of competition.

. . . .

Law used to say to the Regent: 'The sovereign should give credit, not receive it.' This is indisputably one of the most pregnant thoughts ever uttered in political economy. Indeed, it is almost incomprehensible that, after having succeeded in organizing a *unique, central,* and *guaranteed* monetary system, states have voluntarily abdicated an analogous attribute in the organization of general credit and circulation. Governments' right to mint money is one which could not be reasonably challenged; nevertheless, governments have hardly ever claimed the completely analogous right to issue *fiduciary money*. Quite to the contrary, every time that the state finds itself obliged to resort to credit, instead of developing credit within its own bosom – which should be the source and hearth of credit – it goes to seek outside itself and negotiates treasury-bonds like simple commercial stock. The state thus submits itself to the laws of another whereas it is the state which should dictate laws.

There are functions of social life which enter essentially into the attributes of government and whose supreme direction should of all necessity belong to the state under pain of developing abnormally. These functions are those which concern the general well-being; thus, the more a function involves the public interest the greater the necessity of its central-ization. As soon as this centralization is *organic* – and we shall never under-stand it otherwise in the course of this work – far from paralysing or annulling liberty and private activity in any way, centralization on the contrary affirms and corroborates them. Governments are the hearths of society called to exercise a force, not of repulsion or any sort of abrogation but of convergent gravitation and salutory radiation. Governmental inter-vention is thus certainly both natural and beneficial whenever it is a ques-tion not of depressing, forbidding or excluding but of raising the most divergent interests to a higher power and rallying them about a common goal. On the other hand, government should cease or abstain from inter-vention whenever the particular interest does not find itself in direct colli-sion with the public interest; in this case *private* exploitation, whether indi-vidual or corporate, is the most advantageous not only by common and natural *law* but economically too and government intervention would but fetter or deform development. This consideration is the absolute *criterion* of all governmental action in the sphere of political economy. Such evid-ently normal action is precisely the opposite of what is practised in our day, when governmental action instead of being affirmative is hardly more than negative, instead of being general and organizing it is but special and restrictive. In conformity to this principle, the supreme direction, but not the exploitation, of credit is an eminently governmental function.

.   .   .   .   .

Financial assets are the reproductive blood of the social body, its nutri-tive and distributive element, its condition of existence and development. Now conceive, if it is possible, an organic circulation which would be bereft of a heart and which would not have a central organ to transform venous blood, i.e. gross assets, into arterial blood, i.e. circulable and *reproductive* assets. To be sure, in the physical order systems of circulation bereft of such perfect circulation exist and can be found; this is the case at an inferior level of organization, i.e. in plants. So too, credit and circulation have merely vegetated until the present precisely through lack of an appropriate organization. Consequently, if hitherto the circulation of assets has not been comparable to anything other than the imperfect circulation of sap, let us now raise it to a superior level in the scale of organisms and let us make it analogous to that of blood by creating a heart for it.

On the improvement of the condition of rural workers[1] (1845)

We agree with the authors of our programme that, in general, the condition of our farmers since the abolition of personal servitude and compulsory labour services has improved significantly both materially and morally. Thus, we are happy to agree that the position of farm-hands has been raised through appropriate arrangements on large agricultural estates. At the same time, however, we are also forced to remark that the last class of our rural population and, generally speaking, the whole class of day labourers and hand-workers, unlike property owners, is far from capable of significantly improving its condition. Feeling its backwardness this class has fallen into disorder and distemper as oft-repeated complaints and even the preoccupations of our programme attest.

· · · ·

The second point in our programme referring to a careful education of rural youth, especially through the establishment of day-nurseries in the open country, is undoubtedly the most important and the most beneficial of all the proposals heard so far. These establishments are already recognized in all countries and particularly in England and France as so important that people have gone as far as to see in them – and certainly justifiably so – a true instrument of popular regeneration... All in all, I consider them even more important and necessary than schools themselves, for in the latter the child learns some reading, writing and arithmetic but in the day-nursery he learns to *live* and becomes accustomed from the cradle, as it were, to an orderly, social and harmonious mode of life imparting habits which acquired in one's earliest youth stand one in good stead for the rest of one's life.

· · · ·

To be sure, this is only an instrument for the future, since it affects the

[1] An address before the second General Assembly of the Provincial Agricultural Union for the Marches of Brandenburg and the Niederlausitz, 17 May 1845.

growing generation and thus remains more or less without effect for the present, although one cannot help recognizing that parents no longer kept away from work by caring for children can significantly improve their circumstances. However, this instrument always remains pedagogic rather than economic and at the same time we all know – and, for that matter, we could also acknowledge more often within our Association – that human moral and spiritual well-being also requires an immediate material basis, which is certainly the soil on which higher life first develops.

. . . .

As for better remuneration, various ways have been recommended and are also truly recommendable. For example, I know that on one estate in the Grand Duchy of Posen the entire staff is paid a couple of thalers more than on neighbouring estates. The labourer does not receive this extra pay at the end of the year; it remains in the estate administration's till and will only be handed over with interest to the labourer after a good number of years, i.e. in the form of an increased capital. This practice acts as a powerful incentive and prevents the repeated and constant turnover of labour. At this opportunity, I cannot help mentioning another sort of premium which I have already applied in past years: I let the villagers come together and have them choose the best and most orderly workers of both sexes, who are then presented with various prizes according to their place among those chosen and thus according to their degree of merit. The election results have really been very just. Had these individuals been directly rewarded by the estate then the others might have seen this as a particular and unjustified mark of favour, but since I obliged them to recognize merit themselves the moral effect of such prize-distribution should have been considerably raised.

As for the fourth instrument, i.e. the encouragement of thriftiness and the deposit of wage-surpluses in savings banks set up wherever needed, allow me to answer that before one suggests saving as a means one must provide the means to save. Here, it seems to me that we find ourselves in a circle. Saving can improve the position of our country-folk – quite true! – but frankly and generally speaking no savings are possible until the position of our country-folk is improved. To be sure, there are exceptions everywhere: especially favoured regions or, in other regions, particular individuals who find more or less opportunity to accumulate a few pennies in savings. However, I ask the practical farmers of our poorer regions whether even a paltry cash dowry cannot be considered an exception? Furthermore, I ask whether it is at all possible for our day labourers to think about buying a small piece of land? The answer is clearly, no. Thus, before we require that they save properly we must give them the means to save and to find these we must return to the considerations mentioned at the end of our programme.

The encouragement of cottage-work for farm-hands on winter evenings would certainly be worthwhile if it could only be so easily arranged. Unfortunately, this is not the case, and as we go into it more deeply we find that this apparently simple question is connected with a much more complicated one. *Spinning* and *weaving*, which brought wealth to so many areas, have now lost their entire enriching effect because of machinery. Far be it from us to wish to blame machines with this remark. Rather, we are only stating a fact, for however numerous spinners and weavers may suffer consumers as a whole have gained considerably. Thus, we are confronted with the need to look about for arrangements through which the free hand of the worker can find new occupations.

This should be most easily arranged if individuals come together in collective work, for individual work is increasingly losing its importance. With time, this should be all the easier as so many branches of industry will be transferred from the cities to the open country – a phenomenon which now occurs naturally by itself through ever-improving means of communication and circulation making possible what was unthinkable some time ago when people had heard nothing of the railroad and hardly anything of highways. Tying agriculture to more or less industrial occupations is certainly one of the tasks of our day but we must first let mutual interests establish and settle themselves in a natural way.

. . . .

As for the remaining points such as special remuneration for long and faithful service etc., greater conscientiousness in issuing service certificates, requiring attendance at church services, having the employer set a good example – either they pick up what has already been discussed or they speak sufficiently for themselves so that one can only declare oneself in agreement.

. . . .

We can pass over the position of agricultural owners *for the time being* ... They will help themselves because they can, because they themselves have the means to do so more or less. The situation of day labourers and farm-hands is completely different. They still have nothing more than their hands, i.e. what nature has lent them. Society has done nothing for them

93

apart from setting up schools. But what can society do for them? Should the state again offer them property out of lofty considerations? Where should this property be taken from? In a word, should the agricultural population again be *regulated* and *separated*, i.e. the land and soil so fragmented and pulverized that everyone would have something of it? This is impossible and even if it were not impossible, it would be harmful for the national economy. What then is to be done in real and fruitful ways for the improvement of the situation of that class which feels that it is behind?

It can be helped in another way! It is possible to give it a prospect of durable earnings which will spur its industriousness and activity as powerfully as a property grant. Indeed, it is possible to open the road to ever-growing earnings – in a word, to let this class take part in the general increase of capital in agriculture. It only needs a very easily executed arrangement which, generally speaking, should be advantageous to both employees and employers without treading too heavily on anyone.

It is already often acknowledged that most improvements, most important and successful discoveries are usually nothing more than a generalization and large-scale application of facts long known but little noted because of their apparent insignificance. Thus, for example, trains are only the age-old attempt to increase short-range drawing power in factories raised to the level of a general system. Circulation banks too are only a generalization of makeshift practices of individual merchants in the Middle Ages etc. This will be the case here too. Thus, if the practice which we are speaking of had not been previously legitimated through theoretical and practical indications we would boldly throw it out of the house as false, for nothing completely new and previously unheard of exists in the world!

Here, the insignificant fact which is the connecting point with the past is the position of stewards on a large number of estates. As is well known, many stewards and managers draw a portion of the net revenues of the estate administered in addition to their fixed salaries. This share is thus the yield of their industriousness and activity. The wide extent to which this arrangement has been used shows that experience has proven it practical. Now what is to prevent this arrangement from being even more general and *being extended to the other workers*? The orderly administration of an estate requires not only an efficient and interested steward but also efficient and industrious workers. Generally speaking, what is so difficult about rewarding all the workers, i.e. all the participants in the running of an estate, in the same way as the steward is rewarded? What has been found good for one will be good for all. The share which is easily determined in relation to the net income of the steward would be just as easily applied to the most insignificant labourer. One need only take the relation between his hitherto fixed wages and those of the steward as a measuring rod. Thus, the surplus share of the fellow who received only twenty thalers a year in wages will be determined just as easily and, relatively speaking, will be just as important as the share of the steward which comes out to many hundreds or perhaps even thousands of thalers.

What then would be the immediate consequence of such an arrangement? It would be one where both moral and economic effects overlap simultaneously; with one stroke farm-hands and labourers would pass from a relation of external coercion and unconcerned indifference for the interests of the employers (if not actually aversion against the latter, although we should not conceal from ourselves that this is often the case) to one of intimate co-operation and living participation. The hitherto isolated, indeed even more or less contradictory interests of all village dwellers would now find themselves united as if around a focal point; everyone would earnestly wish that the estate prosper because everyone would have an interest in it. Industriousness would thus be spurred on, the constancy of farm-hands encouraged and a truly ethical link established between them and the managers, indeed the estate itself. As culture advances the position of the worker would improve and his outlook broaden. In short, he would no longer feel detached without ties or hope but would find himself bound in a moral and material way precisely through his own interests and his own attachment.

. . . .

When I communicated my project for such a communal arrangement to several friends they drew my attention to an economic plan drafted by the financial councillor of the Duchy of Anhalt-Gotha, Albert, who guaranteed a certain portion of the produce of the soil to workers engaged in production and actually remunerated their labour *in natura* according to the size of the harvest. This plan was based on the perfectly correct principle of a participatory economy and its appearance – with a preface by Adam Müller – caused a certain sensation. Nevertheless, I must describe the way in which this principle was developed as completely wrong. A fleeting glance at the suggestions sufficed to convince me that they put the workers in far too disadvantageous a position; how could they possibly assure their livelihood with one-sixth or one-eighth of their overall production, including statutory labour and hand-work, when it is known that half and even in the case of a favourable tare-principle always more than a third of the whole revenue of the soil must be counted as costs of production?

Moreover, it is admitted that remuneration in kind must work out unfavourably for the worker. Suspicious of this plan from the outset, I went to the spot myself and returned convinced that it was beyond application. I mention this in order to warn of drawing overly hasty conclusions from the failure of similar arrangements and to bring to the memory and the efforts of Herr Albert the recognition which he deserves.

Now I shall turn to a brief discussion of several objections to my plan.

Above all, one may doubt whether the common labourer would really understand such a mode of participation in net revenues and whether a proportional accounting would not exceed his comprehension. I do not believe it would. Even if this were the case, however, the problem would be eliminated by a single year's practice. As soon as the labourers find themselves at the end of the year in possession of some surplus thalers then all their previous hesitations would disappear...

However, a second and completely opposite misgiving might arise: that the workers would understand only too well and that as soon as they realize their interest in the estate they would demand the right to discuss and dispose of it jointly... However, this objection fails to take an important fact into account: that it is only the surplus-share and in no way the fixed and unconditionally guaranteed revenue of the worker which is made dependent on the net revenue of the estate.

To be sure, if the entire livelihood of farm-hands or workers depended on the profits of the estate and if they were subjected to all the fluctuations of the estate, i.e. if they wanted to participate as much in the disadvantages as in the advantages of estate-management, then they should to some extent lay claim to the right of co-administration. In today's circumstances, one need hardly ask what would become of such an enterprise. As long as the worker's present income is in any case guaranteed as a minimum he only stands to gain with this plan and it serves uniquely as a powerful spur to strenuous activity and to the careful protection of all the estate's interests. The more each worker's income rises the greater will be his effort to reduce maintenance costs which can rise very high whether through negligence or wastefulness, misutilization of fixed and variable inventories etc.; consequently, his participation in the net yield will be greater. In any case, he will not receive less than what he draws today so every justification for interfering in enterprise management in any way other than by efficiently executing orders disappears.

Out of these and other considerations I became convinced that this plan would be much better promoted by a moral rather than a strictly legal relation. In fact, I was long undecided whether I would provide for this portion-grant in a legal clause of the farm-hands' and day labourers' contracts or whether I would leave it to the spoken word. After due consideration I have provisionally decided for the latter and here my employees' trust in me proves useful. Although I am certainly aware of the impression immediately produced by a contractual agreement I believe that given the novelty of the arrangement and the impossibility of determining all coming cases in advance I must let the living law rather than dead letters govern, in the constant conviction that allowing this relation to shape itself freely is most conducive to its normal development. To be sure, the portion-grant maintains to a certain extent the character of a gratuity; but what should its character be as long as it has not itself developed rationally and naturally out of life? We should not seek to prejudice living relations in advance, but we should always let them shape themselves, for the reciprocal relation between theory and practice never lets itself be overcome with impunity. Theory if it is to progress normally always first joins an already present practical fact, generalizes it and raises it to the principle which it establishes as such. Then, however, praxis again catches up and, constantly led by thought, it again develops the principle until theory absorbs the empirical in all its breadth, shapes it organically and returns it to life once more, ripe and strong.

On the co-ordination of intellectual aims and works in the Grand Duchy of Posen (1843)

In order to open a hearth of scientific and intellectual life in the Grand Duchy of Posen and to increase the energy and efficacity of efforts capable of contributing to the universal progress of the spirit it would be desirable that a Society of Friends of Progress be established in Posen... The Grand Duchy is too small a country to be able to scatter its aspirations in all directions. Indeed, we are constantly wasting our intellectual work on internal friction among diverse elements whereas we could be attaining the results we seek through their common association where these elements would be mutually *complemented* rather than *excluded*.

. . . .

The immediate means of attaining the ends of the Society would be:

1. Opening the field to both oral and written treatises and debates on all questions of general interest.

2. Publishing a collective journal on a quarterly or monthly basis depending on the abundance of material; this would include texts read or presented at the Society's meetings as well as the discussions to which they gave rise.

3. Founding or maintaining popular courses in the physical as well as the spiritual sciences or those aspects which are most accessible and most necessary for general knowledge, on the model of the numerous English societies founded specifically for this purpose.

4. Establishing competitions and prizes for the solution of tasks which the Society or individual sponsors consider as particularly important and worthy of specific research.

5. Occupying itself with all scientific enterprises which by virtue of their scope or importance would have difficulty in being realized by private means.

Usually when we speak of founding a strictly scientific review complete exclusion of politics from its scope is considered the first condition and indispensable guarantee of its respectability, non partisanship, and purposefulness. We do not share this opinion at all... Our association will make the content of its treatises and debates as political as possible but in the original *classical* sense of that term. That is to say, all scientific inquiry and all intellectual work coming out of the womb of the association should not remain a vain abstraction, a frivolous intellectual game or a sterile investigation but it should always and above all have the good of society and progress of the human spirit as its end.

. . . .

Since both moral and material questions concerning state and society dominate the content of the review and it is these very questions which are the main causes of partisan division the following question would seem to arise: to which party would our review belong? Our answer consists in inverting the question: which party would not belong to us?

. . . .

Parties on a small scale, narrow in scope, and of limited aims, lose their vital elevation and cease being parties to become *coteries*. In truth, the tasks before us are too important to allow us the time for petty bickering. However, it is not only our wish but even our obligation to induce *general* questions from the particular and to look at the particular *side* of each question with the exclusive eye of each *side*. Just as in political parliaments all sides find a place and participate together in forming and clarifying laws, so too in scientific parliaments – as we might call associations of this sort – no party should disregard the binding rules. Whenever the outcome of discussions runs against the wishes of a faction it always has the *negative* arm of defeating or protesting against the measure or the *positive* arm of bringing in a new proposition from another position in order to expose and realize its own views.

Let us note that this co-ordination of parties will not be and should not be a coalition. All coalitions are by nature weak, short-lived, even harmful, because coalesced elements usually cede reciprocally and thus step away from their own positions. This brings about the weakening of these positions and sooner or later their complete rupture. Our concern is not *mutual concession* but *common progress*... Similarly let no one accuse us of wishing to conciliate parties, for however laudable this wish may be it always belongs more or less to the family of *pia desideria*.

We could describe the relation between the so-called reconciliation of parties and the conjunction which we are advocating through the following

99

comparison. It is as if, having heard that steam is formed and thus machines are moved by the concerted activity of fire and water, someone undertook their immediate unification by pouring water on fire thus extinguishing his fire, letting his steam evaporate in vain, and – who knows? – burning himself in the process. This would be the conciliator of parties. Their true unifier on the other hand would first build a cylinder and steam engine and only then put water to act on fire so that these two elements which formerly acted only negatively, i.e. extinguishing or stifling, consuming or destroying, having now been properly united would reveal a great *positive* strength. Pseudo-unification only seeks to abolish parties, their organic co-ordination elevates them.

. . . .

[Regarding the content of the review – AL]. In addition to polemics criticism too will constitute an important part of the review's activity. In our opinion British criticism as found in London and Edinburgh quarterlies unquestionably deserves emulation since it corresponds closely to the concept of this branch of literature and the needs which gave it birth... But polemics and criticism only constitute a *passive* and mostly *negative* element of scientific activity. Our principal concern is the *active* and *positive* element which we consider to be the chief requirement of the present state of the national spirit. Criticism is usually the mark of immature or overripe societies. Nations which have not yet entered the vitalizing atmosphere of social life practise it instinctively and use it as their intellectual whetstone, whereas nations which are more or less withdrawing from this atmosphere again seek reflective criticism as their spiritual surrogate. But societies in an organic state are less concerned with this than with their own creativity. This is why one can consider the question of whether critical or organic literature dominates as one of the surest indices of the spiritual life of a nation.

Unless we are greatly mistaken the organic epoch has dawned for us. The strong development of *poetry* which occurred some years ago and today is ceding to a strictly scientific direction was the harbinger of this epoch... Thus, a scientific association of organic spiritual activity may become a most welcome hearth and its review one of the surest means of attaining its ends... For the force of association acts with accelerated speed and grows geometrically whereas individual efforts can usually only advance arithmetically and at a humdrum rate.

. . . .

Doubtless, in the great family of civilized nations we are still a young tribe; let us not blush at our youth for it is full of strength. Let us not push away an instrument which can give us *consciousness of ourselves* as well as of the vocation to which we are called.

. . . .

In conclusion we should remark that our efforts can not only contribute to furthering the self-education of native elements but that they will also be completely in accord with the general aspirations and needs of the age – and there can no longer be any doubt about the effectiveness of any enterprise which meets the latter condition. Indeed, our age has attained consciousness of the idea of organization. What hitherto developed unheeded, individually, feebly, indifferently by a natural and purely factual process should now form itself and advance towards its directing goal ever more consciously, vitally and actively through the harmonious co-operation of various means... The idea of association is one of the most important manifestations of that organic union of vitality which is to characterize mankind's future deeds; this idea should develop in the scientific field as well as in all others and it should direct humanity's future course.

Prophetic words of a Pole (1848)

The overthrow of Antiquity already shaken in its principles and the erection of the *second* stage of history on its ruins required a new tribe of nations completely alien to the preceding masters of the world and endowed with completely opposite inclinations but possessed of elements proper to the spirit. Today, we again require a new generation of peoples to unite our disrupted world, to unravel its entangled elements, to found its great peace in place of the *sword* brought by Christ, in short, to open the third era of the world; these new peoples must be distinct from those who have hitherto held sway in history but neither completely alien nor opposite to them, nor bereft of any contact with them, for today it is no longer a question of absolutely negating but rather of universally mediating. Now as before, we find an appropriate tribe of peoples in readiness, for mankind lacks neither great men nor great peoples each time they are needed...

.   .   .   .

The tribe called to this new role is already by nature not libertine but possessed of liberty, brave without bravado, ever ready for battle without ever seeking it. It is a tribe which never attacks its neighbours although it is ceaselessly attacked by them. It helps its fellow peoples with enthusiasm and self-sacrifice not only *regardless* of but even *against* its own interests. Its vocation is to transform Christian love from a *private* into a *public* quality and to transfer this virtue from people to peoples.

.   .   .   .

At its origins this tribe knew neither civil nor political servitude. From its very cradle it was *social* and *demo-cratic*, ceaselessly deliberating in councils, diets and assemblies and practising universal representation through its peasants, yeomen and notables. It splendidly developed these early seeds and long stood in advance, both in word and deed, of other tribes which were only adjusting to the condition of free peoples. It loved its *elders* and was docile towards them; it tolerated no master above itself and it rarely made social authority dependent on fate or birth but most often on merit confirmed by election. Indeed, this tribe was most willing to confide authority to people of the lowest estate or of unknown origin and it sought to elevate the oppressed. Like the Romans and their Cincinnatus, so the Slavs found their Premyslav and Piasts at the plough or at work when they came to call them to the highest offices or to announce future dignities. The needs of peace, not war, guided the Slavs in their elections. Consequently, they did not elect the most pugnacious nor carry the elected on shields like a troop of fuzzy-haired Germanics. They sought out the wisest, the most competent and the most honest to rule over them sagely and to judge them justly.

. . . .

Pressed by the needs of the times, the Slavs introduced hereditary authority among themselves, yet they were never capable of completely losing that propensity for *free choice* on which they were virtually weaned and which manifested itself in history at all times and at all levels from the humble master of the primitive Slavic family unto the powerful king of the Polish Republic. In the further course of fate they tasted various forms of government from the most debauched anarchy to the most dissolute despotism, and they came to acknowledge that no exclusive form of government in itself would do and that only the common unification of these forms mutually *moderated* and *animated* by public spirit could assure universal welfare. They convinced themselves at their own cost but with all the more enduring advantage for the future that just as true freedom depends on order so reciprocally true order depends on freedom.

The Slavs often disagreed in their deliberations and yet they were most prone to agreement because they were light-headed but good-willed, contentious but not quarrelsome, as enthusiastic and eager to accept good counsel as they were prepared to place unlimited confidence in the favourites of the nation. They were rightly reprimanded by foreigners for their apparent rather than essential disagreements but wrongly calumniated, because this was not the specific fault of their character but the general ailment of all public life. Such was the Athenian *demos*, the *quiritium turba*, the Anglo-American *mob*; struggles and clashes are life, graven obduracy is death.

. . . .

From their dislike for castles, fortresses and cities, from their repugnance to all medieval formations, it would already be easy to guess that neither vassalage nor burgherdom was allowed to flower among the Slavs. And indeed these fruits of an alien soil could not be adapted to Slavonic fields in spite of the perpetual inflow and outflow of Germanic generations and the later efforts of Slavonic monarchs well-disposed to both Germanic and Latin elements, often to the detriment of their own native character. Yet although this race rejected those grand medieval institutions it did not deprive itself of their spirit. It was noble and knightly in spite of the lack of a feudal knighthood; it was democratic, astute, and civic-minded even though it lacked a middle estate.

What did this race develop which was proper to itself in place of feudalism and burgherdom which it would not accept? What native social structure did it erect in place of alien ones?

It erected none but only laid foundations because the time for its historical activity had not yet come, nor that of the *estate* to which this people corresponds. As history calls successive peoples to the forefront so too it calls different estates of society in turn to the arena of deeds. The *higher* and *middle* estates have already played splendid roles in history and have fulfilled salutary missions for humanity. Today begins the era of activity for the *last estate*; until now this estate was nothing, now it will be everything and the representative of this estate among nations is precisely Slavdom.

This is why among the Slavs one finds neither *feudal* nobility nor a *middle* estate but a naturally *democratic* nobility and a naturally social people. This is why the Slavs were incapable of shaping themselves on the model of former societies; rather, having lived for ages in a *rural* and *communal* manner, from the depths of centuries spent in primitive communes, settlements, villages and habitations, in short, from a whole mode of life based on *unity*, *community*, and *solidarity* they were the harbingers of perfectly fresh relations completely unknown to other tribes. The importance of these relations has not been hitherto realized because the hour of their historical appearance has not yet struck. When these relations have developed in their own proper time they will not only match but outstrip in greatness and splendour the productions of past ages. In this way – and there is no other – the masses of the people will attain that *co-operation*, *co-participation*, *self-government* about which the contemporary world can have only an inkling.

.   .   .   .

It naturally follows from their urge to universal unity and their repugnance to all division that the split between temporal and spiritual authority decreed by the Middle Ages was necessarily contrary to the unifying spirit of the Slavs. Their society was both state and church in one. Their word for priest [*ksiądz*] meant both prince and chaplain; he was both temporal and spiritual leader. Just as formerly Roman *patres familias*, stewards of political and religious matters, themselves performed domestic *sacra* so too the ancient Slavs, 'divine servants', made offerings to God without the intermediary of any spiritual caste. They did not know two *truths* [*prawda*] but only one and this truth was precisely *law* [*prawo*]. This is why their orders were always holy and religious activity was an affair of state. In today's conditions where dead codes rule this would be stultifying; in conditions of spiritual freedom it is invigorating.

· · · ·

Truly God's decrees are just! More is required of those to whom more has been given and those destined for great deeds must merit them by their service. Born in the paradise of freedom and called to realize freedom's social development, the Slav tasted the fruit of the tree of consciousness of good and evil and came to know the greatest evil in the world, the one most contrary to the essence and the vocation of the spirit: he came to know the hell of unfreedom. Most abundantly endowed by God he allowed men to wrong him to such an extent that the name of his nation became the name of slavery. And so it came to pass that today on the whole surface of the earth, so measureless an area of which is covered by this race, you do not have a single corner in which one of these millions could call himself free.

· · · ·

Accept, O hitherto accursed race, the good news of salvation. Know that that nation which experienced injustice and suffered a martyr's death, to redeem the political sins of the world, has descended into the hell of slavery and prevailed over it. Arising in the glory of the spirit it will reveal that the *times have been fulfilled* and that with them thine hour has struck. Thou hast already traversed the purgatory of unfreedom and having suffered excessive suffering thou hast become worthy in God's eyes to announce the era of freedom to the world itself and to lead all humanity to paradise.

· · · ·

Remember that already once slaves saved the world. Today it is the turn of slave peoples. Remember the words of the Truth Teller: 'Blessed are those who are persecuted for righteousness' sake, for theirs is the kingdom of heaven' and 'Blessed are those who mourn, for they shall be comforted' (Matthew 5.10, 5.) and remember too the words of the prophet: 'But the meek shall possess the land, and delight themselves in abundant prosperity' (Psalms 36.11).

Great peace, consolation, such is thy goal, such is the term of thy strivings and sufferings. Remember this and do not seek others though thou be enticed by others. Do not allow thyself to be led into temptation at the decisive hour. The forces of hell are lying in wait but do not renounce thy mission, for today thou art the people of God.

Our Father (1848-   )

THE WAYS OF THE SPIRIT

All secrets of Thought are accessible to the Word. Whatever you think if you only think it through you will express, and whatever you cannot express be sure that you yourself have not understood, that you may have conceived it in pre-sentiment or imagined it in pre-conjecture but that it has not yet ripened unto thought. For the Word is not only the harbinger but the hallmark of all Thought. Where the Word is lacking conjecture and cogitation are insufficient, where thought is wanting vainly will you belabour resounding but hollow sounds for you will not pronounce one substantial word.

Essentially, such an indispensable reciprocity reigns between Thought and Word that neither one would be itself without the other. Indeed, although the Thought signified in the Word is only *expressed* by the Word, imparting an essential *meaning* to a sound or sign which is worthless without it, so too reciprocally the expression of that Thought actualizes it, raising it from the state of a potential, just-established power to that of a precisely designated reality brought into the open and understood by us. It comes down to one and the same *immaturity* whether it be a thought unspoken or a word unthought; it is one and the same absurdity whether a thought is wordless or a word is thoughtless.

. . . .

And the wisdom of all ages never wavered in attesting to this utterance of eternal thought – [i.e. 'Through the Word all things were made which were made and without him was not anything made which was made'; John 1.3 – AL]. Indeed, in the domain of pure knowledge, from the time 'when we began to reason soberly'[1] unto our day, whenever we reasoned

[1] Aristotle's comment on Anaxagoras, whose *nous* was essentially already a pre-conception of ever more perfect intellectual principles such as the Platonic Idea, Neo-Platonic Logos, etc.

107

soberly we always and everywhere recognized the principle or pattern of all things in Thought and Word, that is in their intellectual roots. This is so to such an extent that the history of philosophy finds its greatest pride in the ultimate recognition of the unity, interdependence and reciprocal correspondence of Thought and Being, that communality of the ideal and real order[1] whose accomplishment engendered in the Word and accomplished in the *Deed* constitutes the apex of wisdom and yet is nothing more than the universally abounding resultant and the infinite application within the sphere of all finitude of the truth revealed from above, that 'by God's word all was made' and 'the Word became Flesh'.

INTRODUCTION

What is the 'Our Father'?

I

Holy God! What is happening in the world? How ravishing and repulsive Truth unfolds in all quarters and falsehood prevails everywhere. The world decks itself in festive finery to the funebral sobbing of starved or murdered nations. A sea of indulgence, an ocean of suffering, and in indulgence – tedium, in suffering – despair! The chosen gather about the licentious banquets of life; they relegate the outcasts to grinding their teeth on the ground where an unmarked grave awaits them; for the sages of this world have stated that there is no room for the outcast at the table of life. In public matters – privation, in private matters – disgrace, as vanity shines and virtue idles. The secular arm has become immoral and the spiritual arm has grown decrepit. Everyone uses – or abuses – the divine Word but no one lives in it nor does it live in anyone. The fraternity of people and peoples is proclaimed even as the crimes of Cain have passed from people to peoples! Here progress is vile crime, there crime is progress! Here life is vigorous but sordid; there death is sordid but keen. This life is a sham for it is already infected with death and that death is deceptive for it is already impregnated with life.

Before us are unimagined miracles of industry, undreamt-of treasures of science, continually growing signs of immense and feverish work. Here are luxuries which the Sybarites never dreamt of and strength which the imagination would not dare attribute to the legendary Titan. And yet here too people and peoples hunger, thirst and wail with an inexpressible moan.

---

[1] *Verum et Ens* for the scholastics – *cogitatio et extensio, ordo rerum et ordo idearum* for Descartes and Spinoza – *Identität des Denkens und Seyns* for Schelling and Hegel, etc.

What is all this for? What is it leading to? What has the knowledge of the learned provided? What has the toil of the workers earned? What has the gold of the rich bought? What have the valour and struggles of nations won? What have the tears of so many generations finally washed away? Holy God! what is happening in the world?

For the second time, what has hitherto occurred only *once* in history is re-occurring and will not occur again as long as mankind is mankind. This is the second critical turning point of humanity: the old world is dying, a new one is being born – a *third* world is dawning!

Can this be? Our self-confident, stout-hearted world so rich in vital juices, armed with inexhaustible resources, so overwhelmingly assured in its course – this world so powerful that it is capable of arrogantly over-taxing its forces, so learned that it no longer has either beliefs or doubts, so calculatingly honest whenever honesty pays, sure of itself unto indifference? Can it be that this world is to cede to a new world at the very moment that it is preparing to spread itself out in comfort?

Remember the final days of old Rome, its ancient power and valour, its invincible legions, its well-knit codes of law, all its captured gold, all the grain flowing annually from the granaries of the entire world to feed its citizens, those masters of the world. Remember its roads and aqueducts, its toils and games, and finally, Roman *Fortuna* unmatched by anyone either before or after, and say to yourselves: if such a sun did set, what sun could not set?... Remember too the Balthazarian revelries and the admonitions interrupting them. Finally, recall the clear warnings of the Redeemer, the days of Noah and the 'days of Lot'. Then too people 'ate, drank, married...bought and sold, planted and built...' and had con-fidence in themselves 'unto the day when Noah entered the ark or Lot left Sodom' (Matthew 24; Luke 17). Remember and be watchful!

Is our world to deserve the fate of Rome or that of Gomorrah? Is a flood – a flood of blood or darkness – to cover our earth again?

O no! there will be no flood 'to destroy the earth' (Genesis 9.11). There may be defeats, there may be floods – if you unleash them yourselves. Then, like blind hurricanes, they can sweep away men of good and ill will but they will reach neither peoples nor humanity. It depends on you yourselves if they are to be averted or not. For you shall see that a multi-coloured *rainbow of humanity* is forming, that sign of an ultimate and eternal alliance, a sign of peace and consolation. Look! and ye shall divine the ways and means of the Lord.

It is no longer the weak as of yore but the powerful who call for peace. It is no longer doves but vultures who carry the olive branch, for it is no longer vultures but doves who prepare for battle. What does this mean? That people who seem to chase only after their own profit are working for nations and that nations which seem to undergo suffering only for self-love are working for humanity! We see and weep over them, for the former are ruining themselves by boundless greed and the latter are ruining themselves by boundless sacrifice. Although neither the greed of the former nor the sacrifice of the latter is to prove vain or abortive we still pity the sweet sufferings of the latter and the bitter delights of the former. And we pity those who have hitherto known no delight of the spirit for they are beginning to have an inkling of eternal suffering.

Deliver us, O deliver us O Lord, deliver people and peoples, deliver the masses, deliver humanity!

The salvation of people and peoples, of the masses and of humanity today, depends on themselves and on themselves alone. The age of grace is over, the age of merit has begun. Compassion has been accomplished, compensation has been initiated. The days of free favours have passed, the moment of reckoning has come. Truly, enough *talents* were remitted; let us count what they bought. Woe to the hoarders, glory to the wage-earners!

As long as mankind was a child it was reared under the care of guardians or under the rod of stewards. Today, as mankind approaches maturity may it freely use the forces which it has long experienced, may it live its own life, may it make its own *Promised Land*.

O, poor and weak that we are in spite of all our riches and strength! O, helpless and cowardly that we are in spite of our experience and all our training! Are we ourselves to undertake a task for which centuries have hitherto not sufficed in spite of God's inspired messengers? Where is the required wisdom, where is the required fortitude of spirit? There is but disarray of mind, futility of heart, unfitness of character. Will we, poor orphans, be able to complete this terrible crossing from the old world to the new with our own oars and sails, without a star, without a magnet, without a helmsman?

Your helmsman is Christ, your magnet is His fraternal love, your guiding star is the holy Prayer which He transmitted to you. In this Prayer He included everything *which you still need*. In it He showed you everything which you were to *strive* for until now, which you were to prepare for and which you were to comprehend and attain this very day by the fulfilment of the times. For as He left for the Father He promised that He would not leave you orphans and, watching over you until now with His heavenly eye, from the very beginning He devised and left in your memory the *record* of a future legacy for the time of your maturity. This legacy of

Christ, this eternal Testament of His, this monument left to show you the road to a safe haven, is the ultimate expression of a succession of divine revelations for the human race. It is the completion and fulfilment of all previous revelations. It is the *Revelation of Revelations!*

2

There are monuments of divine thought which contain the guarantee of eternal truth in their own nature and which bear an unshakeable testimony to their divine conception. Neither the intuition of peoples nor the thought of true sages can be misled by them. These are expressions of infinite love, wisdom and freedom, eternal too but revealing themselves in time and in given circumstances. Their meaning is eternal while their intention is temporal. Because they express eternal *truth* at a certain stage of its development these monuments also bear the mark of a certain era of history, a certain social state or upheaval, a certain people or epoch. They thus contain in one or several traits the elements which define their times or reflect in all its force an idea which is governing humanity.

To take an example: great men are the personified expression of all the elements of an epoch or nation and in their own fortunes, their deeds and the consequences of their deeds they give an undisputed guarantee of God's omnipotence to such an extent that each great man may be considered, with due allowance, an envoy of Providence. Similarly, these spiritual monuments which fully reflect a given sphere of the spirit of mankind become the general representations of the nature and direction of an epoch and compel recognition of the importance which historical Providence has given them. If one can rightly say that great men have their own star, that they can neither waver nor perish as long as they have not fulfilled their purpose, as long as they have not completed their mission, then one can also properly say concerning these monuments of mankind's existence that they themselves are like stars guiding the march of a given people or of human-kind, that they are guides both to kings and shepherds and that they will only set or burn out when they have led up to *what was promised.*

．．．．

Such a monument towering above all others, such a star of the first order illuminating the march of mankind and shining with its own particular glitter – such is the *Christian Prayer* transmitted from generation to generation: the OUR FATHER.

3

Millions upon millions of people have recited this prayer for eighteen centuries; millions recite it today and every day; we can count virtually in millions the commentaries, paraphrases, sermons, recollections, comments and considerations – in poetry and in prose – of which it has become and is still becoming the subject. Nevertheless, we must admit that until now it has not yet been understood in its theological, historical and philosophical meaning, that its relation to the past, the present and the future has not been grasped, that its ultimate and hence most important prophecy has hitherto not been perceived – in short, that its eternal meaning and its temporal purpose have not yet been discovered.

At first glance it may appear insolent and even godless to affirm that this universal and daily prayer taught by the Saviour Himself has not yet been grasped, that it has been recited, as it were, blindly. Yet it is so and it even *had to be so for the times were not yet fulfilled.*

· · · ·

Today, however, has come the moment of uncovering that hidden thought of the Spirit, the moment which precedes the Spirit's great deed. Today we need to *know* about this thought in order to *fulfil* it.

· · · ·

Let us thus keep in mind the following: the Lord's Prayer is a series of social appeals, hence the expression of the needs and aspirations of all society. It was given to us by the Saviour Himself in order to show us the essential *aims* of humanity and to give us at the same time a guarantee of their attainment, as He said: 'Ask and ye shall receive.' It thus constitutes the veritable divine revelation since it reveals not that *which is but that which will be,* not the aspirations of the individual Christian but those of all humanity. In this it is an extraordinary prophecy soaring above all ordinary prophecies, more important precisely because it was not imparted to the world in the form of an individual prophecy but as a universal requirement, as a social appeal.

· · · ·

4

Here the question could arise as to why this revelation was granted to us in the form of a *prayer* and not in the apparently more simple and precise form of a direct *prophecy*? If the Saviour's concern was to show us what was later to ensue, then surely He could have imparted the immediate consciousness of that future to us through some clear prophecy instead of hiding this secret in the entreaties of a prescribed prayer. Then we would have known precisely what to expect and acted accordingly without having to await the fulfilment of the times to uncover these concealed truths.

. . . .

When we expect the fulfilment of some prophecy we behave merely passively; often we even doubt its fulfilment for we do not feel in ourselves the immediate guarantee of its accomplishment. In truth, however, when praying we no longer doubt, for otherwise we would not pray or we would pray only with the lips and not with the heart or the whole spirit; indeed, in prayer we are both sure and unsure. If we really pray we already begin to *act*, to operate on the future, for we kindle our will with our yearning and the will is the mother of the deed and of reality... Consequently, Christ required of us that we yearn and strive towards the end which He had indicated, that we have this end before our eyes every day and even every moment until it is attained by our own deed and our own merit. It is not enough to ask and pray; we must accomplish and *fulfil our aim by ourselves*, for the fulfilment of the *prayer* itself is *labour* (*orare et laborare*).

. . . .

OUR

Social solidarity. The natural consequences of divine paternity

. . . .

4

Verily, in its simplicity and fullness this single invocation, 'Our Father', comprehends everything contained in that justly celebrated but now unfortunately notorious slogan, 'liberty, equality, fraternity'. Indeed, it contains a hundred times more because it speaks to the heart, the mind and the will more feelingly, more truly and more effectively than a slogan which however laudable and essentially right has been dissipated and transformed into an ironical phrase since it has begun to be scribbled about on city walls or on any common scrap of paper even while being frenziedly eradicated from our hearts. If in a social storm we lose our compass, this conscience of any vessel, then the splendid but frail flag which we hoist will not suffice to lead us into port, for being neither a sail nor a compass it gives neither strength nor direction. Unless, aroused by the breeze of faith, hope and charity, we look above to a guiding star which will give us an infallible direction because it has shone for ages over the same haven where Christ's compass needle has shown us the way. This star will reveal to us that divine fatherhood is both *cause* and *proof* of our freedom, our equality and our fraternity, for as one cannot do without the other so too whenever we neglect causes we deprive ourselves of the consequences.

. . . .

13

Now, you who today abuse the fine name of socialists! You are not in the least socialists plotting *coups* with fire and sword rather than thinking of healing a contorted society with spirit and love. Listen, you so-called red socialists! If you were really what you call yourselves you would be *building* society instead of demoralizing it whether through your example or your principles. Since either your thought or your life is anti-social how can society have confidence in you? How is it to seek the drops of a doubtful medicine in a multitude of obvious poisons? Where is your authority? Where is the pragmatic sanction of your sociability?

There was a time when you were rightly distinguished from blind communists or fanatical demagogues. There was a time when, perceiving everlasting beams among the evanescent flickers of your theories, one rejoiced at the richness of sentiment and conjecture – however unripe and peculiarly entangled in peculiarities – which abounded in your endeavours. You then constituted a slender but compact band warmed by good thought, preparing for construction, not destruction. Although the world hurled derision and heaped abuse at your hopes you in turn had the right to smile at these mockeries. For wherever good faith, good thought or good will flourish sooner or later they will merit respect and sooner or later they will be blessed with fruit.

. . . .

For know ye this, that the awaited social state, more perfect than all known in history, that state of harmony and concord of which you dream and for which the ages before you have yearned, is nothing but and can be nothing but the promised Kingdom of God materially *pre-figured* in the earth of Canaan and morally *pre-figured* in the Church of Christ. Having attained this Kingdom you shall receive everything else in addition and in turn, for this is the fulfilment of the destinies of humanity, peace and joy in the Holy Spirit. But if you pass it by or solicit something else on the side, obviously you shall attain nothing.

. . . .

14

'You are the salt of the earth; but if salt has lost its taste, how shall its salt-ness be restored? It is no longer good for anything except to be thrown out and trodden under foot by men' (Matthew 5.13). Yea, you could be the salt of the earth as activators and inspirers of upright progress, as fomentors and sowers of the holy elements of the world. You could be 'the light of the world... Nor do men light a lamp and put it under a bushel, but on a stand and it gives light to all in the house' (Matthew 5.14, 15). Instead, what are you? You are Jesuits of progress. What do you seek most? You seek the office of inquisitors of temporal salvation.

These so-called companions of Jesus used and abused the most holy name on earth to carry out designs against Jesus not caring in the least about the sacredness of the means but only anxious to attain pseudo-sacred ends. Unmindful of the Master's precepts they did not hesitate to hide the light under the bushel and, bloated with pride, planned to ensnare the world, having allowed themselves to be ensnared by the spirit of servitude. So too you, whose usurped name designates you as advocates of society, insult the name which unites you by paying homage to dissoluteness. In spite of your Master's numerous reminders you do not hesitate *per fas et nefas* to detach the world from religion instead of re-attaching (*religare*) it. Without blanching before the wantonness of the world you entangle yourselves in sinister licentiousness whose inevitable issue is servitude. And even exter-nal signs involuntarily betray 'whose spirit you are'. As the others donned blackness, the cloak of darkness and night where even dirt is invisible, so you have assumed crimson, the colour of blood, that 'strangest juice' craved by 'the eternal negating spirit' which well knows what it still needs for its outrageous task.

To be sure, Christian virtues have sometimes bloomed in Loyola's or Dominic's assemblies where to this day merits worthy of admiration sprout in spite of the bleak suffering left in their wake. So too posterity will not overlook the noble ore of your fiery but sooty smithies in spite of the red rust which devours it. However, the Last Judgement will be harsh both for you and for them, for you lie to yourselves and society just as they have lied to themselves, the world and the Redeemer.

Verily, verily neither the blacks nor the reds shall inherit the Kingdom of Heaven and cross its gates. Indeed, they will halt humanity in the swelter of the desert and cause hunger of the spirit. For this Kingdom is inaccessible to any corruption (cf. 1 Cor. 15.50) and if doubt alone can retain us at its gates how much more will depravity hinder us! Yea, the gate to the Kingdom of God is the *Rainbow of Reconciliation*, as clear and pure as love, full of universal tones, like the countenance of the One blessed among women.

This nuptial link between heaven and earth, this divine sign of unification and covenant, this likeness of divine glory, is also the symbol of our reconciliation on earth. This is our emblem of concord, the badge of peace and consolation, because in it coincide all the tones and splendours of the world moderating each other and multiplying them out of themselves without number or limit, without excluding or condemning any, for it requires them all. Indeed, it proves to each that none can live without the other, that each evokes its own complement; only the universal plenitude of all colours, like the universal plenitude of all tones, constitutes harmony. It proves that these sisters require each other as they run and melt into a single, opalescent white.

THY KINGDOM COME

I: 1

After the invocation referring to the Supreme Being ['Hallowed be Thy Name' – AL] follows an appeal concerning the relations of humanity; the issue of God Himself is followed by the social question of the world. Obviously, God is the highest good, the highest aim, the aim above all others; consequently, the primary request naturally had to have God as its aim. Similarly, the Kingdom of God is the greatest among worldly goods and human aims so it is right that the second request should deal with this Kingdom. Since it is the greatest of all human goods it is their condition and fulfilment, for Christ has prophesied: 'Seek first his Kingdom and his righteousness and all these things shall be yours as well' (Matthew 6.33).

And so the *Kingdom of God* is the object of the next request ['Thy Kingdom come' – AL]. His justice is the object of the following one ['Thy will be done' – AL]. What the Redeemer tells us to seek in the preceding part of His Prayer is precisely what He enjoins us to request in the second part even as He shows us its condition in the third part. Since He orders us to pray for all this, He has obviously not yet endowed us with these gifts but only *promised* and *brought them closer*; otherwise, He would not have ordered us to seek or to pray for them.

It is also obvious that this request has not yet been fulfilled in the *second* Christian epoch of the world but can and will be fulfilled only in the *third* epoch which is to follow the *middle ages*. It is enough to look at the state of social relations to date, at the strife and disruption which have reigned in the world, at the deprivation and illnesses which mankind has hitherto suffered, to convince ourselves that the Kingdom of God has truly not yet come, for clearly the state of the world does not as yet correspond in the least to the concept of the Kingdom of God. It suffices again to mention Christ's words – 'My Kingdom is not of this world' (John 18.36) – to be convinced that the Kingdom of God on earth *was not to come* throughout the whole Christian era.

On the other hand, it is equally and unquestionably obvious for anyone in the least versed in Scripture or Church history that Christ most clearly promised mankind the *coming* of the divine Kingdom on earth and that faith in this approaching occurrence was the universal *orthodox* conviction of all Christianity in the first centuries of rebirth. We shall presently sort out Christ's principal statements as well as the testimonies of the Fathers and Doctors of the Church in this regard. At this point, we may remark by way of introduction that it would be enough to reflect without prejudice on the following request of our universal prayer, where Christ enjoins us to pray not for the Kingdom of God in general or its development or such like but explicitly for its coming, to find besides the inadequacies of the present the promise of a definite future occurrence along with a guarantee of its attainment. Later, some began to affirm that this Kingdom was never to come into *our world*, remaining the eternal privilege of *another* world. Still later and quite contradictorily, others tried to explain that the Kingdom had already been transferred to earth by Christ. If this was so, why would Christ have enjoined us to pray 'Thy Kingdom come'? In either case, this prayer would be an absurdity, for one does not request what one has already received or what one will definitely never receive; one does not summon or call for the *coming* of that which can never come or what has already come.

. . . .

I: 2

If we admit faith in the coming Kingdom of God on the basis of this prayer an important difficulty confronts us from another perspective. How can this request concur with Christ's declaration invoked just above:

'My Kingdom is not of this world'? This stands in fundamental contradiction to the present prayer, for the hopes raised by the entreaty under examination are just as firmly dashed by this declaration; what the former clearly affirms, the latter clearly denies. Why then did Christ order us to request the coming of this Kingdom, prophesy its coming so often, and promise it so firmly if He Himself ultimately acknowledges that the Kingdom is 'not of this world'? What does this dreadful contradiction mean?

. . . .

I: 3

Distingue tempora et concordabit scriptura. In the Christian epoch the Kingdom of God was not and could not yet be of *this* world, for Christian salvation and regeneration depended precisely on mankind's detaching itself from the sensuous and visible world, on turning away from the alluring earth. It depended on *negating* this merely external world in order to break decidedly with it, on awakening in the spirit of humanity the internal, infinite world, invisible to the corporeal eye, and on establishing it in place of the damned world – in short, on directing all mankind's life to an ideal heaven. This repudiation of the external world and foundation of an internal world, this rupture of present relations and disruption of existing circumstances, this foreshadowing of eternal conditions, was also an elevation of the spirit to a higher scale and a higher power.

. . . .

Thus, throughout the present, middle ages which began with our era and last unto this day, the Kingdom of God *was not* and could not be *of this world* but was only approximated, sowed, prophesied and related. In other words, *its concept* was only *founded in ourselves*, the Word (*logos*) of the Kingdom of God had appeared but the Word had not yet become flesh (*Verbum Regni*; Matthew 13.19). We shall see in the texts themselves what Holy Scripture means by this and similar expressions of a detached, invisible, extra-terrestrial *ideal* state, hence of an as yet unreal kingdom. We shall again see, as in the first entreaty, that Christian revelation has only contributed the foundations and building materials of the Divine Kingdom, leaving the real construction of these ideal nuclei to the *third* revelation and the third epoch in history. Here, however, let us first bear in mind that whatever is only *conceptual*, in the state of thought and word and not yet of the deed, by this same token is not yet perfected and completed for it lacks an appropriate reality – the Word has not yet become flesh. Thus, for us any *other-worldly* kingdom would be only an abstraction, a subjective thought and not essential reality, objective nature, being. Thence it follows that this Kingdom which has as yet only been thought needs to be *fulfilled and incarnated*.

.　.　.　.

I: 7

The early Christians did not waver in appraising these words of Christ [Matthew 24.30 and 26.29 and others prophesying a worldly Kingdom of God – AL], and their relation to explicit promises. Neither did they doubt for a moment, in the opening centuries of our era, the *secular* imminence of the Kingdom of God after a 'brief' period of oppression and trial. They obviously noticed and painfully recognized that then as well as now this Kingdom was not of this world, for they were not yet so thoroughly trained in theological fictions or so schooled in the artificial dissection of expressions as to argue against the obvious in the manner of later inventions which have persisted. They believed all the more strongly and sincerely in this future coming and attributed its 'divine delay' only to their own imperfections and their own impatience.

.　.　.　.

The hopes of early Christians awaiting the return of the Lord and the coming of His Kingdom as the Jews await their Messiah had to be vain. But they were vain not in the least because they were false but because they were too sudden, too *impatient*. The whole Christian epoch had to be an epoch of patience and suffering, for He who revealed it was a suffering Messiah. The science which *He* brought was precisely the science of detachment from the world, the Kingdom which *He* founded was not yet to be of this world. Together with this revelation He also prophesied that a unification would occur between this broken world and the ensuing Kingdom of God on this earth. This would not occur through a New Word but through new, complementary words of this revelation which 'the world was not yet capable' then of accepting or comprehending.

.　.　.　.

Thus, later tradition did not err in rejecting all chiliastic reveries as fantasies. Indeed, the chiliasts themselves erred in expecting to reach their *end* without taking an indirect road strewn with hardships. Christ and all Christianity is precisely this *road*.

II: 1

The social state is the destiny, the nature, the essential condition of human life. Man is created for society, without it he would not even be a person, for only the social state coincides with this concept.

In saying that man is a political animal, Aristotle expressed a real and fundamental truth. Later came others who proposed to correct Aristotle, saying that man is a *'religious* animal'. We have no objections if by 'religious' they meant that eternal community and cohesion of all spirits, that solidarity with God and men, the not merely blind or involuntary but self-conscious and voluntary recognition of dependence, hence of free spiritual *dependence* and *belonging* – in short, that absolute *connection* and *obligation* which lies at the root of the word 'religion' and even more so in its eternal meaning and destiny. Indeed, we emphatically accept this complementary definition and willingly recognize it as a correction appropriate to the great progress brought by Christianity into the world. Only let us note that this is precisely what Aristotle, from his standpoint, that is, at the level of pre-Christian representations, understood by *politicity*, for among the ancients *politeia* was always *theothen* and their political life naught else but religious life.

· · · ·

II: 2

Thus, it is not surprising that mankind's absolute state of nature could never exist anywhere, except perhaps on paper as the fruit of vacuous theoreticians' fancies as they sophisticate on the social state and try to extract some sort of sociable agreement, *contrat social*. Certainly, the human race had a certain state of nature proper to itself but this state was already highly social, although characterized by merely mechanical and innate community. We saw this state in the first volume as the state of nature of society itself, not that of persons, for the person as person already carries society with himself. No wonder then that even the so-called savages live in a certain state of society, for wherever there is a body there too must be gravity.

· · · ·

It is not therefore the individual as individual but society itself as society which finds itself in a state of nature, that is to say, in a state inappropriate to itself. The destiny of society is precisely to disengage itself and to slowly develop out of this *given* and *innate* state. Indeed, the threefold task of the social state is first, to *grow* out of the state of nature, to be shaped in its very womb; second, definitively to overcome the state of nature, abolish it and to cast it away; third, to reappropriate this state of nature, that is, not to regress to it by any means but rather to lift it through assimilation to one's own level, *to use it as one's own organic element* rather than as a power foreign to oneself, and to harness this reborn nature to oneself. These are the *three periods* of mankind's grand life-span and the three principal stages of history.

Society is the universal person and just like a person it is a spirit joining the sinews of the body and the soul. As in a person, it is first the body which develops most during the period of infantile growth; then it is principally the soul during the period of adolescent upbringing; finally, and only after having come of age, a person begins a full and proper life developing the whole reality of his spirit in a period of virile civic valour. So too every society and indeed all humanity, that universal collective person, must traverse similar stages of life before attaining its mature and proper state.

. . . .

II: 6

Are these two separate spheres, the religious and the political, exclusively Christian products? No, it is only their separateness, their antagonism, their *reflection in themselves* which is the innovation of the new world. In the ancient world religion and politics dozed in undisturbed oneness and common indifference. It is Christianity which wrought their very division into two opposite camps, their stepping out of and against themselves, and thus definitive manifestation...

. . . .

II: 8

These two opposite poles constitute, as it were, two opposite electricities and as long as they were in a dynamic state they formed the living streams of the Middle Ages. Since their destiny is to penetrate each other, can they long maintain themselves in a division so indifferent to each other, in the separate tension in which we see them today? Indeed, they can for a while, that is, as long as they are separated from each other as if by the glass of a Leyden battery, and this is precisely their position today. But this *pane of indifferentism* is treacherous; as long as there is still electricity in the battery the tension lasts – but the first carelessness can discharge it.

Aye, if you are no longer concerned about one of these separated electric charges supposing that with time or the humidity of the social atmosphere it has been drained away or evaporated, O poor physicists, do not try to deceive yourselves. Know ye that the second charge has also disappeared, for each is the necessary condition of the other and as soon as one disappears the other is no more. Behold! your whole battery is dead. So too your politics are without a soul whenever religion atrophies in them.

Having glimpsed this, perhaps you will come to doubt completely in electricity? Nonsense, electricity always *is*; it lives in nature; it embraces the universe. But the electricity which you carefully separated and, as it were, gathered into your batteries, possessed and wished to indifferentiate not knowing how to use it, has flowed together to its universal source. It is in the universe and enlivens the universe but you do not have even a trace of it in your offices! Be thankful too that premature discharging has not yet shattered the battery and has not pulverized you with its bolts.

. . . .

II: 10

As the *natural indifferentism* of the social state of Antiquity had to disintegrate into the *ideal differentism* of the social state of Christianity, so too the latter must rise to the *spiritual unity* of the third world. The hitherto detached generality of Christianity aims for completion through the factual particularity of the antique world. The world comes to recognize one spiritual humanity, to join its hitherto distinct religious soul to its hitherto mangled political body. The formerly *disiecta membra* of humanity desire a vitalizing breath for their common unification, for life in, for and through themselves. The *ideal Republic* revealed in Christianity yearns for realization in nations and through nations. This *logos of the social world which until now was only in God becomes flesh and dwells among us.*

Peoples, (*gentes*), the ancient ethnic element, are the very organs of that incarnation, means to that end, diverse elements of its diverse functions called to unification. The solidarity of humanity, hitherto only *subjective, invisible to the senses*, founded within thought and ideally grasped, becomes flesh. The Word of the divine Kingdom (*Verbum Regni*) today appears *objectively* and visibly in the external and public relations of the world. Formerly *inborn* and innate nations are themselves *regenerated*. They cease to be exclusive and limited as in the pagan world, rising rather to general association and living communion. No longer separate and mechanically interacting they become co-agents of the universal organism. They coincide not lifelessly but vitally uncovering and discovering their proper office in the organism of humanity.

This regeneration, this *palingenesis*, this *resurrection in the spirit* only constitutes their own transition *from the state of nature to the state of civilization of societies*, to the state of citizenship of nations, to the *Commonwealth of Peoples*. As until now only the particular individual was citizen of his own particular nation, so today any nation as a collective person becomes a citizen of this republic of the world, this assembly above assemblies, this universal ecclesia which the Lord's great apostle calls the plenitude of peoples, *plenitudo gentium* (Rom. 11.25).

This commonwealth can embrace the most diverse forms in accordance with the most diverse dispositions of peoples from the strictly monarchical unto the purely democratic just as until now diverse estates have communed with each other and the most diverse rungs of the social hierarchy have existed in individual states. Instead of fighting with each other about borders, influence or supremacy states are to lie down together and help each other like individual estates in a healthy republic.

This commonwealth's destiny is no longer exclusive or temporal, limited or self-seeking like pagan societies; nor, on the contrary, is its aim detached, extra-worldly, postulatory, potential rather than real, eternally infinite and hence unattainable – negative and abnegating – like Christian society. It is precisely the plenitude and unity of these two positions, the socialization of the world, the accomplishment of the destinies of the spirit of humanity, the attainment of its entreaties and the elevation of its members to true concord, to the harmony of being, thought and the deed. It is this very harmony, this unison of universal diversities, this peace and agreement among previously stormy and mutually repelling elements which constitutes *the Kingdom of God on earth*.

· · · ·

II: 11

Thus, it would be a grave mistake for anyone to seek a pre-cast, *a priori* form of this Kingdom and having found one to his fancy to think that he could pour the conditions of the world into this mould, for he would only add a new utopia to the quite sufficient number of existing ones.

· · · ·

The Kingdom of God cannot come *here* or *there*, *this way* or *that way* but precisely both here and there, both this way and that way since it is the very attunement of the universal elements of the world which constitutes this Kingdom. Hence it is said: 'The Kingdom of God is not coming with signs to be observed nor will they say, Lo, here it is! or There!' (Luke

17.20, 21). To compare it further, the Kingdom will absorb the whole horizon like lightning, for it is nothing but the electrification of the world with the spark of common life and the assimilation of temporal states through the eternal bonds of universal fraternity among peoples and the universal community of institutions.

As long as we thought that this Kingdom could be *one* of the kingdoms of our globe singled out from among others – so to speak – as the capital of God, we were deceiving ourselves with the basest, traditional Jewish illusions. As long too as we judged that the Kingdom cannot be of this world at all, that all the kingdoms of our world 'have nothing in common with it', that it will always remain within us in the ideal element of thought and will always have only future life as its aim, we were deluded by a lofty but most one-sided abstraction. Both these opposite illusions need to be abolished and discarded together. The task of the Kingdom of God is to develop the eternal life of the Spirit on earth and the aim of humanity is to realize this Kingdom not in a detached future life but in the present which is a participant of the eternal. For mankind does not die; it is only re-generated, and eternal life is but the universal plenitude of present elements and the universal continuity of succeeding ones. The Kingdom of God is nothing but the *organic state of societies, the unification of the world, the harmony of nations, the political church of humanity*!

. . . .

II: 12

Let us reflect more closely on this definitive passage from the Christian epoch into the epoch of the future and let us analyse the reciprocal relation of their social states.

After having abolished all the real commonwealths which it found on earth and after having uncovered their nullity and volatility, Christianity brought its own ideal commonwealth into the world, its Church of the Word, that gathering of Kindred and Faithful joined to each other not yet through any real but uniquely ideal and moral ties, only striving for a state of peace, unity and consolation. Certainly, this was already a Church of God but only a *struggling* Church. This ideal, invisible commonwealth just founded in us was precisely the word (*logos*) of the perfect society but not yet its body. Hence, the Kingdom of the Word was – as the Gospel calls it – only the *word* of the Kingdom of God (*Verbum Regni*).

. . . .

But the love and brotherhood of all men, brought by Christ as a nucleus of consolation and stimulating root of society, was only founded subjectively within each man's spirit and thus could not yet pervade the world. This foundation was only an indication, a postulate which the world's external conditions did not allow to be fulfilled. It was only an abnegating, hence one-sided, precept, for it was only individually *moral* and not publicly *social*. To be sure, this *internal regeneration of man himself* was necessary, this stepping into oneself was needed as was the stepping out of the external world because without it the pagan would not have been worthy or capable not only of attaining but even of *approaching* the Kingdom of God. Today, however, this is not enough. *The internal rebirth of the person* does not yet suffice without the external rebirth of the circumstances of the world itself, without the rebirth of societies themselves – but more on this in the third entreaty.

. . . .

Thus it turns out that 'the Kingdom of God on earth' is related to the Christian kingdom which 'was not yet of this world' as the deed is to knowledge, reality to the concept, fulfilment to possibility.

. . . .

II: 15

Thus, we see that one of the conditions and characteristics of the divine Kingdom on earth is this unification of humanity in eternal and universal peace. The theoretical conceptions of virtually all profounder publicists instinctively strove toward this end. Present relations of diplomacy and the law of nations gravitate toward this aim in practice, albeit blindly and unwittingly for them and visibly only for us.

. . . .

II: 16

Nations have been and will be incapable of accepting the idea of eternal peace and carrying it out in reality as long as they are not joined to each other *religiously*, born of the Spirit, and affirmed in the *sociability of the Holy Spirit*. Without this connection, rebirth and affirmation, existing states glued together or carved up in defiance of the elements of the Spirit, in defiance of the holy and inviolable laws of nationality, and in defiance of truth and social good, will never be capable of falling together nor of ever creating a truly universal and vital body of humanity. There can never be universal peace among these states because in them peace itself is either an exception or a sham and a lie. Although their lips say 'peace, peace', they have no peace (Jeremiah 6.14; 8.11).

. . . .

Eternal peace among peoples cannot be produced by any little tract or diplomatic conference, fakery or *tinsel*; in short, by any artificial paste or ruse or *untreated lime*. It is only through the true idea of the life of humanity, reborn of the Spirit, joined in a holy alliance and religiously developed in its real members. Glory to the Slavonic monarch who first thought of the *Holy* Alliance, for however unripe and quickly warped it was nonetheless a vital idea. Thanks to him at least for this noble desire and shame to those political pharisees who from the outset smiled ironically at the sight of such a *queerly intended* political freak and who later, unable to escape it, twisted, wounded, distorted and aborted it.

. . . .

II: 19

Whoever believes in liberty, equality and fraternity among men – not in the manner of revolutionary demagogues who scribble these words on the walls even as they drive them out of their hearts and minds – but as these words flow from the revelation of our Father who is in heaven, may he also believe in liberty, equality and fraternity among peoples, for one is the condition of the other. Whoever does not grasp this, whoever does not feel this with all his heart, has not yet been reborn in the Spirit. He is not only himself unworthy of entering into the Kingdom of God but in addition he obstructs his brothers' entry. But whoever denies to any nation its sacred independence, whoever hypocritically pretends to deplore the injustice inflicted but does not dream of refusing to acknowledge this *fait accompli*, dooms himself. To be sure, the injured nation will not revenge itself, for a just God will mete out punishment in His own time.

. . . .

III: 1

For religion is not merely catechism, symbolic rites or moral rules. In short, religion is not 'merely' anything but indeed the whole fullness of feeling, knowledge and will directed to the absolute aims of the Spirit. Thus, religion is the absolute association and obligation of the universe. It is absolute harmony and universal harmonization. If we abolish this connection, if we abolish this vital, unifying force we shall disintegrate into dust. If we take away the unifying soul then the body having become a cadaver will begin to decompose. Since we are aiming at nothing other than harmony and organic association we are penetrated with religion through and through for without it we would not have any common aim. All that is common, all that is harmonious, all that is united is *ipso facto* already religious. Hence, Christ's words are marvellously beautiful and truthful: 'Where two or three are gathered in my name there am I in the midst of them' (Matthew 18.20). Just as man cannot be comprehended without society so too society cannot be understood without religion. Such a society would be nonsensical and completely absurd for it would not be a community, a society, and hence it would be something other than what it is.

Those who affirm that we no longer need religion, that *it has been good for nothing*, by the same token unwittingly affirm that we do not need society for society itself is already religion. Religion is the universal union of people and peoples, their mainspring and essential strength. The whole life of humanity is a great religion and religion is its whole life. Religion is *all for all*.

. . . .

Thus, religion *as soul* and the political state *as body* have always co-incided with each other, but once *without consciousness of their oneness* and a second time with *consciousness of their division*. Only today is recognition of their full *unification* and harmony in the Spirit approaching; only today is the soul *being materialized* in the body and the body in the soul.

. . . .

III: 3

Let us now pass from this genealogy of the Kingdom of God to a closer delimitation of its essence. It embraces religion conceived as the absolute association of the universe not only for immediately visible, temporally limited, contingently innate ends as in pagan societies nor for the ends prevailing in Christian society – ideal, extra-worldly, here completely invisible, perpetually merely eternal hence never temporal, or present, always only transcendent and never immanent. The true end of the world and humanity, the highest good of the Spirit, requires both material and ideal fulfilment, for the Spirit is the fullness of body and soul.

The Kingdom of God thus embraces the organic development of all the resources and all the gifts of the Spirit, all the treasures of the universe, all the elements of humanity, their union in ever more perfect life, their culti-vation and elevation to an ever more noble and more stalwart state. It comprehends the conscious realization of the freedom of the Spirit not merely uniformly and exclusively but completely. It contains a conception of the unity of social order and religious observance and the concept of government as a principal and active organ of these demands, this association, this religion, as an instrument and hearth of the organic life of peoples and humanity.

The Kingdom requires the organization of this government in such a way that all those capable of acting are called to it and *really act*, that is to say, are themselves participants in this government and ministers of the reigning Spirit. Wherever and however he can, each member accepts and accomplishes some public charge from the lowest level of the primeval horde or hamlet – *commune*, *Gemeinde*, *mir* – that primary molecule of the social body – *molecule primitive*. From here on, the principle of *self-government* reigns and opens innumerable public and social vocations calling on *each* member to participate in public affairs. This participation begins with the tiniest and most numerous units at the base of the social pyramid of capacities and rises ever higher on the rungs of the hierarchy, this holy order, as these tasks themselves acquire an ever wider and loftier character up to the highest point of centralization intended to assemble the entirety and universality of social matters. This constitutes a *sensorium commune* of society and all societies, a hearth of both its active and passive movements, like the brain for the nervous system and the heart for the circulation of blood.

The Kingdom of God requires recognition of public activity and participation at all levels of social life not only as a right but as a *social* and utmost *religious duty* and thus as virtue itself. It requires that participation in government be recognized as a religious observance, as a duty and sacred practice, as a means and condition of salvation. Where God Himself is king any partaking in government is already by this very token divine service. Thus, the Kingdom requires that this *public service*, this service to humanity to the extent of one's capacities, in the area of one's capacities, and to the best of one's capacities, be recognized as truly *divine* service, as a *priesthood of the Spirit*, as the vocation and consecration of social man. It requires the conviction that the higher one's authority, the more one serves, the more one is *servus servorum*, the greater is one's social duty but also the greater one's merit. It requires the conviction that there is no higher merit than this absolute, *divine service in humanity* from the smallest to the greatest spheres; that before God and for God this is the greatest merit; that God desires only this and nothing else, hence no futile ceremonies or dead practices – honourable as approximations but incapable of exhausting His aims, for God is Spirit and desires above all the *cultivation of the Spirit*.

The Kingdom of God requires the conviction that whoever *does not serve* in any manner in this universal kingdom of which God Himself is king, whoever does not work at all in this vineyard of the Lord, whoever does not sacrifice himself and thus does not consecrate his life to maintaining, developing and perfecting the life of his family, community, nation, humanity, those lower and higher churches, is but an empty weight on the earth (*inutile terrae pondus*), 'like a trumpet sounding'. Indeed, he sins against the Holy Spirit, for he removes himself from its sociability, and 'sins against the Holy Spirit will not be forgiven either in this age or in the next'.

The Kingdom requires one to pay heed that this *social sacrifice* be no longer a futile and abstract sacrifice for sacrifice's sake, that is, a means rather than a goal, a useless mortification of self as ascetics had formerly prescribed, but rather that it be a *fertile sacrifice* for a common and vital aim, a completion and a sanctification of life.

These are the main principles of this Holy Commonwealth, which thus becomes both state and church, both a worldly and a divine institution, quite literally: *the divine reign on earth*.

. . . .

III: 5

. . . .

Who today does not see that one of the main causes of social *fermentation* is the *need* for and *right* to public activity in communities and suitable participation in public affairs, a need and right which evokes continual protest against all that happens in government without the concurrence of the governed? The governors deplore this stormy and fanatical ambition which stirs up individuals in society and ceaselessly cuts across all governmental policies and makes government virtually impossible through the very lack of a will to govern. They take refuge in various narcotics to assuage this hitherto little-understood social irritability, from individual scaffolds or general martial hecatombs to despondency and discouragement. But see! this social irritability and fermentation turns out to be nothing else than the required ferment of social peace, the condition of higher life.

. . . .

III: 6

. . . .

Today in individuals and nations, in particular associations and in the great company of humanity, this impulse towards auto-sufficient and auto-regulating activity, towards autonomous direction of both individual and general affairs – in short, towards the right of active citizenship (*droit de citoyen actif*) – stalwartly reveals itself. People, peoples and humanity have hitherto found themselves relatively under age in a state of tutelage or, as St Paul says (Gal. 4), 'under stewards', and hence subordinated to an alien law (*heteronomy*). Only passivity was universally shared; *active citizenship* was not a universal right but still an exclusive privilege, not a rule but an exception. From now on the exception will become the rule and the duty of *blind obedience* will be transformed into a duty of *conscious participation*. Today humanity celebrates its moment of emancipation. Today people, peoples, and humanity are casting off all alien yokes, desiring henceforth to live and march under their own laws. This desire is both right and de-served. It is right because the characteristic of all Spirit is independence, freedom, *life through itself*; it is deserved because through the vicissitudes, experiences and labours of past life – in short, through the *progress* of childhood and youth – mankind has come of age and so has truly deserved its emancipation.

. . . . .

III: 8

And in reply to the question [of how the offices and officials of the Spirit are to be born and reborn – AL], the Church of Christ, this approximate figure of the Kingdom of God, gives us an answer precisely by advancing an approximate example. Thus, in the organism and history of the Church we have the likeness of the organization of the Kingdom of God. We see that the great soul of the great body of the faithful developed simul-taneously with the autonomy of the early Christian communes – unity in diversity and diversity in unity, an ever more centralized administration, an ever stronger and more universal government, an ever more perfect organization, in short, the admirable Catholic hierarchy.

If anywhere it was there that objective God-given authority (*auctoritas*) was recognized. Yet in spite of this or rather *precisely because of it* this authority was based on the subjective *participation of members*, that is, it derived from their own choice, their free election. God's choice was indicated by the very choice of the faithful, and you have not nor cannot have a more appropriate indication and a stricter *criterion* for the Spirit. In this way the *vox populi* was legitimized as the true *vox Dei*, as the instrument for the revelation of God's designs.

In the course of centuries the forms of election were diverse and of varying excellence, inasmuch as they were only approximations, for the true *age of election* had not yet come but had only been forecast and was only becoming *likely*. Nevertheless, whether at higher or lower levels of the hierarchy, whether directly and actively or indirectly and passively, whether firmly or gradually, externally or internally, always and everywhere we see that in the last analysis the substantial authority of the Church rests on this democratic principle. Only in further inner transformations, as if in ever higher sublimation of the original elements, the Church developed its aristocratic and monarchical components provoking an aristocracy from within itself... Even today, after so many vicissitudes, the outstanding relic of this essential form of the life of the Catholic Church remains the election of its head, the pope, by Church magnates assembled in a college of cardinals – the impoverished *caput mortuum* of a once living organism.

As in Christ's Church so in the Kingdom of God objective social authority is born of *free election*, but as soon as it is founded and begotten it acquires form by *God's grace*, resolution and inspiration. Yet how often, particularly in modern times, has the true and simple formula 'by the grace of God' been lapidated! 'All authority comes from God' and hence is really by the grace of God.

Thus, the Church itself indicates the solution to this in the weighty question: *whence are to come all offices in the community of the Spirit, from God or from the people?* Our answer is that they are to come *from God through the people and from the people through God*. When an election truly comes from the people it is by the same token inspired by God and when it is truly inspired by God by the same token it must be expressed by the people.

· · · ·

III: 9

When however, we say that election is the definitive *principle* of social authority we by no means affirm that it must be so uniquely and *invariably*. This government, this hierarchy would itself be excessively one-sided and abstract if that which constitutes its own nucleus were forced to penetrate its every dissemination and ramification, repeating itself and preventing any other formation at all.

. . . .

Thus, if we were to apply only a single principle unilaterally to the organism of humanity we would underestimate this organism by committing precisely the same error as if we were to reason in embryogenesis that, since the basic cell is an egg and all organic life originates in the basic cell which is an egg, therefore all organic bodies are composed only of eggs. Just as elementary cells give birth to other and further formations so too the organism of the social body requires similar transformation and regeneration.

In fact, the needs of the hierarchy are manifold and its functions most diverse. Thus, if the body is not to ail, its organs must correspond to and be adjusted to its functions. Let us not then arrest the self-generated life of societies in any way. Let them beget themselves by various means and form various members in various ways by their own means. Let us be sure that the harmony of purposes will flow precisely from this self-begetting.

. . . .

III: 10

In the very formation of individual governments, not only in their daily administration, but in their most essential arrangements, the principle of self-government, of free and autonomous self-constitution is to reign. At the same time these governments are to fulfil the essential condition of participation in a universal organization which is to be composed of:

1. a central government – the highest executive authority;
2. a universal council of humanity (*concilium oecumenicum humanitatis*) – the highest legislative authority;
3. a universal tribunal of nations – the highest judicial and regulatory authority.

. . . .

Then we shall not ask, what and where is humanity? Whither is it unfolding? Is it but an empty generality, a chimera of our thought, nowhere possessing either body or basis? We shall then see it and acknowledge it already in the deed. It will act as a living being; we shall count and point out its organs instead of speaking as if it were the iron wolf whom no one has seen or *experienced*. As long as humanity *qua* humanity did not have its own organs it was only incorporeal spirit (*spiritus incorporalis*) which is but a phantom (*fantasma daemonium incorporale*). Humanity was thus like a people without government, authority, or social organization. Such a people would not be a people; it would not *be* at all. For this reason humanity *was not* until now but from now on it will be.

. . . .

III: 11

This *participation* both of members of an individual community in public affairs of their own scope and of individual communities in the public affairs of humanity has been shown to constitute not only the essence of self-government, that is, each citizen's political freedom in his own sphere, but, over and above this, the essence of the social order itself, the *principle* and goal of the office and government of the Spirit. We acknowledged free choice (*election*) as the principle and source of government and office. We acknowledged organic communion, unification in ever higher communities, in ever more excellent churches (*ecclesiae*) as their end and goal.

We first acknowledged the right of individual citizens to self-determination, participation in public affairs and a share in government. This government, which we originally considered in opposition to self-government as the objective foundation of subjective impulses, turned out to be a collective citizen also endowed with the right of participation in ever higher levels of the hierarchy so that the hierarchy itself is nothing but a grand replica of primitive communal self-government. Thus, our point of departure was participation and we returned to it completing *subjective* with *objective* participation. This order, this hierarchy which we first considered a completely opposite condition of freedom and self-government, as different as heteronomy is from autonomy, turned out to coincide completely – to *come out to the same thing*. Government is influenced by citizenship and citizenship is moulded by government.

. . . .

What then is to unify the freedom of individual citizens and the general order; what will secure their strict identity? What enables subjective right to be objectively applied and objective institutions to be grounded subjectively? Nothing other than what constitutes the highest unification of the world, what is at the same time a means and an end, true universal unity: the *Spirit* and the manifestation of its life on earth, *Religion*. In particular, since we are speaking of social and political matters, the condition of their unification is the existence of a strong social spirit, what we call a *living public spirit*.

. . . .

It has long been recognized that the principle of true democracy is civic virtue, that the condition of elective governments and self-governing republican institutions is a strong and vital public spirit. This recognition is certainly real but formerly it was intuitive rather than conscious. For it was not and could not be known that public spirit could not be *complete* as long as the revelation of the Holy Spirit had not been fulfilled... This is why all elective governments, all republican institutions *attempted* before the advent of the community of the Spirit, could only succeed more or less, that is, to the extent that public spirit reigned in them, and, before the full manifestation of the Spirit, it reigned only partially and approximately.

. . . .

That the elective system, for example in Greece, Rome or Poland, could give birth to evil consequences proves nothing other than that election was not the proper element of these ages. In fact, election could only become a proper part of the third epoch, the epoch of the Holy Spirit, the epoch of the will and freedom. In previous epochs, it had grown – so to speak – on a field which was not its own, where it could easily run riot or waste away; whereas there it was only an instalment, an announcement, a first flush of day, here it will appear in its own light, in suitable fullness and in healthy fruitfulness. Indeed, the intuition of the Christian Church that each election is a religious act, *a specific act of the Holy Spirit*, was both deep and accurate and this is why before proceeding with an election it sought to evoke the hitherto buried forces of the Holy Spirit with a separate mass to the Holy Spirit as well as the splendid hymn *Veni Creator Spiritus*.

. . . .

III: 13

What then are the characteristics of this public spirit's existence? To say that 'we shall know it by its fruits' is certainly true, but insufficient, for we would expose the commonwealth to sinister tests and harsh experiments and we would only be *groping* where we should be consciously advancing.

. . . .

The mark of public spirit's existence is *just* and *social* activity in all relations of life coupled with the abandonment of written law or statutes. It is absorption by the thought and aim of law, recognition of law as salutary, and fulfilment of its prescriptions through one's own impulses and not through external coercion, whether physical or moral. This means the replacement of dead law or statutes with living social *customs*. It means inscribing law in the hearts of one's compatriots so that they carry law within them and walk in it rather than confront it as if it were an alien and awkward regulation. In short, public spirit is that state which has hitherto revealed itself only exceptionally at the most heroic moments in the life of formerly existing societies, in everyone who 'sponte sua, sine lege fidem rectumque colebat' (Ovid, *Metamorphoses*).

. . . .

Written law is the more excellent the less one needs to read it. The rise of written law was one of the first advances of social groupings; dispensing with it and forsaking it will be among the last. The written law or statute or *lex* is always dead and frozen, its justice is only vain and barren, but the Spirit requires living law and living Spirit is the master of dead law.

. . . .

III: 15

. . . .

Of all the approximated states of the Spirit the most venerable, the greatest and the richest in resources for the future is certainly the Church of Christ. For the Church of Christ constitutes that great *general figure* of the Holy Commonwealth of nations or harmonious community of the Spirit which *divina institutione moniti, audemus Regnum Dei dicere*. On the other hand, all hitherto existing states, governments, institutions etc. – in short, all secular components – constitute only single *moments, disiecta membra* so to speak, which only the universal organism will be able to unify.

It thus follows that the constitution, components and history of the Church as it has existed so far give us an indication, but only an indication, a *figure*, a *model* of the constitutions, components and history of the Kingdom of God. All institutions, laws, roots, forms, customs – in short, all manifestations of life of the old Church – developed, elevated, fulfilled and applied to the life of humanity, will become precisely those of the universal Church of humanity, but always only to the extent to which the characteristics of a lower position can be applied to a situation of fullness and universality. Thus, these merely approximated types are to be seen in the perspective of an approaching Kingdom. It is now up to humanity to educe mature and suitable organs out of these approximated types... [For instance – AL] although the hierarchy of secular priesthood corresponds to and has found its worldly application in the political administration, monastic organization still awaits its appropriate development in socio-economic organizations, leagues, associations, fraternities, trade unions, friendly societies, etc.

· · · ·

III: 16

Just as the Christian Church had its history and experienced various vicissitudes in the course of the ages so too one should not imagine this great Church of organic humanity as a frozen and hence lifeless state. It too will live and develop; it will even have to undergo conflict both *within* and *outside* itself. Now, this truth may not seem immediately obvious, for if harmony is the mark of the state of the future, how is one to accept conflict in the womb of the divine Kingdom, and not only external but internal conflict? Where there is conflict there is no harmony or peace and so, one might say, the Kingdom will no longer be one of harmony, no longer one of peace.

On the contrary! Harmony would cease with the very exclusion or stifling of conflict, for conflict itself would then *conflict* with this one-sided, apparent, unlikely *harmony*. Indeed, harmony without conflict is an abstraction and fantasy, for in the divine Kingdom conflict is to *serve* harmony itself by maintaining and developing its life. The whole difference is that conflict as the *negative–progressive* element will no longer exist *for itself* and through itself, but *for peace*, that is, conflict will cease to be goal in itself in order to become a means out of itself. By the same token, its character and manifestation will be completely changed; it will be *overcome* and perfected and, in this way, it will be a *harmonious struggle*.

· · · ·

We thus see that certain organic constituents of today's political conditions, for instance the judiciary, the public guard, will be transferred in an elevated and perfected form to the Kingdom of God, to the state of universal humanity. Reciprocally, the constituents which are proper to this state and which are to reveal themselves only in it will not be limited to a general presence within the federation of humanity but will also be internally shared by individual nations. The governing characteristic of today's state of society is still conflict; it prevails over everything; it sets the tone in everything; or rather, it attunes everything to its own false note. The reigning disarray, the struggle of all against all, creates a division in *society* itself which by its nature must necessarily be a *community* and a unity. Hitherto, the social state has been an anthill of internal disputes, contradictions of both public ambitions and demands and private interests among themselves; private interests and aspirations in general against public interest and ambition in particular, the governed against governments. There is ceaseless friction of both the governors and the governed among themselves and of governors against the governed. If there is any unity anywhere it is only out of war-weariness (*de guerre lasse*), the faintness of strength, the armistice of the dead.

· · · ·

III: 17

Our civilization as it existed until now, however lame and lazy, was nevertheless able to far outstrip the barbarian peoples of both hemispheres in the development of social life. This civilization as the one closest to true civilization thus has the right and capacity to accomplish a definitive passage and therefore the initiation of the new era of the world belongs to it. To be sure, with the Christian renewal of the world the initiation of a new order of things could fall to peoples retarded in civilization, since the very mark of this renewal was the retreat from existing relations and the abolition of formerly existing societies. With the present rebirth of the world it is no longer a question of abolition but of elevation. The Christian community by its nature was the enemy of preceding societies. The community of the Holy Spirit is precisely their reciprocal amity, unification and plenitude. The former was an unsocial society; the latter is the society of societies. Consequently, the unification of nations which are to constitute the Kingdom of God will first embrace those peoples who have already passed the Christian epoch socially and have become participants or at least tasted of the present approximation of civilization. There is no doubt that nations which have hitherto been barbarians will next become the staunchest members of the Kingdom, that they await precisely the fullness of peoples in order to develop socially. On the other hand, it is equally certain that they require this *ferment* which is to draw them to sociability.

· · · ·

III: 18

We thus see that Christian missions were only the pre-figuring and the foundation stone of the great missionary work of the Kingdom of God, that this element of Christian propaganda, when it merges with the ancient element of colonization, and the *collegium de propaganda fide*, when it is reborn as a *collegium de propagando summo bono*, will finally accomplish the great Christian task of leading our earth to the state of one flock with one shepherd. It is only here that the whole inherent truth will be revealed of that famous and infamous axiom of the old Church: *extra ecclesiam nulla salus*. To be sure, this is a great truth but until now it was only approximated; it will be completed only in the future. For it is evident that outside this great Church of Humanity there can be no salvation, for only here will the unification, harmony and happiness of society be realized. Every person, every people is and certainly will be free, under condition of not interfering with the community of one's neighbours, to withdraw from the Church of Humanity, from the community of the Holy Spirit, not to enter into the association of peoples and people. But who will want to separate, who will want to visibly *deprive himself of salvation*? Hitherto, salvation was a matter of faith, a matter for the ideal future, today it is becoming a question of the real and present moment, of visible conviction. When all persons in society and all peoples in the society of societies recognize the satisfaction of their vocation and their obvious salvation, or, as the Apostle said, 'perceive *justice, peace and joy* in the Holy Spirit', then, we ask, who will want to separate from the great Church of Humanity?

. . . .

III: 19

We neither desire nor are entitled to determine in advance how humanity and peoples are to organize themselves, how the Kingdom of God will develop in the future course of history, what its internal order, its discipline, will be. This is a matter for future tradition, for future customs, for future vitalizing progress; to state it in advance would be to prejudge history, it would be to curb or constrict the freedom of the Spirit. For freedom depends on *essential* and therefore *necessary principles* being embodied in an infinite *possibility of contingent manifestations*.

. . . .

We said in the first entreaty that the religion of the Holy Spirit is not a *new* religion but Religion itself, essential and eternal, which has hitherto revealed itself page by page, has successively though one-sidedly shaped individual spiritual elements and today stands full-blown. Similarly, here we are saying that we do not bring a new political form, a freshly baked constitution with a given number of articles to be put down on paper and solemnly administered to someone condemned to the role of constitutional monarch.

. . . .

THY WILL BE DONE ON EARTH AS IT IS IN HEAVEN

1–6

The object of the first entreaty was God, the object of the second was Humanity, the object of the third is freedom... For our freedom is one and the same (*unum et idem est*) as the fulfilment of God's will on earth. Freedom is the highest attribute of the Spirit; we could even say that it is not only the highest but even the only essential attribute, its absolute predicate, its meaning, and its destination. Freedom is for the Spirit what weight or length is for any body, what illumination and understanding are for any thought.

. . . .

True freedom requires not merely possibility but reality, not abnegation but affirmation, not disarray but order. The fundamental act of resolution does not suffice; it requires *free life*, completed process, harmonious reality. It must be a deed and not only an intention. The most voluntary abdication of one's will cannot be freedom, for the will by its very nature does not *want* to be abdicated, it *wills* to be free, it wants to live, to be determined and realized in this life and to be constantly in harmony with its destination... But the *lack* of freedom in the Christian world stems not only from its voluntary abdication. The masses did not abdicate or cede freedom; they lacked freedom by virtue of its inaccessibility. Why? Because man conceived of himself only as a subject and not yet as a person; that is to say, man attained consciousness of his own abstract dignity as an inner person but not of his concrete entitlements as a member of the community. He was already conscious of his eternal rights and duties but not yet of his *temporal* ones. Since these eternal laws and duties were only eternal and not at the same time temporal they were only ideal–abstract and hence inauthentic, as yet unreal products of unripe thought, of primary representation. For we know that an eternity which does not contain temporality within itself and which excludes the present is by this very fact not true reality, for it limits itself, extricates itself from the womb of all reality, abandons a vitalizing atmosphere for the futility and emptiness of some ideal land.

.　.　.　.

As an individual, man is only a specific, contingent man; he is such-and-such. He *feels and finds himself* in external circumstances; here he tries as he can to establish and organize himself. As *subject* man is already a universal but still *abstract* man; he apprehends and recognizes himself in his interior and only endeavours to shape and order this interior. The individual man was only concerned about his being, his existence, his right to exist. The subjective man is only concerned about his thought, his essence, his *intention*. There he was abstract in his particular reality; here he is abstract in his universal reality. Both positions require completion.

This completion is found in the concrete completed man, in the *person*. It is no longer as a contingency that the person finds and feels itself in the world; it no longer knows *of itself* merely as an *ego* necessarily endowed with rights, it also *wants to develop its essence and existence out of itself*. It acts *through itself*, it affirms itself effectively and not only intentionally *out of* itself, creates its own cause in society, itself organically contributes to the organic life of humanity.

As a legal individual, man is only demarcated from others and crystallized in himself. He guards his rights and his own existence while others have only the negative duty of respecting these rights, that is, of not affronting them. As a moral subject, man merely melts in abstract universality, sacrifices himself, thinks not of his rights but of his duties, respects only his essence and intentions. As a social person, man acts and interacts and participates in real, full, social life. The social person is both individual and subject raised to a higher power. It has rights, it is not merely an idle universality, a zero without figures, nor is it only a single, separate figure unconnected to the great computation of the world. The person is the real *member of society*. Its position here comprises both its independence and dependence, its being-through-itself and its co-activity in the universal, its passive and active participation, its function.

Right and duty are two opposite sides of one idea and this consolidating idea is virtue. Right is virtue in the state of dead being, unconditional prescription; duty is virtue in the state of detached thought, still unfulfilled intention. Only virtue itself is the living fulfilment of right and duty, the satisfaction of the conditions and strivings of their constituent elements. It is right and duty passed from being and thought to autonomous life, it is the *Deed*. Right and duty are in constant conflict with each other as long as virtue is not born of them and absorbs its parents into itself. In and through virtue, however, right becomes duty and duty right. Only in and through virtue are the execution of right and the fulfilment of duty a delight and joy. Thus, for example, in civic virtue the execution of civic rights and the fulfilment of civic duties in short, serving the *res publica* – is the delight, the ardent desire, the goal and reward of the upright citizen's endeavours.

. . . .

7

Statutes as well as legal, moral and social institutions are thus the objective realization and substantial fulfilment of the will. They are for the will what knowledge is for thought, what the fine arts are for feeling. They are both the highest *creations* of the Spirit and the highest objects for the Spirit.

. . . .

9

Truly, there is a very strange harmony, a very strange measure in the progress of the spirit of mankind. Just as we come to the absolute knowledge of God, when God fully and finally reveals Himself to us, when we no longer imagine Him by approximations but know Him as what He is, the Holy Spirit and the absolute Spirit of the universe, at that very moment this knowledge ceases to be the ultimate aim of the spirit and a new, *active*, *free* and absolutely *practical* aim emerges. The *concept* of the absolute is no longer absolute as was hitherto thought; the active and free realization of its will – and the will is its whole essence and existence – becomes the new absolute, the *absolute absolute*. This task will no longer be purely scientific but *ethical*. In fulfilling it, we shall no longer be striving only toward absolute truth but toward absolute good. Truth, however, and good are essentially and distinctly one and the same, only at different levels of development; that is, truth remains merely within thought and this theoretical state is its satisfaction. Good, however, develops in the world of the Deed and passes into social life.

. . . .

To live according to our destinies, according to the nature of the Spirit, according to the indications and impulses which manifest themselves in the Spirit itself and call for normal development, fulfilment and completion – this is the goal of humanity and also the will of God. God *wants* what He has *established* and what He has established is *good*. Thus, the nature of the human spirit is fundamentally good; it is only a question of man developing it well, that is, in accordance with the divine will.

. . . .

All inclinations are related to three sources or, rather, three chief inclinations exist:

1. *love of oneself*, the first and most direct, corresponding in the sphere of objective spirit to the idea of *law* since law in its abstract sense is founded on this psychological principle;

2. *love of others*, which constitutes a complete contradiction of the first, the sphere of reflection, objectively corresponding to *morality*;

3. *love of the species*, the speculative, synthetic unification and justification of the two former ones and the abolition of their immanent contradiction, the highest position to which impulses rise, the psychological source of *sociability*. This is the broadening of individuality to ever wider spheres, the feeling and recognition of one's *ego* in others and the concentration of others' egos in one's own, and it is this which constitutes the very representation of the species. Only in this sphere is the ostensible incompatibility of self-love and love of kin abolished since in the spheres of family, nation and all humanity the individual recognizes and feels himself an integral member of the organism.

. . . .

Why does the divine will not agree with the will of man? Why have they hitherto always been in antagonism? Precisely because until now man's will was not free but coerced by some limited and limiting, external or internal impulse. The divine will is the *good of the universe, universal happiness*, the spiritual excellence of all.[1] Man's individual will is also happiness, it is also the good but conceived in an individual, limited way. Eventually, man comes to grasp that a limited, individual good cannot be *the good* for by its very nature the good is harmony, agreement and accord and there can be no one-sided harmony (this would be a *contradictio in adiecto*). Therefore, the good of man is dependent on the good of people and humanity, on the good of nations and tribes, on the *community of goods*. We do not mean that abstract and hence false *community* about which befuddled communists daydream, those *contradicting* spirits who think they are on the track of humanity's true progress when in fact they *con-*

---

[1] 'God the Saviour who desires all men to be saved and to come to the knowledge of the truth' (I Timothy 2.4).

tradict all freedom and true community, which consists of co-participation, reciprocal ties and duties, the harmonious unification of individual sides. Only when man has grasped this does man's will become divine will and vice versa. God wants naught but that all elements of the spirit ring fully and harmoniously. This constitutes the *happiness*, this constitutes the *health* of God Himself.

. . . .

GIVE US THIS DAY OUR DAILY BREAD[1]

No passage in the prayer has become the cause of more superficial and woolly comments than this expression, which encompasses such an important truth and a principle so rich in consequences. Commentators rightly felt that in its complete simplicity this entreaty would be diametrically opposed to the whole spirit of Christianity, where an absolute detachment from the world and abnegation of all sensible considerations constitute the essence of normal life and where all strivings for physical or temporal goods are either condemned or barely tolerated. According to their conception, the daily, most universal prayer of the Christian should not contain or at least should not accord equal dignity to an entreaty aiming only at a worldly good, the daily bread about which Christian preachers specifically prohibit the faithful to be concerned. Thus, these commentators took refuge for the most part in figurative translations affirming that the bread in question is mostly moral and spiritual, that is, divine teaching, and thus avoiding contradiction with the general spirit of the faith.

. . . .

Thus, we see that Christian preachers and commentators were certainly right in feeling a contradiction between our entreaty and the spirit of their faith and, from their point of view, quite correct in trying to twist this entreaty by force into Christianity by bestowing a more figurative and ascetic meaning upon it. But even as we recognize the relative or *temporal* correctness of the attempt by no means can we accept it as absolutely, that is *eternally*, justified since it is precisely this entreaty which *does not at all*

---

[1] The translation of the expression *sēmeron* by the expression *today* is completely erroneous since this Greek expression means not only *today* but *always*, i.e. every day, not only *hodie* but also *quotidie, semper*, and is used in Scripture exceedingly often in this final sense . . . The translation of the expression *epiousion* by 'daily' would also be subject to criticism. *Indispensable, sufficing, ample*, would be more accurate and would convey quite faithfully what St Jerome wished to express by *supersubstantialis*.

need to accord with the spirit of Christianity. As we have so often mentioned, all these entreaties refer to a later epoch which is to succeed and complete the Christian epoch, that is, they aim at the attainment of the fundamental characteristics of the future epoch and not in the least at the determinations which are already our lot within the ambit of Christianity itself. Moreover, not only do these entreaties not need to agree with the spirit of Christianity but indeed as partial abolition of the latter they must find themselves more or less in contradiction. This is why if we were to reply to the question of the Roman catechism we would reply most clearly that it does not become *Christians* as Christians to ask for temporal things since for them all temporality is unbecoming. But for post-Christian man, for organic humanity, the community of the Holy Spirit, it is not only fitting but necessary to be concerned with temporal things and precisely because it is *necessary*, because it is *fitting*, the Saviour Himself has enjoined us to pray for them.

. . . .

Let us recall those important words of Rousseau, in whose writings we so often find both the past's blind pre-sentiment and the throbbing pain of the present's irritated nerve: 'Tous les animaux ont exactement les facultés nécessaires pour se conserver. L'homme seul en a de superflues. N'est-ce pas bien étrange, que ce superflu soit l'instrument de sa misère?' To be sure, this is true now, but with the establishment of the normal order of things this excess of human abilities will convert itself from an instrument of misery into the very instrument of happiness. Just as, for example, with every animal the formation of teeth and all physiological organs is a condition and sign of the mode of life which it is to lead, so too the formation of the human spirit is the condition and sign of the normal mode of life of humanity. These superfluous abilities which Rousseau mentions are only superfluous in respect of today's social state, just as the strength and organs of the lion are superfluous in the cage of the menagerie. But just as the menagerie is not the destination of the lion so too the present state of society is not the destination of humanity. The moment is approaching when mankind will be able to use these superfluous forces and abilities to lift itself to a higher level of life. We cannot suppose otherwise without blaspheming against God and the wisdom of His resolutions.

. . . .

Mere reflection on the present situation proves that the entreaty which occupies us today, just like all others in the Prayer, refers to the future awaited state of society. Our institutions, instead of reducing the misery of the lower classes and providing them with their *daily bread*, do not even stop at a stagnant and indifferent attitude; quite the contrary, they even tear this bread out of the mouths of the poor. I shall only mention the fiscal arrangements and onerous taxes governing basic necessities which are not felt in the least by the well-to-do even as they crush the whole life of the poor. For example, are not the Corn Laws in England which raise the price of bread so significantly, and the heavy duties imposed on bread in other countries, really and literally tearing the bread out of the mouths of the humblest day labourer? Is not meat, this indispensable condition of health and strength for working people, almost everywhere saddled with a tax restricting its consumption? Is not salt, one of the most acute needs of the people, everywhere the source of enormous treasury revenues which often make it inaccessible to the people? etc., etc. Moreover, as if public monopolies were not enough, do not private monopolies exist in virtually all countries under the most diverse forms, whether *de iure* through feudal law or only *de facto*, and apply themselves to administering a final blow to proletarians? It would seem as if all institutions were conspiring to trample upon the proletariat; can the effect be called anything other than tearing the *daily bread* out of the mouth of humanity?

It is not enough that all these clearly onerous creations produce such lamentable effects. What shall we say, how shall we adequately express our horror when we realize that arrangements introduced with the most laudable intentions, for the good of humanity, make a similar or often worse impact? Taxes on the poor, for instance, shelters or workhouses in their present-day organization, as well as all present-day philanthropical schemes, instead of remedying a recognized evil, magnify it a hundredfold. Not only do they not correspond at all to their aim, being unable to provide man with the means capable of lifting him to the dignity of a citizen and member of the community, since only the next paracletic epoch can bestow this dignity with all its attributes, but they also deprive him even of the abstract dignity of moral man with which Christianity had already endowed him. It would be superfluous to repeat here what has been already so often and so emphatically demonstrated regarding the deplorable influence of those measures and half-measures with which contemporary statesmen have expected to cure this social disease and the poisonous medicines administered upon society to this very day. Generally speaking, today's institutions, instead of applying themselves to the spiritual progress and growth of the human race, have led it backwards and knocked it down from positions already attained. They have become the source of corruption and the scourge of morality, not only failing to furnish external goods men lack but even snatching away the internal good gained by the faith of Christ. Idleness, drunkenness, loathsome dissipation, vengeance, arson, prostitution, frauds and crimes of all sorts, the trampling and destruction of all moral feelings and the consequent spread of venom onto physical organization – in short, the poisoning of all life in all its relations – these are the results which we encounter in studies on the social state of the lower classes in the most civilized lands. Brotherly love, this fundamental virtue of Christianity, here reveals all its impotence and itself proves that a cure is not to be sought here. Instead of bringing salutary results it manifests itself in untimely alms-giving or exercises and exhausts itself in clumsy half-measures. It is only oil cast into the fire, acid exacerbating a wound.

．　．　．　．

This fundamental rule of social morality – 'consider each an end and no one as a means' – will attain apodictic and universal realization only in the next social organization; in Christianity it could only be a *private postulate*, being grounded in *subjective* morality and not in *objective institutions*. This rule itself suffices to bring into the open the whole contradiction inherent in the concept of the proletarian, a person deprived not only of necessity and reality but even of the possibility of developing what is potentially within him.

Two great men whom humanity will soon count among its saints in spite of their errors are the heralds of this great reform foretold in the present entreaty: Saint-Simon and Fourrier. Already Saint-Simon and his sect have directed the inquiries of the friends of humanity onto the deplorable state of proletarians, and this is undoubtedly the loftiest point in their teaching and the one which deserves the deepest attention. Almost all conscientious political economists were already actively occupied with this question; the brilliant Fourrier had clearly showed the futility and frailty of all attempts at establishing true freedom and a better worldly existence without what he calls the *proportionate minimum*, that is, that each member of the community, without exception or condition and by virtue of his very membership, should constantly and unfailingly be assured of the means to maintain himself adapted to his individual needs and the degree of their evolution. Only then will each individual become a true and concrete person, for he will no longer work to live but rather will live to work, that is, in order to develop and shape his life normally. Otherwise, work will not depend negatively on the ceaseless replenishment of a constantly renewed penury but positively on the universal growth and progress of the spirit in accordance with its destination. Henceforth, we shall consider working in order to live as social blasphemy and living in order to work as the goal of humanity.

Moral evil will be abolished by a new science and new principles when formerly existing ones have revealed their ineffectiveness and shrivelled up. Physical evil, the source of this state, will recede through the organization of work and the establishment of the proportionate *minimum* which will complete what is missing in the *concept of social man*. Precisely this minimum is the daily bread which we implore from God. The very term *daily* bread indicates to us that we are not requesting luxuries or abundance but the essential needs of our being so that we may be capable of attaining man's innate goals and fulfil our destination on earth in the normal harmony of all the elements of our nature. We find the symbolic foreshadowing of this minimum in the *manna* with which God supplied the Israelites.

Through the progress of humanity the sphere of excess settles ever more into the sphere of needs. In other words, what was still an excess yesterday, *today* becomes a need and *tomorrow* will become our daily bread. For instance, what could have seemed more superfluous than postal communications some years ago, whereas today what are they compared to railways and the electric telegraph if not a need and even a daily bread!

We shall doubtless be rebuked at this point. On the one hand, we recognize that the palliatives with which Christian brotherly love wants to soothe today's evils are harmful since they set people on the road to idleness, indifference to their fate and – by the same token – to vice, that they plunge people into an even more lamentable state instead of delivering them from their misery. On the other hand, we propose as a radical medicine an instrument which can only bring about the same results in a considerably intensified and more perniciously universal form. What can be a greater enticement to absolute idleness and blind thoughtlessness than the universal and constant guarantee to each of his means of subsistence? What can more assuredly give an impetus to his greed and bode a more pernicious dissolution of its elements for any company?

We must reply immediately to this specious argument. Let us overlook the specific but exceedingly important reply that it is precisely the lack of bread which mainly drives people onto the road of vice and crime and that by abolishing this scarcity we shall, with very few exceptions, deprive prisons and gallows of their victims. Let us mainly turn the attention of our critics to the following principle: if something may seem inapplicable in regard to the present but contains the guarantee of truth within itself, we must first inquire whether the source of this inapplicability is not to be found in external circumstances and whether a principle which cannot be realized at a low and immature position is not awaiting a higher position for its normal growth. Now, it is true that in today's social organization, or rather disorganization, such medicine as I have recommended seems incomprehensible or paradoxical. This does not empower us, however, to acknowledge it as specious in itself. How many things which we see today would have been incomprehensible for our ancestors? For example, what Greek or Roman at any period before our era could have understood the purely spiritual and ascetic life of the Christian and recognized in it the only means of his own reintegration? Before Gutenberg or Watt, those great prophets of the renewal of the world, were sent down to earth, who could have imagined the moral and physical miracles of print and steam? Further examples abound. I shall even go further: what seems to us now to be improbable may be one hundred times more probable in the future than what really exists or has existed. For instance, if history had not unearthed the factual proofs and historiosophy the speculative causes of numerous conditions in Antiquity could we have acknowledged their verisimilitude? In respect of the past, who today would consider that social folly which was the Roman empire as mighty? – and so on. In regard to the present, who would be capable of supposing that after nineteen centuries of Christianity, human slavery, this enormous and horrible perversity, this social absurdity, would still exist in a significant part of our globe alongside the civilization and political conditions of the world? In the face of these shrieking witnesses who would dare deny that improbability itself is probable?

．　．　．　．

Yea, truly, all will become new just as with Christ's coming the figure of the world was completely renewed. We have already concurred in the meaning of this revival and some of its separate aspects in our earlier considerations; the following ones will add even further clarification. As for the entreaty under discussion, it suffices to remark that through the realization of God's will on earth, through the elevation of humanity's religious, intellectual and moral state to the position at present required by the identification of impulse with duty, effects today uncomprehended will appear natural tomorrow.

When work which is now constraint and compulsion becomes alluring and pleasurable through industrial organization[1] and attraction, then certainly no one will stop at his guaranteed minimum but will listen to the concordant voice of both his impulses and his duties. The perfect grandeur of God's ways will be manifest precisely in that work, which was designated as a punishment for humanity upon its retreat from paradise, will become mankind's prize upon its return.

. . . .

At this moment, an immense majority of society, all those classes whose state we have just acknowledged as so deplorable, is equally bereft of spiritual and of material bread. With momentary anguish but with the comfort of hope we must acknowledge that the moral degradation which necessarily precedes every important crisis even as it foreshadows new social momentum presents us with a doubly distressing scene: lack of that which is to be and the poisoning of that which was. Through Christianity humanity was already endowed with spiritual bread. However, a number of causes have sapped the nourishing properties of this bread: the fall and corruption of religious feelings, indifference to eternal laws so forcefully expressed by one great writer, and above all, conceptual effervescence, which introduced the nucleus of ferment into Christianity, as well as the immemorial mould and fog of prejudice for whose dispersal a sufficiently strong sun has not yet risen. Moreover, these factors have not stopped at

---

[1] Listening to today's economists deliberate the organization of work and routinists reject the expression itself as purportedly smelling of utopia, one would think that it is something never, but never, heard, seen or imagined. However, here it will be shown that until our times work was not bereft of organization. What is slavery among the ancients if not a certain form of organization of work proper to that age but afterwards considered improper and replaced by the development of other relations? Indeed, it was in the very interest of the master to care about the life and condition of slaves etc. Later, rural serfdom and lordship, medieval urban corporations and monopolies again constituted a certain organization of work which alongside numerous indignities and limitations at least had the advantage of assuring a certain order in industries and preventing those working-class ills which have only appeared in our days. Today, however, under the deceptive slogan 'freedom of industry and work' a real disorganization of work has taken place: everyone for himself and on behalf of himself – but no one will suffice to himself, even less so to others. We can thus paraphrase Madame de Staël and declare that it is not the organization of work but precisely its disorganization which is a fresh invention. The former is old as the world and precisely because it is vital and necessary to humanity, it was constantly transforming itself into ever newer and higher forms. We admit that these numerous forms of organization of work were not only approximate and imperfect but even clearly evil and unbearable as is most obviously proven by their abolition. They were not only evil from a physical, material point of view but also often *wicked* from a moral point of view. We must acknowledge, however, that they *were* because they had to be, for work cannot survive without organization under pain of social death.

stripping this bread of good; they have even poisoned it by infecting it with a strong measure of evil.

Here, as in the material relations of society, we see a similar phenomenon: we cannot even console ourselves with a *zero* or indifferent state, for not only have we lost salutary influences but corruption has emphatically taken the upper hand. A double task awaits the reform: to abolish evil, to realize good; to tear the poison away from humanity and to give it nourishing bread. This end must be attained:

1. *morally–religiously* by revealing and establishing the new religious relations which we have spoken of in other chapters.

. . . .

2. *purely intellectually* by opening the road to real knowledge to humanity, enriching it with a mass of elementary concepts, making even higher concepts ever more accessible. The right to a minimum here is as undeniable as that which we recognized from a material point of view. Each individual should thus enjoy unpaid elementary learning; in the further course of his education he should find only facilities instead of the present obstacles. . . As the education of society is universalized the efforts of social administration will be directed to providing the constant means of further education and satisfying intellectual needs once awoken. This will be done through elementary books, public and periodical publications – some very cheap – as well as by installing useful and generally accessible books throughout communes. A strong impulse will thus be given to the progress of the human spirit without which any attempts to improve the material state of humanity would be a futile illusion and clumsy effort.

3. *intellectually–practically* by the establishment of professional and normal courses not only for the young who are to devote themselves to industrial crafts but even for adult workers and craftsmen, to keep them abreast of progress and inventions and to clear the way for them to acquire the practical knowledge of which distance or inaccessibility deprive the industrial class almost completely; moreover, by imparting a greater range of information relating to practical life through elementary education than was hitherto the case.

I do not believe there is any flimsier reproach than that learning will deter the worker from work and give him improper ambitions. In fact, there is nothing easier than proving that precisely without the mental education of workers labour will never succeed in dragging itself out of the state of debasement in which we still see it today; it will never cast off the stigma of coercion, compulsion, negligence and abhorrence which suck its nourishing juices, deprive the world of so many positive advantages, and brand as imperfect those of its positive elements which it cannot eradicate. It is high time that one ceased to attach a denigrating connotation to the image of the craftsman, time for the craftsman to feel himself an artist and approach his work with the enthusiasm of art, with rational love. It is high time that he replaced mechanical with organic work, that he experienced the same pride and joy in work accomplished as the soldier in victory. For in the future the industrial class will be the true army of humanity constantly winning ever new conquests from nature under the banner of the spirit, and these conquests will never be connected with defeat, will never wring tears; even as they assure innumerable advantages to those present they will establish the happiness of future generations. Suffice it to understand this position to foresee from afar the whole magnitude of the fountain of well-being which will gush forth.

Thus, the request for daily bread is a request for removing all the anomalies and obtaining all the salutary effects which we have touched on in this chapter. We have seen that the necessary result of today's state of humanity is the guarantee of a material as well as an intellectual minimum to each individual in order to provide him with the capacity for his own independent progress. This minimum will not consist only of those objects which we today consider as basic necessities; there are others now considered superfluous which will soon appear indispensable, for the *sphere of needs* will broaden ever further at the cost of the *sphere of the superfluous*. This is not in the least regrettable since everyone's well-being depends not, as has been erroneously affirmed, on divesting oneself of all needs and thus retreating into and closing up in the shell of hideous indifference but rather on multiplying, refining and perfecting these needs more and more after having assured oneself of the means to satisfy them. Thus, we must not include only such things as nourishment, heating, shelter, the teaching of reading and writing as well as basic knowledge, under the general expression 'daily bread'; with the progress of humanity we shall draw ever more elements into the area of this minimum. For instance, we shall make the establishment of free baths and gymnastic facilities as well as the introduction of public entertainment and more or less spiritual spectacles equally indispensable conditions of this minimum.

We have chosen precisely these examples from among many others because they are less susceptible to sceptical denials and because we have already seen them realized in Antiquity – witness the Greek *palaestra* and Roman *thermae* as well as Olympics, circus, theatre, field and martial games etc.; the people thus satisfied *gratis* what cannot be called minor pleasures but true needs of life. This demand is neither illusory nor exaggerated since it has already been fulfilled in reality and now only awaits its reintegration and regeneration. I shall even say that many similar demands will yet be awoken in the further development of future institutions and this will not be a frightful but a delightful sight for the friend of humanity as well as a proof of humanity's rapid progress. That the need for physical and moral recreation lies deeply rooted in the nature of man is proven by today's degenerated popular amusements, those carnivals and revelries which are mere debauchery but which could lead, if given a higher and better orientation, even beyond the lofty position at which they stood to a certain extent in the classical world.

One more doubt, one more direct and palpable difficulty may still creep in. Where will the means to assure this minimum be found? Whence the funds for these expenses? Is it the social administration which is to assume them, and if so, whence will it draw the funds? Our first reply is another question: whence does today's administration draw the means for its own costly maintenance and considerable expenses in some branches, such as the army which will prove if not completely unnecessary *in this shape* at least quantitatively superfluous; admittedly, some soldiers would be needed for civilizing missions, so to speak, against peoples who have not yet been incorporated into the society of the world and who could threaten that society. On the other hand, would such a strong impulse injected into industry not promise immediate sources of production more than capable of compensating this organic consumption?

Labour, the element of wealth dependent on ourselves, and nature, the objective undepleted source of wealth whenever galvanized by work, leave us with more than adequate means for attaining social ends. I repeat: however difficult it might seem to some to form a clear picture of future human relations from today's perspective, let them not be discouraged by this difficulty but let them boldly strive to invent absolutely true principles, and having concurred in these, we are convinced that their realization in the deed will quickly follow their grounding in consciousness.

Finally, resuming the postulates developed in this chapter, we reach an understanding of three branches of institutions which are indispensable for the consolidation of the coming position:

1. a system of universal *insurance* to guarantee each individual *what he* already *possesses* and thus to shield him from *adverse* losses;

2. a system of universal *guarantee* to assure each individual of what he does not but should possess, i.e. the minimum, and in this way shield him from a position of complete starvation, from being a social nullity;

3. the system of universal *association* to assure each individual's attain-

ment of *what he can possess* and to obtain that to which he has the right, ability, and even obligation, economically as well as spiritually, to open an easier – nay, the only – way of galvanizing him into seeking *positive* ends so as to confirm the words 'Behold how good and pleasant it is when brothers dwell in unity' (Psalms 133).

AMEN

Having delivered ourselves of the preceding petitions, with what joy we pronounce this last word, which is but the most complete guarantee of their future fulfilment. Christ often used this word to support and strengthen his revelations and St Cyprian rightly called it the most perfect seal of prayer, for it means: *in truth it will be so*. Not only did the Redeemer teach us what we should request, thus showing mankind what it lacks, guiding its desires and pointing to the goal which mankind is to attain and whose conquest is to become the reward of its exertions. He also added this important word and thus conferred apodictic certainty to what was already a strongly founded hope. If He said, 'Believe that whatever you shall ask in my Name will be given to you', how could we doubt that we would be denied what He Himself orders us to request, what He considered indispensable for our happiness, what we request, after all, not only in His Name but in His own words? We may add convincing scientific reasons to our confidence based on the authority of religion. Philosophy and history – *a priori* and *a posteriori* – prove to us that the present social cataclysm of which we are passive and active witnesses is nothing but a chaotic preparation of that new configuration of the world and its many characteristics touched on in our analysis of the petitions. Therefore, if at this point *faith* and *knowledge* abandon their long quarrel for a speculative identity would it not be blasphemy against God and reason if someone were – I shall not say to doubt, for doubt is passive and negative and thus does not extend so far – but if someone were to stubbornly refuse to recognize this obvious certainty?

Finally, let us cast a glance at the essence and the entirety of the Prayer whose details we have just analysed, to convince ourselves that the principles laid out at the beginning in all their continuity and individual traits have been confirmed. This is a prayer intended for Christians; its petitions can be summarized as signifying the expectation of a new state of society where barriers to Christianity have been removed and its inadequacies completed. Each of the elements composing the prayer is a beam of light cast on the future and even confining ourselves only to these elements we could compose a fairly precise image of the future. Accordingly, its principal traits are the following:

We shall not set God up as an other-worldly being directing us but rather as living and participating in humanity. We saw this prepared and mystically prefigured in the momentary and temporal life of Christ on earth. It will now take place absolutely through the reign of the Holy Spirit in the spirit of time and society. This is the realization of the heralded return of the Messiah and the descent of the Holy Spirit no longer on individuals alone but on humanity as a whole.

The true, not abstract, unity of faith prophesied by Christ will be realized. Only the speculative concept of God will bring about the universal sanctification of His Name, because what we do not understand we may be forced to dread through violence or fear but we can never love or adore.

All the prophecies found in the New Testament, those of the Old Testament whose predictions are not limited to Christianity alone but reach unto our day, as well as the burning faith of the early Christians in the coming of the Kingdom of God, will be fulfilled. This Kingdom of God will embrace a new social order where the legal and moral state of society will be determined not through external violence or internal struggle but through the harmony of natural instincts with the essence of duties, where all the most lofty aims of humanity in the sphere of family, society and state will have a free course and the ideas of beauty, truth and the good will find their ultimate realization in the absolute spheres of art, science and religion.

The will of the highest Being no longer finds itself in collision with the will of these worldly individuals; it will reveal itself not only in the whole course of history *par excellence* but also in private relations. Mankind will be freed from the stigma which to this day disfigures the supposedly self-confident civilization of our days and which Christianity could only partially remove by abolishing slavery. The condition of proletarians, men without bread and consequently incapable of higher aspirations, will disappear from society. Thus, a long-awaited equality among members of humanity will come about. Verily, this equality will not depend on those abstract, one-sided and exaggerated fancies of the end of the last century which cost so much blood and inflicted so many calamities on the world. It will be an equality founded on the effective *capacity* of achieving all the loftiest aims whose seeds lie in the essence of the human spirit and whose realization has previously been impossible, an equality based on possession of the means of achieving these goals and an open road to their attainment.

Faith in a just and merciful God will be most thoroughly strengthened by the certitude that we ourselves are the authors of our own happiness or misery through our own conduct. Man, having passed through external coercion and internal struggle, will feel the bliss of a harmonious activity uninterrupted by discord and refractoriness among the elements with which God endowed him, elements which will no longer be placed in mechanical resistance or chemical antagonism to each other but will collaborate in organic life.

In short, mankind will be freed from all evil which is necessarily dismembered and self-contradictory. Having attained the third, synthetic sphere of its development, in the harmony which is characteristic of this stage, and enlivened by an equally regenerated spirit and matter, mankind will again begin to traverse the internal determinations contained within this sphere until it has attained the final state of bliss mentioned by St John in Revelations (11.11, 21–4 and 14.3).

Having entered such a future we shall no longer recite this great prayer because the petitions it contains will have been fulfilled. Nevertheless, it will always remain one of the most precious memories and relics of the life of humanity as well as one of the most important monuments to the divinity of Jesus Christ, Redeemer of the human race. If anyone could then still doubt His divine mission this prayer would be sufficient proof, for who if not God Himself would be able to incorporate the secret of so distant a future in so few words and in such a way that consciousness of this secret would only be disclosed as mankind is to enter the promised future? Now, however, that we have unlocked its meaning the eyes of mankind will reopen to understand Scripture and everyone will realize that this prayer was that Book of Daniel closed until the times were right. We possessed it for almost nineteen centuries but the time had not yet come for its enclosed hidden meaning to be uncovered, for this unassuming book of the future to be opened. As long as we have not yet extracted the future revealed in it we recite this prayer with the utmost fervour worthy of the petitions it contains, with all the love which we owe its author, with the full conviction required by the truths it contains, with the perfect religious spirit which should inspire us so that we may become worthy of the heralded Kingdom of God. And when it comes about, then in place of this prayer we shall raise a hymn of praise and thanksgiving to the Pre-Eternal, a hymn which the vigour of our feeling and the fervour of our faith will put into our lips.

Amen! so be it – and it shall be so.

Bibliographic Essay

Cieszkowski's writings are dispersed and relatively inaccessible. After Cieszkowski's death in 1894 his son published, republished and translated several individual works. There have been a few more recent contributions but, for the most part, one is obliged to consult either the rare original editions or those prepared by August Cieszkowski junior, which date from the turn of the century. All the selections presented here have been freshly translated from their original version – German, French or Polish. With the possible exception of some parts of the *Our Father*, where an abridged English translation exists, all the selections in this volume are appearing in English for the first time.

Cieszkowski's first work, *Die Prolegomena zur Historiosophie*, (Berlin, Veit, 1838) was reprinted in its German original (Posen, Leitgeber, 1908) and as a Kraus reprint (Nendeln, Liechtenstein, 1976) and translated by the author's son as *Prolegomena do Historiozofii* (Posen, Leitgeber, 1908). This Polish translation has now been reprinted in full with some minor modifications in August Cieszkowski, *Prolegomena do Historiozoi, Bóg i Palingeneza, oraz mniejsze pisma filozoficzne z lat 1838–1842*, edited by Jan Garewicz and Andrzej Walicki (Warsaw, Państwowe Wydawnictwo Naukowe, 1972), pp. 1–106. Quite recently, the first French translation has appeared as August von Cieszkowski, *Prolégomènes à l'historiosophie*, translated by Michael Jacob (Paris, Editions Champ Libre, 1973). The selections translated here correspond with some omissions to the following pages of the original German edition: pp. 1–34, 43–8, 61–71, 78–92, 95–102, 108–23, 128–33, 146–54.

Cieszkowski's doctoral thesis, *De philosophiae ionicae, ingenio, vi, loco*, was submitted at Heidelberg in 1838. The thesis itself has been lost but Cieszkowski's thoughts can be gleaned from his unfinished article 'Rzecz o filozofii jońskiej jako wstęp do historii filozofii' ('Material about Ionian philosophy as an introduction to the history of philosophy') in *Biblioteka Warszawska*, I, I (1841), pp. 287–306 and 536–61, as well as from the fragment 'S. 9–16 des deutschen Manuskriptes Cieszkowskis für seine Dissertation über die jonische Philosophie 1838' published in pp. 431–40 of Kühne's book discussed below.

Gott und Palingenesie: Erster kritischer Teil. Erstes kritisches Sendschreiben an den Herrn Professor Michelet auf Veranlassung seiner Vorlesungen über die Persönlichkeit Gottes und die Unsterblichkeit der Seele, (Berlin, E. H. Schröder, 1842) was reprinted (Posen, Leitgeber, 1911) with an annex containing C.-L. Michelet's *Epiphanie der ewigen Persönlichkeit des Geistes*, vol. III (Nürnberg, T. Cramor, 1852), pp. 99–135, which purportedly presents Cieszkowski's positive views on the same subject. The second part of *Gott und Palingenesie* never appeared, so this appendix and the fragments published in Kühne, pp. 440–4, 'Nachgelassene Materialen Cieszkowskis zu *Gott und Palingenesie*' and pp. 446–54, 'Fragmentarische Abhandlung Cieszkowski's über Diesseits und Jenseits zur Ergänzung von *Gott und Palingenesie*' are the sole guides to the possible content of the second, positive part. The 1911 edition was translated with its appendix into Polish by August Cieszkowski junior (Posen, Leitgeber, 1912). The translation has been reprinted in full with only minor changes together with a Polish translation of the fragments in Garewicz and Walicki's edition cited above, pp. 107–244 and 302–22.

Cieszkowski's principal economic work, *Du crédit et de la circulation* (Paris, Treuttel et Wurtz, 1838), underwent a second and a third revised edition (Paris, Guillaumin et Cie., 1847 and 1884). In both cases these revisions consisted of lengthy footnotes in reply to criticisms made of the original work. Moreover, the third edition contained two of Cieszkowski's articles as appendices: 'Du crédit immobilier, rapport fait au congrès central d'agriculture' and 'Sur l'extinction progressive de l'agiotage'. The former had originally appeared in *La Phalange*, March 1847, as 'Du crédit agricole mobilier et immobilier, rapports faits au congrès central d'agricul-ture par M. A. Cieskowski et J. Duval', as well as in the *Journal des Economistes*, XVII (June 1847), under the title 'Du crédit foncier, rapport fait au congrès d'agriculture'. The second appendix had appeared in the *Journal des Economistes*, XXXVI (October 1866). The third edition of the work, complete with appendices, was translated into Polish by the author's son (Posen, Leitgeber 1908) as *O kredycie i obrocie*. Walicki, in *Oxford Slavonic Papers*, II (1969), p. 104, mentions a Russian translation of 1893 which I have been unable to find. The selections translated here correspond to the following pages of the third French edition: pp. 1–2; 4–6; 9–11; 33; 41; 46–9; 60–4; 99–101; 105–10; 120–1.

De la pairie et de l'aristocratie moderne (Paris, Amyot, 1844) was

republished (Paris, Société Française d'Imprimerie et Librairie, 1908) with
a foreword by the author's son. This edition was translated into Polish by
August Cieszkowski junior and appeared (Posen, Leitgeber 1908) as *O
izbie wyższej i arystokracji w naszych czasach.*

In addition to the articles mentioned above Cieszkowski published a
number of other pieces on social and economic matters. Among the selections here is virtually all of *Zur Verbesserung der Lage der Arbeiter auf dem
Lande; ein Vortrag gehalten in der zweiten General-Sammlung des landwirtschaftlichen Provinzial-Verein für die Mark Brandenburg und die Niederlausitz, am 17 Mai 1845* (Berlin, E. H. Schröder, 1846), which appeared
in French in the *Journal des Economistes*, xv (October 1845), as 'Sur les
moyens d'améliorer le sort de la population des campagnes, discours
prononcé au congrès agricole de Berlin le 17 mai 1845, traduction de M. A.
Julien' and in Italian in 1891 as a separate brochure published by Ferrari
Kirchmayer in Venice and translated by 'M. A. C.', presumably Cieszkowski junior or senior. Another important article not included here is 'O
ochronach wiejskich' ('On village shelters'), *Biblioteka Warszawska*, II, 2
(1842), pp. 367–411, translated into German as *Antrag zu Gunsten der
Klein-Kinder-Bewahranstalten als Grundlage der Volks-Erziehung. Beitrag
zur Bestimmung und Feststellung der Aufgabe des Staats in Beziehung auf
Volkswohlstand,* (Berlin, W. Moeser, 1855/56). Also of theoretical interest
is 'Organizacya handlu drzewem i przemysłu leśnego', ('The organization of the wood trade and forest industry'), *Biblioteka Warszawska*, II,
2 (1842), pp. 112–43, as well as a topical comment 'Uwagi nad obecnym
stanem finansów angielskich' ('Remarks on the present state of English
finances'), *Biblioteka Warszawska*, II, 1 (1842), pp. 377–418.

Cieszkowski put out several statements and proposals of a political
nature. In this category one might include the crypto-political article
translated virtually in its entirety for this volume, 'O skojarzeniu dążeń i
prac umysłowych w Wielkim Księstwie Poznańskim', ('On the co-ordination of intellectual aims and works in the Grand Duchy of Posen'), from
Rok, 1 (1843), pp. 132–43. Other contributions are Cieszkowski's legal
memorandum *Zusammenstellung von Staats- und Völkerrechtlichen Urkunden, welche das Verhältnis des Grossherzogtums Posen zur preussischen Krone
betreffen,* (Berlin, Unger, 1849), and the texts of two speeches, *Zwei
Anträge des Abgeordneten August Cieszkowski die Posener Universitäts- und
Unterrichtsfrage betreffen,* (Berlin, n.p., 1853).

Other articles of varying importance are the following: 'O drogach
Ducha' ('The Ways of the Spirit'), *Roczniki Poznańskiego Towarzystwa
Przyjaciół Nauk*, II (1863), pp. 735–76, which was to constitute an intro-

ductory essay to the *Ojcze Nasz*; a small part of this article has been translated in the selections from the *Ojcze Nasz*. *Słowa wieszcze Polaka wyrzeczone roku MDCCCXLVI* ('Prophetic words of a Pole uttered in the year MDCCCXLVI') appeared as a brochure at the Prague Pan-Slavic Congress (Prague, Haase, 1848). It was reprinted almost integrally in volume I of the *Ojcze Nasz*. Excerpts from this brochure have been translated separately here. 'O romansie nowoczesnym' ('The modern novel'), *Biblioteka Warszawska*, VI, 1 (1846), pp. 135–66, is an interesting exercise in Hegelian literary theory. Minor articles include 'Uwagi na temat mowy Schellinga' ('Remarks concerning Schelling's speech'), *Biblioteka Warszawska*, II, 1 (1842), pp. 424–6 (signed A.C.); as well as two more personal travel reports, 'Kilka wrażeń z Rzymu' ('Some impressions from Rome'), *Biblioteka Warszawska*, II 1 (1842), pp. 642–57, and 'O wystawie berlinskiej' ('the Berlin exposition'), *Biblioteka Warszawska*, IV (1844), pp. 704–9.

Cieszkowski's major work is generally considered to be the *Ojcze Nasz* ('Our Father'). Volume I, the Introduction, appeared anonymously in 1848 (Paris, Maulde et Renou) and was reprinted in 1870 (Posen, Żupański). The rest of the work came out posthumously in two separate editions. The first edition, published by Leitgeber in Posen, consisted of four volumes: I (1899), the Introduction as in the previous editions, with 'O drogach Ducha' as postscript; II (1899), the Invocation; III (1903), the first entreaty, 'Hallowed be Thy Name'; IV (1906), the second entreaty, 'Thy Kingdom Come'. The second edition, published by Fiszer i Majewski in Poznań, was more extensive even though it contained only three volumes: I (1922), the Introduction preceded by 'O drogach Ducha'; II (1922), Invocation and the first entreaty; III (1923), the second to seventh entreaties and the Amen.

In both cases the text was established by the author's son, who contributed a brief preface to each volume of the first edition; the first volume of the second edition contained a preface by Adam Żółtowski. For reasons of availability the selections from the *Ojcze Nasz* translated here are drawn from both editions and correspond to the following pages: vol. I (2nd edn), pp. iii, viii, 1–5, 9–10, 14–16; vol. II (1st edn), pp. 142, 296–8, 300, 304–6, 310; vol. III (2nd edn), pp. 1–5, 7–8, 21–7, 30–4, 47–59, 68–72, 78, 83–8, 92–112, 117–24, 127, 130, 155, 171, 175–8, 185–97, 201–17, 283–6.

The *Ojcze Nasz* was translated into French as *Notre Père*. Unfortunately, this translation is exceedingly rare; volume I of *Notre Père* was translated by W. Gasztowtt and the author's son (Paris, Société Française d'Imprimerie et Librairie, 1906) from the first volume of the first posthumous edition. Volumes II to IV were translated by Paul Cazin and the author's son and published between 1927 and 1929. They too were based on the first posthumous edition, with the exception of volume IV, where the second to seventh entreaties were translated from the second Polish edition. For further details about this translation see Teresa Garnysz-Kozłowska, 'Z dziejów francuskiego przekładu *Ojcze Nasz* Augusta Cieszkowskiego', *Archiwum Historii Filozofii i Myśli Społecznej*, XVI (1970), pp. 173–83. There is apparently a translation of the 1848 edition of volume I in Italian prepared by Aurelio Palmieri (Bologna, Zanichelli, 1923). An abridged English translation by William J. Rose came out as *The Desire of All Nations* (London, Student Christian Movement, 1919) and its preparation is described in *William J. Rose's Polish Memoirs*, edited by Daniel Stone (Toronto University Press, 1975).

Apart from these published works and in spite of the destruction of Cieszkowski's *Nachlass* in Warsaw during the Second World War, a number of other sources are available. The most valuable is Walter Kühne, *Graf August Cieszkowski, ein Schüler Hegels und des deutschen Geistes: Ein Beitrag zur Geschichte des deutschen Geisteseinflüsses auf die Polen*, Veröffentlichungen des Slavischen Instituts an der Friedrich Wilhelm Universität Berlin, vol. XX, (Leipzig, O. Harrassowitz, 1938). This work contains several unpublished fragments mentioned above as well as the following short pieces: 'Entwurf Cieszkowskis zu einem Curriculum vitae, 1838', pp. 426–7; 'Nicht veröffentliche Vorrede Cieszkowskis zu seiner Schrift "Prolegomena zur Historiosophie" ', pp. 444–5. All, with the exception of the curriculum vitae, have been translated into Polish in Garewicz and Walicki's edition, pp. 293–302. Moreover, Kühne's book contains the Cieszkowski–Michelet correspondence, forty-five letters over almost sixty years, pp. 353–425. This too is translated in Garewicz and Walicki, pp. 325–433. Kühne's book has recently been reissued as a Kraus reprint (Nendeln, Liechtenstein, 1968).

Cieszkowski's Diaries (*Dzienniki*) are an equally valuable source. These two unpublished notebooks contain commentaries, ideas, lists of readings and personal encounters between approximately 1831 and 1839. They are deposited in the Manuscript Division of the Poznań University Library, (Wydział Rękopisów, Biblioteka Uniwersytecka, Uniwersytet im. Adama Mickiewicza, Poznań). Dr T. Kozanecki, Director of the Parliamentary Library in Warsaw (Biblioteka Sejmu), has prepared a typescript of most of the Diaries which, it is hoped, will soon be published.

There are several other sources worth mentioning. Cieszkowski's 'Address to the Representatives of Free Peoples' written at the Breslau

Congress was first published in *Gazeta Polska*, 93 (14 July 1848), and as a separate brochure. It has been included in Władyslaw Tadeusz Wisłocki, *Jerzy Lubomirski 1817–1872* (Lvov, 1928), pp. 46–53. Cieszkowski's statements in the Polish Circle of deputies in Berlin during the Circle's first years have been conveyed in Z. Grot's edition of the minutes of the Circle, *Protokoły posiedzeń koła polskiego w Berlinie*, vol. I (1849–1851), (Poznań, Poznańskie Wydawnictwo Naukowe, 1956). Cieszkowski's commentaries in the Philosophische Gesellschaft on topics ranging from the law of progress in history to differential tariffs have been quoted and summarized in Kühne, pp. 159–69, pp. 218–49, pp. 340–7. Some of these later comments were originally published in *Der Gedanke*, I, 3 (1861), p. 235; II, 4 (1861), p. 38; II, 6 (1861), pp. 246–7; V, 2 (1864), pp. 101–2; VI, 2 (1865), pp. 107–14. Finally, Cieszkowski's poems of 1830/31 are published in Janina Znamirowska, 'O nieznanych wierszach Augusta Cieszkowskiego', *Ruch Literacki*, IV, 2 (February 1929), pp. 44–7.

Very little of Cieszkowski's extensive correspondence remains; much of it, including apparently an exchange with Lamartine, was burned during the Second World War. Apart from the Cieszkowski–Michelet correspondence already mentioned Kühne also published several letters, notably from Varnhagen von Ense, Ferdinand Lassalle, and several Hegelians, in 'Neue Einblicke ins Leben und Werke Cieszkowskis: aus unveröffentlichem Nachlass', *Jahrbücher für die Kultur und die Geschichte der Slaven*, VI, 1 (1930), pp. 54–66, and VII, 1 (1931), pp. 3–36. Kühne's *Graf August Cieszkowski*, pp. 87–8 also contains the draft of a letter to Schelling which Cieszkowski apparently never sent but which may be compared to his 'Uwagi na temat mowy Schellinga' cited above. The most important collection of letters to Cieszkowski is *Listy Zygmunta Krasińskiego do Augusta Cieszkowskiego*, vols. I and II, edited by J. Kallenbach with an introduction by A. Żółtowski, (Cracow, Gebethner, 1912) covering the years 1841 to 1859. See also 'Listy Konstantego Gaszyńskiego do Augusta Cieszkowskiego', edited by S. Brydzinska-Osmolska, *Rocznik Koła Polonistów Słuchaczy Uniwersytetu Warszawskiego* (1927), pp. 181–204.

Scholarship on Cieszkowski has produced a number of items of varying importance. I refer the reader to the most complete listing, which is to be found in the *Bibliografia filozofii polskiej*, vol. II, edited by the Instytut Filozofii i Socjologii Polskiej Akademii Nauk, (Warsaw, Państwowe Wydawnictwo Naukowe, 1961), pp. 34–52, items 304 to 496. This bibliography is particularly valuable in noting reviews of Cieszkowski's writings as well as short biographical items. Unfortunately, in addition to being now somewhat out of date, this bibliography omits Cieszkowski's non-philosophical works and stresses Polish-language references. Here, I shall attempt to supplement this bibliography by pointing out some of the most important studies, particularly those in Western languages or of recent date, and by giving some indication of trends in the growing literature on Cieszkowski.

Book-length studies have concentrated on Cieszkowski as religious thinker. This is the case with A. Jakubisiak, *Principes de la morale d'après Auguste Cieszkowski* (Paris, 1914); J. Keller, *Czyn jako wyraz postawy moralnej Augusta Cieszkowskiego* ('The deed as expression of August Cieszkowski's moral stance'), (Lublin, Towarzystwo Naukowe Katolickiego Universytetu Lubelskiego, 1938); M. Klepacz, *Idea Boga w historiozofii Augusta Cieszkowskiego na tle ówczesnych prądów umysłowych* ('The idea of God in the historiosophy of August Cieszkowski in the light of the intellectual currents of his times'), (Kielce, 1933). K. Kowalski, *Filozofia Augusta hr. Cieszkowskiego w świetle zasad filozofii św. Tomasza z Akwinu. studium porównawcze* ('The philosophy of August Count Cieszkowski in the light of the principles of the philosophy of St Thomas Aquinas'), (Poznań, Nakład Księgarni Św. Wojciecha, 1929). There is also one book dealing with Cieszkowski's social and economic views, A. Roszkowski, *Poglądy społeczne i ekonomiczne Augusta Cieszkowskiego*, Poznańskie Prace Ekonomiczne, II (Poznań, Fiszer i Majewski, 1923), as well as a thesis concerned with Cieszkowski as philosopher, A. Żółtowski, *Graf August Cieszkowskis 'Philosophie der Tat'. Die Grundzüge seiner Lehre und der Aufbau seines Systems* (Posen, 1904). Moreover, there are two attempts at a comprehensive analytical and biographical study of Cieszkowski: Kühne's work discussed above and my own *Between Ideology and Utopia : the Politics and Philosophy of August Cieszkowski*, Sovietica, XXXIX (Dordrecht, D. Reidel, forthcoming).

In recent years, Cieszkowski scholarship has developed in two contexts. In Poland, scholars have subjected Cieszkowski for the first time to serious examination freed of both the pietism of the earliest discussions and the hostility of the first post-war studies. In the West, the 're-discovery' of Cieszkowski has resulted in increasingly frequent reference and citation of his works. In both cases, there has been an effort to extent analysis beyond the traditional reference point of German idealism and to treat Cieszkowski's writings as a whole. This trend is amply illustrated by Andrzej Walicki's seminal article on the French sources of Cieszkowski's thought, 'Francuskie inspiracje myśli filozoficzno-religijnej Augusta Cieszkowskiego', *Archiwum Historii Filozofii i Myśli Społecznej*, XVI (1970), pp. 127–

71, as well as by the first English-language article to appear on Cieszkowski, Benoît Hepner's 'History and the Future: the vision of August Cieszkowski', *Review of Politics*, XV, 3 (1953), pp. 328–50. Above all, debate has centred around two broad questions: the *Prolegomena zur Historiosophie* and its influence on the development of Hegelianism and Marxism; the *Ojcze Nasz* and its relation to Polish messianism.

The debate on the *Prolegomena* was inaugurated by George Lukács's 'Moses Hess und die Probleme der idealistischen Dialektik', *Archiv für die Geschichte des Sozialismus und der Arbeiterbewegung*, XII (1926), pp. 103–55. Lukács acknowledged the work's influence on Hess but stressed the limitations of Cieszkowski's notion of *praxis* and refused to recognize any influence on Marx. A quite different assessment was put forward in Auguste Cornu's monumental *Karl Marx et Friedrich Engels*, vol. I: *Les années d'enfance et de jeunesse. La gauche hégélienne, 1818/1844*, (Paris, Presses Universitaires de France, 1955), p. 142, which argued that Cieszkowski's 'revolutionary transformation of the philosophy of Hegel' had necessarily affected the formation of Marx's ideas. Two important English-language studies have taken a similar view: Shlomo Avineri, *The Social and Political Thought of Karl Marx* (Cambridge University Press, 1968), pp. 124–31 and, to a lesser extent, David McLellan, *The Young Hegelians and Karl Marx* (London, Macmillan, 1969), pp. 4–7. This same idea has been far less convincingly argued by R. Lauth, 'Einflüsse slawischer Denker auf die Genesis der Marxschen Weltanschauung', *Orientalia Christiana Periodica*, XXI (1955), pp. 413–48, and somewhat less unconvincingly by J. Ostrowski, 'A Christian contribution to the origins of Marxism', *Kongres współczesnej Nauki i Kultury Polskiej na Obczyźnie*, vol. I, edited by M. Sas-Skowroński, (London, 1970), pp. 45–57.

The difficulty of establishing a direct relation between Marx and Cieszkowski has moved the debate about the *Prolegomena* to a discussion of its impact on the Hegelian milieu. Even in this context, however, the question of Cieszkowski's possible influence on Marx is rarely far from the forefront. The following studies situate Cieszkowski vis-à-vis his contemporaries and conclude by supporting the notion of an indirect debt or, at the very least, a coincidence of views: N. Lobkowicz, 'Absolute knowledge and praxis: Cieszkowski', which is chapter XIII in his *Theory and Practice : History of a Concept from Aristotle to Marx* (Notre Dame and London, University of Notre Dame Press, 1967), pp. 193–204; L. S. Stepelovich, 'August von Cieszkowski: from theory to practice', *History and Theory*, XIII, 1 (1974), pp. 39–53; my own 'Prolégomènes à une théorie de la praxis', *Economies et Sociétés*, cahiers de l'I.S.E.A., VIII, 10 (1974) (series S, no. 17), pp. 1487–1506. This assessment is also shared by Leszek Kołakowski, *Głowne Nurty Marksizmu : powstanie-rozwój-rozkład*, vol. 1, Biblioteka Kultury, no. 262, (Paris, Instytut Literacki, 1976), pp. 89–92.

On the other hand, Jan Garewicz in 'August Cieszkowski w oczach niemców w latach trzydziestych i czterdziestych XIX-go wieku' ('August Cieszkowski in the eyes of the Germans in the 1830s and 1840s'), *Polskie Spory o Hegla*, edited by the Instytut Filozofii i Socjologii Polskiej Akademii Nauk (Warsaw, 1966), pp. 205–43, has minimized the possible influence of the *Prolegomena* by pointing out that Cieszkowski could not be considered a 'left' Hegelian and that he was quite isolated in the Hegelian milieu. Finally, two studies have succeeded in looking at the *Prolegomena* with primary reference to Cieszkowski's Hegelian predecessors and the Hegelian school independently of Marx: J. Gebhardt's chapter, 'Der Übergang von der akademischen Schule zur politischen Bewegung', in his *Politik und Eschatologie: Studien zur Geschichte der Hegelschen Schule in den Jahren 1830–1840*, Münchner Studien zur Politik, 1 (Munich, Beck, 1963), pp. 130–52; H. Stuke, 'August Cieszkowski und die Begründung der Philosophie der Tat im absoluten Spiritualismus', in his *Philosophie der Tat; Studien zur 'Verwirklichung der Philosophie' bei den Junghegelianern und den Wahren Sozialisten*, Industrielle Welt, III (Stuttgart, E. Klett, 1963), pp. 83–122.

Whereas the debate about the significance of the *Prolegomena* has continued both in Poland and in the West, discussion about the nature of the *Ojcze Nasz* and its place in the context of Polish messianism has been largely confined to Poland. Essentially, this discussion has involved a critical re-examination of two competing interpretations of the messianic phenomenon which both tend to assimilate Cieszkowski as a typical messianist in their respective understanding of the term. The traditional view, exemplified in J. Ujejski, *Dzieje Polskiego Mesjanizmu* (Lvov, 1931) has tended to see messianism as the suffering expression of a collective yearning for national and religious integrity. This has also been the judgement of non-Polish thinkers such as Nicholas Berdyaev, *The Russian Idea* (New York, Macmillan, 1948), pp. 212–14, who specifically discusses Cieszkowski as 'the greatest philosopher of Polish messianism' in support of this view. The second view involves a somewhat self-conscious and schematic Marxist approach typified by T. Kroński in 'Koncepcje filozoficzne mesjanistów polskich w połowie XIX-go wieku', *Archiwum Historii Filozofii i Myśli Społecznej*, II (1957), pp. 81–125, and 'Reakcja mesjanistyczna i katolicka w Polsce połowy XIX-go wieku', in *Z Dziejów Polskiej Myśli Filozoficznej*, vol. III, edited by B. Baczko, (Warsaw, 1957), pp. 271–

94. This interpretation stresses the inseparability of messianism from other forms of reactionary ideology by insisting on the Catholicism, the class origins and the class interests of leading messianists.

The inadequacy of traditional approaches has provoked some interesting and fruitful attempts to subject the phenomenon of Polish messianism to a critical inquiry which would recognize its ideological autonomy vis-à-vis both progressive and reactionary thought systems and which could situate the phenomenon in the broad context of millennarianism and secular messianism elsewhere. Studies such as B. Gawecki's 'Próba interpretacji zasad polskiej filozofii romantycznej w terminach nauki współczesnej', *Sprawozdania Polskiej Akademii Umiejętności*, XLVI, 6 (1946), pp. 202–6, and A. Walicki's 'Milenaryzm i mesjanizm religijny a romantyczny mesjanizm Polski', *Pamiętnik Literacki*, LXII, 4 (1971), pp. 23–40, are examples of this attempt, which has often confirmed previous interpretations but in a dispassionate, rigorous and systematic manner.

In the case of Cieszkowski the two traditional approaches have converged in distorting the content of his world-view as well as the originality of his ideological posture. The first interpretation has consistently exaggerated Cieszkowski's mysticism and romanticism even as it has misunderstood his cosmopolitan nationalism and reforming pragmatism. The second interpretation has been unable to free itself from absorption with Cieszkowski's class position and ostensible religiosity and has thus failed to examine the contradiction between his distrust of revolutionary rhetoric and his social radicalism. It would now seem, however, that nuances in the assessment of messianism are being reflected in studies on Cieszkowski such as A. Walicki's 'Cieszkowski: Filozoficzna Systematyzacja Mesjanizmu', in *Filozofia Polska*, vol. II, edited by B. Baczko, Seria Myśli i Ludzie (Warsaw, Wiedza Powszechna, 1967), pp. 289–313, and particularly his 'Dwa Mesjanizmy: Adam Mickiewicz i August Cieszkowski', in his *Filozofia a Mesjanizm: studia z dziejów filozofii i myśli społeczno-religijnej romantyzmu polskiego*, (Warsaw, Państwowy Instytut Wydawniczy, 1970). Unfortunately, the abridged English translation of the article, 'Two Polish Messianists: Adam Mickiewicz and August Cieszkowski', *Oxford Slavonic Papers* (N.S.), II (1969), pp. 77–105, omits some of the original's interesting theoretical discussion of messianism. Walicki has also recently published an article in English entitled 'August Cieszkowski's philosophical works of 1838–1842 within the intellectual context of their times', *Dialectics and Humanism*, 3 (summer 1975), pp. 197–209.

Index

Cambridge Studies in the History and Theory of Politics

Editors: MAURICE COWLING, G. R. ELTON, E. KEDOURIE, J. G. A. POCOCK, J. R. POLE and WALTER ULLMANN

A series in two parts, studies and original texts. The studies are original works on political history and political philosophy while the texts are modern, critical editions of major texts in political thought. The titles include:

TEXTS

Liberty, Equality, Fraternity, by James Fitzjames Stephen, edited with an introduction and notes by R. J. White

Vladimir Akimov on the Dilemmas of Russian Marxism 1895–1903.
An English edition of 'A Short History of the Social Democratic Movement in Russia' and 'The Second Congress of the Russian Social Democratic Labour Party', with an introduction and notes by Jonathan Frankel

J. G. Herder on Social and Political Culture, translated, edited and with an introduction by F. M. Barnard

The Limits of State Action, by Wilhelm von Humboldt, edited with an introduction and notes by J. W. Burrow

Kant's Political Writings, edited with an introduction and notes by Hans Reiss; translated by H. B. Nisbet

Karl Marx's Critique of Hegel's 'Philosophy of Right', edited with an introduction and notes by Joseph O'Malley; translated by Annette Jolin and Joseph O'Malley

Lord Salisbury on Politics. A Selection from His Articles in 'The Quarterly Review' 1860–1883, edited by Paul Smith

Francogallia, by François Hotman. Latin text edited by Ralph E. Giesey; English translation by J. H. M. Salmon

The Political Writings of Leibniz, edited and translated by Patrick Riley

Turgot on Progress, Sociology and Economics: A Philosophical Review of the Successive Advances of the Human Mind on Universal History. Reflections on the Formation and Distribution of Wealth, edited, translated and introduced by Ronald L. Meek

Texts concerning the Revolt of the Netherlands, edited with an introduction by E. H. Kossmann and A. F. Mellink

Regicide and Revolution: Speeches at the Trial of Louis XVI, edited with an introduction by Michael Walzer; translated by Marian Rothstein

Georg Wilhelm Friedrich Hegel: Lectures on the Philosophy of World History:
Reason in History, translated from the German edition of Johannes
Hoffmeister by H. B. Nisbet and with an introduction by Duncan Forbes
A Machiavellian Treatise by Stephen Gardiner, edited and translated by
Peter S. Donaldson
The Political Works of James Harrington, edited by J. G. A. Pocock

STUDIES

1867: Disraeli, Gladstone and Revolution: The Passing of the Second Reform Bill,
by Maurice Cowling
The Social and Political Thought of Karl Marx, by Shlomo Avineri
Men and Citizens: A Study of Rousseau's Social Theory, by Judith Shklar
Idealism, Politics and History: Sources of Hegelian Thought, by George Armstrong
Kelly
The Impact of Labour 1920-1924: The Beginnings of Modern British Politics, by
Maurice Cowling
Alienation: Marx's Conception of Man in Capitalist Society, by Bertell Ollman
The Politics of Reform 1884, by Andrew Jones
Hegel's Theory of the Modern State, by Shlomo Avineri
Jean Bodin and the Rise of Absolutist Theory, by Julian H. Franklin
The Social Problem in the Philosophy of Rousseau, by John Charvet
The Impact of Hitler: British Politics and British Policy 1933-1940, by Maurice
Cowling
Social Science and the Ignoble Savage by Ronald L. Meek
Freedom and Independence: A Study of the Political Ideas of Hegel's 'Phenomen-
ology of Mind', by Judith Shklar
In the Anglo-Arab Labyrinth: The McMahon-Husayn Correspondence and Its
Interpretations 1914-1939, by Elie Kedourie
The Liberal Mind 1914-1929, by Michael Bentley
Political Philosophy and Rhetoric: A Study of the Origins of American Party
Politics, by John Zvesper
Revolution Principles: The Politics of Party 1689-1720, by J. P. Kenyon
John Locke and the Theory of Sovereignty: Mixed Monarchy and the Right of
Resistance in the Political Thought of the English Revolution, by Julian H.
Franklin
Adam Smith's Politics: An Essay in Historiographic Revision, by Donald Winch